WORDSWORTH AND THE
LAKE DISTRICT

Wordsworth
and the
Lake District

——

A GUIDE TO THE POEMS
AND THEIR PLACES

David McCracken

Oxford   New York

OXFORD UNIVERSITY PRESS

Oxford University Press, Walton Street, Oxford OX2 6DP

Oxford New York Toronto
Delhi Bombay Calcutta Madras Karachi
Petaling Jaya Singapore Hong Kong Tokyo
Nairobi Dar es Salaam Cape Town
Melbourne Auckland

and associated companies in
Berlin Ibadan

Oxford is a trade mark of Oxford University Press

First published 1984
First issued as an Oxford University Press paperback 1985
Reprinted 1985, 1988, 1990

British Library Cataloguing in Publication Data
McCracken, David
Wordsworth and the Lake District: a guide to The Poems and Their places.
—(Oxford paperbacks) 1. Wordsworth, William, 1770–1850
—Homes and haunts—England—Lake District. I. Title
821'.7'09 PR5884
ISBN 0–19–281396–X

Library of Congress Cataloging in Publication Data
McCracken, David.
Wordsworth and the Lake District.
(Oxford paperbacks)
Bibliography: p. Includes indexes.
1. Wordsworth, William, 1770–1850—Homes and haunts—England—Lake District.
2. Wordsworth, William, 1770–1850—Settings.
3. Literary landmarks—England—Lake District. 4. Lake District (England) in literature.
5. Lake District (England)—Description and travel—Guide books. I. Title
PR5884.M35 1985   821'.7   84-20707
ISBN 0–19–281396–X (pbk.)

Printed in Great Britain by
Richard Clay (The Chaucer Press) Ltd.
Bungay, Suffolk

For Marcia, Peter, Janet, Stephen, and Michael

PREFACE

William Wordsworth—landscape designer and gardener, traveller and travel writer, and, not least, poet—has become, through this constellation of interests and his own genius, perhaps the greatest poet of place in the English language. There is much in his poetry about his home country, the Lake District, though the poems themselves usually do not say which places they are associated with, or how, or why. Conversely, much in the landscape and life of the Lake District can illuminate his poetry, if we make an attempt to see something of what Wordsworth saw. In this book I have tried to supply the connections between the poems and their places. Since it is primarily about poems and places rather than about the poet's life, I have begun with places along the main road through Wordsworth Country, from Ambleside to Keswick. But the story of Wordsworth's poetic interest in place is a part of his biography, and I have reserved the places where Wordsworth lived along this road for the second section in order to consider them in the context of his successive homes in the Lakes. The final two sections of Part I are devoted to the places Wordsworth wrote about to the east and west of the main road through the central Lake District.

That Wordsworth himself was interested in the connections between poems and places is most clear in the notes he dictated to his friend Isabella Fenwick in 1843, when he told her in some detail about the actual people, episodes, and places that suggested particular poems. These notes have provided a beginning point for my research, and I have quoted many of them here. In addition, I have used his prose works, Dorothy Wordsworth's journals, letters of the Wordsworths and friends, memoirs of his contemporaries, early travel writers, Wordsworth scholarship of the late nineteenth and twentieth centuries, and my own observations in the Lakes. Part I, containing the essays on the poems and their places, and Part II, containing the maps and guides to and about places, are interlinked by key letters, A, B, etc. I have separated the two Parts to make the first more readable and the second more convenient as a guide, but I hope that the essays will send readers to the maps and that the guides will send travellers—armchair and otherwise—to the essays and poems.

My largest debts are to three extraordinary Wordsworth scholars: William Knight, Ernest de Selincourt, and Mary Moorman. For Professor Knight's pursuit of Wordsworthian places in two books (1878 and 1887), Professor de Selincourt's (and Miss Darbishire's) edition of the poems, and Mrs Moorman's biography, I am most grateful. I am also indebted to many scholars who have followed them—the editors of the Oxford *Prose Works* and *Letters* and of the Cornell edition of the poems, Mark L. Reed for his chronology, T. W. Thompson and Robert Woof for their studies of local history, and many others who have written about Wordsworth.

When quoting from Wordsworth's poems, I have used the text in the de Selincourt and Darbishire edition of the *Poetical Works* (5 vols.) and of *The Prelude* unless an earlier version of a poem is more specific about its place. In quoting from *The Prelude*, I have sometimes quoted from the 1805 version (cited '1805 *Prelude*') when it is more detailed in its description of places than the revised version published in 1850. References simply marked *The Prelude*, with no date, are to the 1850 text, which is the more readily available one.

I gratefully acknowledge the help I have received from the following: Dr Peter Laver, Dr Terry McCormick, and the Trustees of Dove Cottage for allowing me to use the library and museum; the staffs of the Cumbria County Record Offices at Kendal and Carlisle, the Ambleside County Library, the Armitt Library, the Kendal County Library and Cumbria Collection, and the University of Washington Library; the University of Washington Graduate School Research Fund; Mr and Mrs B. Blake, Mrs Lena Parker, Mrs R. Calvert, and Miss Margaret Hayes for their information about Grasmere, Broad How, and Hallsteads; David Streatfield, Jack O'Connell, and Louise Hirosawa for making me think about literature and places together; Don Bialostosky for innumerable conversations about Wordsworth; and Martin and Angela Clark of Bainriggs, Grasmere, for their friendship and hospitality, as well as their knowledge of the Lakes. I should also like to thank Peter Bicknell for his generous help in suggesting illustrations for various chapters and for obtaining photographs of them. For permission to include the illustrations I gratefully acknowledge the Trustees of Dove Cottage (p. 21) and the Tyne and Wear County Council Museums (p. 128). My warmest thanks go to my wife Marcia, who has helped and encouraged at every stage of this book.

CONTENTS

ILLUSTRATIONS

MAPS

ABBREVIATIONS

De Quincey	Essays originally appearing in *Tait's Edinburgh Magazine*, collected in a Penguin paperback, *Recollections of the Lakes and the Lake Poets*, edited by David Wright (Harmondsworth, 1970).
Grosart	'Conversations and Personal Reminiscences of Wordsworth', in *The Prose Works of William Wordsworth*, edited by Alexander B. Grosart (London, 1876), vol. iii.
Guide	Wordsworth's *Guide to the Lakes.* Available in an Oxford paperback, edited by Ernest de Selincourt, or in *Prose Works*, vol. ii.
I.F.	Notes on the poems dictated by Wordsworth to Isabella Fenwick. Printed in the notes in the five-volume *Poetical Works* (*PW*).
Letters	*The Letters of William and Dorothy Wordsworth*, edited by Ernest de Selincourt, second edition revised by Chester L. Shaver, Mary Moorman, and Alan G. Hill (Oxford, 1967—).
Prose Works	*The Prose Works of William Wordsworth*, edited by W. J. B. Owen and Jane Worthington Smyser (Oxford, 1974), 3 vols.
PW	*The Poetical Works of William Wordsworth*, edited by Ernest de Selincourt and Helen Darbishire (Oxford, 1940–49), 5 vols.
W.W.	William Wordsworth.

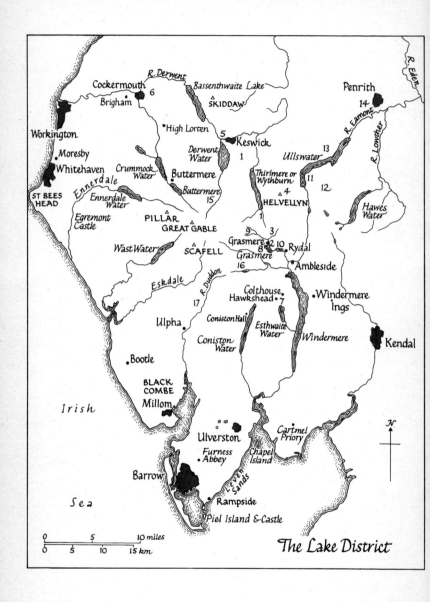

The Lake District

INTRODUCTION

In the mid-eighteenth century, the poet Thomas Gray and a few other travellers made adventurous forays into the remote corner of England known as the Lakes. In the following decades more travellers followed; some wrote books about the extraordinary scenery, some sketched it, and some painted it. But it was not until the early nineteenth century that it became a popular destination for travellers. By that time and continuing to our day, seeing the Lakes has been coloured by the presence of William Wordsworth. A century and a half ago, many went to see Wordsworth himself as well as the country he wrote about. When his reputation was established, hundreds of strangers arrived each summer at Rydal Mount on what Charles Lamb called 'gaping missions'. They were greeted or shown about by the gardener or servant, a member of the family, or often Wordsworth himself. It is not surprising that they should have associated seeing the Lakes with seeing the poet, or that the area should come to be known as Wordsworth Country. Wordsworth is *the* English poet of place, and the Lake District was his home for the first twenty and the last fifty years of his life. In the 1790s—the only decade when he did not live continuously there— he was a wanderer, travelling or living in Cambridge, France and Switzerland, London, North Wales, back in the Lake District, Dorset, Somerset, Germany, and Yorkshire. We may say in retrospect that his first volumes of published poetry, in 1793, present him as a poet of place in these two senses—Lake District devotee and wanderer. His first publication was called *An Evening Walk* ('Addressed to a Young Lady, from the Lakes of the North of England') and the next *Descriptive Sketches* ('Taken during a Pedestrian Tour in the Alps').

Today the Lake District is still, perhaps more strongly than ever, steeped in Wordsworth's presence. His childhood, schoolboy, and adult homes are preserved, three of them open to the public and seen by thousands each year instead of by hundreds, as in his day. The place names we find throughout his poetry—Grasmere,

Skiddaw, Dungeon Ghyll Force, the River Duddon—are the names still on the maps, part of the daily speech of shepherds, mountaineers, and tourists. And our collective sense of the spirit of the place—whether we know it or not and whether we have even read Wordsworth or not—is to some extent the result of Wordsworth's poetry. His excellent travel book, *Guide to the Lakes*, although less well known than his poetry, tells us not only where to look but how to see. The poems, on the other hand, say little about looking but a great deal more about seeing. A naïve clergyman, according to Matthew Arnold's story, professed great admiration of the *Guide* and asked Wordsworth if he had, by any chance, written anything else. He had indeed. No other great poet has influenced our consciousness of an English place as much as Wordsworth has done of the Lake District; no other has written so extensively, perceptively, and fruitfully about a particular landscape; and no other has devoted so much attention to travellers.

In 'The Brothers' it is not Wordsworth but rather his character, 'the homely Priest of Ennerdale', who takes a dim view of tourists:

> 'These Tourists, heaven preserve us! needs must live
> A profitable life: some glance along,
> Rapid and gay, as if the earth were air,
> And they were butterflies to wheel about
> Long as the summer lasted: some, as wise,
> Perched on the forehead of a jutting crag,
> Pencil in hand and book upon the knee,
> Will look and scribble, scribble on and look,
> Until a man might travel twelve stout miles,
> Or reap an acre of his neighbour's corn.
> But, for that moping Son of Idleness,
> Why can he tarry *yonder?*—In our church-yard
> Is neither epitaph nor monument,
> Tombstone nor name—only the turf we tread
> And a few natural graves.'

He is judging, as he comes to realize, 'most unkindly'. It happens that the Stranger he is eyeing has brought something with him that makes even the bare churchyard, without a single monument, a place of impassioned interest to him, for it is where his brother is buried. The Priest is wrong not only about the Stranger, who is in fact a native, but also about travellers. Some may of course be butterflies or sober scribblers, but the genuine traveller, in Wordsworth's view, is not classifiable as one of various types of 'Sons of Idleness'. The traveller, like the Brother, brings something to a spot—whether it be to Ennerdale's churchyard, Blea Tarn, or Helvellyn—and receives something from it. 'After all,' he wrote in the *Guide*, 'it is upon the *mind* which a traveller brings along with him that his acquisitions, whether of pleasure or profit, must principally depend.' Far from idleness, travel is an action, or rather an interaction between two living things, the traveller and the landscape. For Wordsworth the landscape *lives:* that belief, knowledge, act of imagination—call it what you will—underlies both his poetry about place and his travel writing.

Wordsworth was a confirmed traveller, not only in his youth, but for most of the fifty years after he went back to the Lake District as home. He explored the Lakes thoroughly, often walking thirty and more miles a day, as poet, traveller, Stamp Distributor, or some combination of them. He made various excursions to Scotland, several to the Continent, and many visits to London and other places in England and in Wales. '*Books*', he said of Southey, 'were in fact *his passion;* and *wandering*, I can with truth affirm, was *mine.* . . . Had I been born in a class which would have deprived me of what is called a liberal education, it is not unlikely that, being strong in body, I should have taken to a way of life such as that in which my Pedlar [in *The Excursion*] passed the greater part of his days' (I.F.). Walking for him was not just a personal passion; it was a public passion. He championed public footpaths with a spirit that should warm the hearts of modern walkers and conservationists. Travelling with Coleridge's nephew, John Taylor Coleridge, to a social gathering at Lowther Castle in 1836, he walked to a friend's house through private, enclosed property. The Hon. Mr Justice Coleridge reported his qualms and the aftermath:

I remember well, asking him if we were not trespassing on private pleasure-grounds here. He said, no; the walks had, indeed, been inclosed, but he remembered them open to the public, and he always went through them when he chose. At Lowther, we found among the visitors, the late Lord W——; and describing our walk, *he* made the same observation, that we had been trespassing; but Wordsworth maintained his point with somewhat more warmth than I either liked, or could well account for. But afterwards, when we were alone, he told me he had purposely answered Lord W—— stoutly and warmly, because he had done a similar thing with regard to some grounds in the neighbourhood of Penrith, and excluded the people of Penrith from walking where they had always enjoyed the right before. He had evidently a pleasure in vindicating these rights, and seemed to think it a duty.

(Grosart, iii. 425)

His *Guide to the Lakes*, too, is a public-spirited undertaking—informative, eloquent, full of love for its subject, and addressed to the reader bringing to the Lakes a mind and a heart, as well as wheels and a pair of legs. He was perhaps the first person and certainly the first writer to take a long-range view of the beauty of the Lakes. He wrote his *Guide*, he said, from 'a wish to preserve the native beauty of this delightful district' and he concluded the book in 1810 with the remarkably early and prescient notion that the Lake District is 'a sort of national property'. This wish and prophecy the National Trust, the National Park, and others now work at fulfilling.

It is then much to be wished, that a better taste should prevail among these new proprietors; and, as they cannot be expected to leave things to themselves, that skill and knowledge should prevent unnecessary deviations from that path of simplicity and beauty along which, without design and unconsciously, their humble predecessors have moved. In this wish the author will be joined by persons of pure taste throughout the whole island, who, by their visits (often repeated) to the Lakes in the North of England, testify that they deem the district a sort of national property, in which every man has a right and interest who has an eye to perceive and a heart to enjoy.

(*Prose Works*, ii. 224–5)

The way we perceive the Lake District's native beauty is now different from how Gray and his relatively few fellow-travellers perceived it over two centuries ago, and not the least important difference is that it is now Wordsworth Country. Wordsworth, along with other poets and painters, has led us to see landscapes in different ways, and this is especially true of the Lakes where and about which many of Wordsworth's poems were written. He said that genius in the arts widens 'the sphere of sensibility'. That is precisely what his poems have done. Considering particular poems that Wordsworth wrote about particular places will, I hope, help the eye to perceive and the heart to enjoy the poetry, the landscape, and the connections between them.

PART I

Poems and Places

O Soul of Nature! that, by laws divine
Sustained and governed, still dost overflow
With an impassioned life, what feeble ones
Walk on this earth! how feeble have I been
When thou wert in thy strength! . . .—giving way
To a comparison of scene with scene,
Bent overmuch on superficial things,
Pampering myself with meagre novelties
Of colour and proportion; to the moods
Of time and season, to the moral power,
The affections and the spirit of the place,
Insensible. . . .
In truth, the degradation . . . was transient; I had known
Too forcibly, too early in my life,
Visitings of imaginative power
For this to last: I shook the habit off
Entirely and for ever, and again
In Nature's presence stood, as now I stand,
A sensitive being, a *creative* soul.

The Prelude, xii. 102–207

i. The Waggoner and Other Travellers

1

From Ambleside to Keswick[1]

In a draft for a travel book which he never published, Wordsworth imagined a group of travellers stopping at the Salutation Inn in Ambleside for fresh horses and for information from the innkeeper about the local sights:

'From Ambleside to Keswick', explains the bustling leader of a party of Tourists, glancing his eye carelessly on the map in his hand or casting a look towards the clouds for information concerning the state of the weather, 'is how far?'

'Sixteen miles.'

'Is there any thing worthy of notice on the road?'

'Nothing but what all Travellers see as they pass along'—will probably be the answer of mine host of the Salutation if the question be asked at the height of the season and he is anxious to have his horses back again for a fresh job. The Post boy will confirm the asseveration if necessary, it being a point of feeling with him to hate all stoppages for which he does not receive extra pay.

'But are there not some celebrated Waterfalls not far from the road?'

'Oh yes, Sir, I had forgotten them', replies the veracious informant, apparently thankful to be set right. 'You must alight in the Village of Rydal and they may be seen in half an hour.'

That half hour is given to the purpose, for usage and fashion require it. For the rest of the journey the Party are contented with what they can collect by their eyes—some from the barouche box, others from their seat in the open Landau, with occasional upstandings upon especial summons, or with the presentations through the windows of a close Chariot, as the several vehicles are whirled along at the rate of 7 miles an hour.[2]

[1] Map on p. 198.

[2] I have edited the passage, especially the punctuation, and omitted a part. The manuscript version may be found in *Prose Works*, ii. 340n–41n.

'THIRLMERE BRIDGE, LOOKING NORTH, CUMBERLAND'. This view looks from Armboth across the old causeway, now under more than fifty feet of water, since Thirlmere was made a reservoir. Great How is in the centre, Raven Crag at the far left, and Helvellyn at the right.

'Whirled along at the rate of 7 miles an hour'! What would the poet think of tourists trying to see the Lake District in modern close Chariots at the rate of 40 to 60 miles an hour? The rate that constitutes *whirling* to Wordsworth seems a snail's pace to us, offering a glimpse of the difference between his age and ours. We have made stunning progress in our ability to whirl faster, but at the risk of seeing even less than the bustling and duped tourists at the Salutation. The road that they travelled, and that we still travel, is no ordinary road through pleasant scenery: 'A more interesting tract of country is scarcely any where to be seen, than the road between Ambleside and Keswick', Wordsworth wrote in his *Guide to the Lakes*, and he did not make such claims idly.

Wordsworth's sister, Dorothy, knew what was of interest along this road: she walked. On a Sunday in February 1802, she left Dove Cottage for an evening stroll over White Moss. In less than a mile she started down the hill toward Rydal Water and met a group of travellers struggling up a hill that we can now glide up effortlessly. She stopped to watch, for travellers at that time were by no means abundant and negotiating the hill up White Moss was by no means easy.

About 20 yards above glowworm Rock [B][3] I met a Carman, a Highlander I suppose, with 4 carts, the first 3 belonging to himself, the last evidently to a man and his family who had joined company with him and who I guessed to be Potters. The carman was cheering his horses and talking to a little lass about 10 years of age who seemed to make him her companion. She ran to the Wall and took up a large stone to support the wheel of one of his carts and ran on before with it in her arms to be ready for him. . . . There was a wildness in her whole figure, not the wildness of a Mountain lass but a *Road* lass, a traveller from her Birth, who had wanted neither food nor clothes. Her Mother followed the last cart with a lovely child, perhaps about a year old, at her Back and a good-looking girl about 15 years old walked beside her. All the children were like the mother. She had a very fresh complexion, but she was blown with fagging up the hill with the steepness of the hill and the Bairn that she carried. Her husband was helping the horse to drag the cart up by pushing it with his Shoulder.[4]

---

[3] The capital letters in brackets refer to the maps and guides in Part II. See pp. 198 ff.

[4] *Journals of Dorothy Wordsworth*, ed. Mary Moorman (1971), p. 91.

Wordsworth had written his description of tourists in their
barouche, landau, and chariot before 1810, when such things were
still rare in the Lakes. Indeed, any wheeled vehicles, except the
carts that Dorothy describes, were rare. The road was built in the
1770s as a turnpike, with a toll gate at Town Head, but it was used
mostly by pedestrians and pack animals. In 1801 Dorothy noted in
her journal, 'Today a chaise passed'—an unusual event. Within the
next decade, however, travel to the Lakes increased, and in 1811 a
regular coach service passed through Grasmere: the 'Good Intent',
a coach holding four passengers, stopped three times a week on its
way between Kendal and Whitehaven. Scheduled whirling, though
to us in slow motion.

Even in that first decade, however, when the pace was necessarily
slow, the Wordsworths were by no means isolated; they received
mail, fuel, and merchandise by cart. Near the end of 1805,
Wordsworth sent a copy of *The Prelude* to be available for Coleridge
to read when he returned from Malta, but it fell off the carrier's cart
and was not found until late January, 'soaked with rain'. Perhaps
this episode partly triggered the writing of Wordsworth's splendid
comic poem *The Waggoner*, the first version of which was 'thrown
off under a lively impulse of feeling' during the first two weeks of
January 1806. It is Wordsworth's most thoroughly topographical
poem, covering the high road through the heart of Wordsworth
Country and relating in four cantos the story of Benjamin—no
ordinary carrier with a one-horse cart, but an expert driver of an
eight-horse wagon team. 'The characters and story', the poet told
Miss Fenwick, are 'from fact.' Most carriers, no matter how much
they whipped a team, could not get a heavy wagon and eight horses
up the rough roads and steep hills between Ambleside and
Keswick. This is how Benjamin, walking by the side of his wagon,
manages the hill where Dorothy had watched the carman and potter
struggle with their carts:

> Along the banks of Rydal Mere
> He paces on, a trusty Guide,—
> Listen! you can scarcely hear!
> Hither he his course is bending;—
> Now he leaves the lower ground,
> And up the craggy hill ascending

Many a stop and stay he makes,
Many a breathing-fit he takes;—
Steep the way and wearisome,
Yet all the while his whip is dumb!

   The Horses have worked with right good-will,
And so have gained the top of the hill;
He was patient, they were strong,
And now they smoothly glide along,
Recovering breath, and pleased to win
The praises of mild Benjamin.

(i. 30–45)

Later, on the way up Dunmail Raise [G], Benjamin recalls to his team the time when another carrier had tried to get them up that slope, beating the horses which 'between rage and fear' could move no further.

As chance would have it, passing by
I saw you in that jeopardy:
A word from me was like a charm;
Ye pulled together with one mind;
And your huge burthen, safe from harm,
Moved like a vessel in the wind!

(i. 130–5)

'The fact of my . . . hero's getting the horses out of a great difficulty with a word, as related in the poem,' Wordsworth added in a note, 'was told me by an eye-witness.'

   Benjamin, alas, likes strong drink, and the road from Ambleside to Keswick is a series of temptations which jeopardize his job. The *horses* do not care:

   . . . this they know . . .
That Benjamin, with clouded brains,
Is worth the best with all their pains;
And, if they had a prayer to make,
The prayer would be that they may take
With him whatever comes in course,
The better fortune or the worse;
That no one else may have business near them,
And, drunk or sober, he may steer them.

(iii. 10–19)

But the master will not tolerate drunken drivers.[5] Benjamin's first temptation, now called Dove Cottage [C], proves to be easy enough: it had once been an inn (which is true of Dove Cottage, and the source of its name) but now was the home of a water-drinking bard—Wordsworth himself.

> For at the bottom of the brow,
> Where once the DOVE and OLIVE-BOUGH
> Offered a greeting of good ale
> To all who entered Grasmere Vale;
> And called on him who must depart
> To leave it with a jovial heart;
> There, where the DOVE and OLIVE-BOUGH
> Once hung, a Poet harbours now,
> A simple water-drinking Bard;
> Why need our Hero then (though frail
> His best resolves) be on his guard?
> He marches by, secure and bold;
> Yet while he thinks on times of old,
> It seems that all looks wondrous cold;
> He shrugs his shoulders, shakes his head,
> And, for the honest folk within,
> It is a doubt with Benjamin
> Whether they be alive or dead!
> *Here* is no danger,—none at all!
>
> (i. 52–70)

Just one mile beyond it, however, is a more serious temptation, with a sign crudely painted by the owner (now, Wordsworth lamented in a note, 'supplanted by a professional production') [D].

> Who does not know the famous SWAN?
> Object uncouth! and yet our boast,
> For it was painted by the Host;
> His own conceit the figure planned,
> 'Twas coloured all by his own hand;
> And that frail Child of thirsty clay,
> Of whom I sing this rustic lay,

[5] The owner of the wagon and horses that actually travelled this route was probably William Jackson, Coleridge's landlord at Greta Hall in Keswick.

> Could tell with self-dissatisfaction
> Quaint stories of the bird's attraction!
>
> (i. 88–96)

Benjamin triumphs, the wagon rolls past, and the team begins the 'long ascent of Dunmail-raise'.

Soon the sky turns black and a storm appears, with a lurid light

> Above Helm-crag [E]—a streak half dead,
> A burning of portentous red;
> And near that lurid light, full well
> The ASTROLOGER, sage Sidrophel,
> Where at his desk and book he sits,
> Puzzling aloft his curious wits;
> He whose domain is held in common
> With no one but the ANCIENT WOMAN,
> Cowering beside her rifted cell,
> As if intent on magic spell;—
> Dread pair that, spite of wind and weather,
> Still sit upon Helm-crag together!
>
> (i. 168–79)

With much effort they reach the pass, where the last king of Cumberland is said to have been killed in battle and buried under the huge cairn [G]:

> And now have reached that pile of stones,
> Heaped over brave King Dunmail's bones,
> He who had once supreme command,
> Last king of rocky Cumberland;
> His bones, and those of all his Power,
> Slain here in a disastrous hour!
>
> (i. 209–14)

Here the good Benjamin allows a woman and child to take refuge on his wagon under a blanket; the husband, a sailor with a model of Nelson's ship *Vanguard* mounted on wheels, follows behind with his ass. At midnight they pass Wythburn Chapel [H]:

> IF Wytheburne's modest House of prayer,
> As lowly as the lowliest dwelling,
> Had, with its belfry's humble stock,

> A little pair that hang in air,
> Been mistress also of a clock,
> (And one, too, not in crazy plight)
> Twelve strokes that clock would have been telling
> Under the brow of old Helvellyn. . . .
>
> (ii. 1–8)

In those days, not far beyond the Chapel was an inn, The Cherry Tree [1]. The lights, sound of music and gaiety, and the Sailor's urgings prove too much for the carrier, and 'soon, of all the happy there, | Our Travellers are the happiest pair'.

Two hours and many tankards of ale later, the pair emerges, splendidly drunk, singing 'many a snatch of jovial song' as their entourage moves along Thirlmere—Benjamin, the Sailor, eight horses, a wagon with its cargo plus the sailor's wife and child, the *Vanguard* on wheels, and the sailor's ass, now tethered to the wagon next to the wagon-owner's dog, which receives a humiliating wound from the ass's hoof. They have one more steep hill, Castlerigg, to surmount before reaching Keswick. But by the time they are at 'Castrigg's naked steep', Benjamin is 'Sickening into thoughtful quiet', 'Drooping is he, his step is dull'. Worse yet, at the top of the hill is his master, the wagon-owner,

> Who from Keswick has pricked forth,
> Sour and surly as the north.

Poor Benjamin,

> When duty of that day was o'er,
> Laid down his whip—and served no more.—
> Nor could the waggon long survive,
> When Benjamin had ceased to drive:
> It lingered on;—guide after guide
> Ambitiously the office tried;
> But each unmanageable hill
> Called for *his* patience and *his* skill;—
> And sure it is that through this night,
> And what the morning brought to light,

> Two losses had we to sustain,
> We lost both WAGGONER and WAIN![6]
>
> (iv. 185–96)

The poet's Muse, who is responsible for making this sad tale a great deal of fun, does not accompany Benjamin to the bitter end but leaves him at the end of Thirlmere and wanders into St. John's Vale, looking back at

> the awful form
> Of Raven-crag—black as a storm—
> Glimmering through the twilight pale;
> And Ghimmer-crag, his tall twin brother,
> Each peering forth to meet the other. . . .
>
> (iv. 18–22)

When morning comes she sees, with 'her unsuspecting eye',

> Red, green, and blue; a moment's sight!
> For Skiddaw-top with rosy light
> Is touched—

and then flies up to the ridge of Nathdale Fell [L], from where she sees Threlkeld and 'beyond that hamlet small | The ruined towers of Threlkeld-hall . . . at Blancathara's rugged feet' [N,O]. Looking in the other direction, she sees the bizarre entourage making its way up the last steep hill to meet the 'moody man' who has sallied forth to seal Benjamin's fate.

The poem is a wonderful comic *tour de force*, reminiscent of the spirit of Burns in the story and characters of Benjamin, his tolerant beasts, and his outlandish companion, the striking descriptions of such things as the June thunderstorm or the pair's intoxicated visions, and the good-humoured, mock-heroic spirit in which the

---

[6] Wordsworth appended this note to the poem: 'Several years after the event that forms the subject of the poem, in company with my friend, the late Mr Coleridge, I happened to fall in with the person to whom the name of Benjamin is given. Upon our expressing regret that we had not, for a long time, seen upon the road either him or his waggon, he said—"They could not do without me; and as to the man who was put in my place, no good could come out of him; he was a man of no *ideas*."'

narrative is told.[7] It is suffused with Wordsworth's sense of particular places along the road from Ambleside to Keswick, making it unimaginable apart from them. One thing that stands in the way of its being more widely appreciated is the abundance of local allusion. Wordsworth in fact hesitated to publish the poem for this reason, but his friend Charles Lamb—no Lake District dweller but a Londoner by birth and nature—urged him to it. Hence the Dedication in 1819 to Lamb, in which Wordsworth hoped that 'since the localities on which the Poem partly depends did not prevent its being interesting to you, it may prove acceptable to others'. Lamb was delighted with the poem and with its 'spirit of beautiful tolerance'. It was a favourite, too, with Wordsworth himself. Coleridge's nephew told of Wordsworth's reading much of the poem to him. 'It seems a very favourite poem of his, and he read me splendid descriptions from it. He said his object in it had not been understood. It was a play of the fancy on a domestic incident and lowly character: he wished by the opening descriptive lines to put his reader into the state of mind in which he wished it to be read. If he failed in doing that, he wished him to lay it down.'[8]

On that occasion Wordsworth also read a suppressed passage of the poem which he later added in a note—the passage about the famous Rock of Names [J], an actual rock on the Thirlmere road where Coleridge, coming south from Keswick, often met the Wordsworth group, coming north from Grasmere. Into the face of the rock they carved their initials: W.W., M.H., D.W., S.T.C., J.W., S. H., for William Wordsworth, Mary Hutchinson, Dorothy Wordsworth, Samuel Taylor Coleridge, John Wordsworth, and Sara Hutchinson. The rock was, Justice Coleridge said, 'about a mile beyond Wythburn Chapel', and therefore half a mile beyond The Cherry Tree, where the eight patient horses waited while Benjamin drank. When he and the Sailor emerged and took the road again, with 'throat on fire', they needed a drink of water. The Rock of Names had, as Benjamin well knew, a stream of spring water running down its surface:

[7] The entire poem is printed in *PW*, ii. 176–205, 499–501, and in the Cornell Wordsworth, *Benjamin the Waggoner*, edited by Paul F. Betz (1981).

[8] Grosart, iii. 429–30.

But Benjamin, in his vexation,
Possesses inward consolation;
He knows his ground, and hopes to find
A spot with all things to his mind,
An upright mural block of stone,
Moist with pure water trickling down.
A slender spring; but kind to man
It is, a true Samaritan;
Close to the highway, pouring out
Its offering from a chink or spout;
Whence all, howe'er athirst, or drooping
With toil, may drink, and without stooping.

Cries Benjamin 'Where is it, where?
Voice it hath none, but must be near.'
—A star, declining towards the west,
Upon the watery surface threw
Its image tremulously imprest,
That just marked out the object and withdrew,
Right welcome service!

The passage about the rock itself is Wordsworth's tribute to those he loved best and to the 'monumental power' of a spot cherished by them all:

Rock of Names!
Light is the strain, but not unjust
To Thee and Thy memorial-trust
That once seemed only to express
Love that was love in idleness;
Tokens, as year hath followed year
How changed, alas, in character!
For they were graven on thy smooth breast
By hands of those my soul loved best;
Meek women, men as true and brave
As ever went to a hopeful grave:
Their hands and mine, when side by side
With kindred zeal and mutual pride,
We worked until the Initials took
Shapes that defied a scornful look.—
Long as for us a genial feeling
Survives, or one in need of healing,

> The power, dear Rock, around thee cast,
> Thy monumental power, shall last
> For me and mine! O thought of pain,
> That would impair it or profane!
> Take all in kindness then, as said
> With a staid heart but playful head;
> And fail not Thou, loved Rock! to keep
> Thy charge when we are laid asleep.

Who could 'impair it or profane' in the face of the poet's plea? The Local Authority kindly skirted King Dunmail's pile of rocks when a new road was built over the Raise, but the Manchester Water Authority blasted the Rock of Names in the 1880s to make way for a new road and to gather rubble for the Thirlmere dam. Canon H. D. Rawnsley, his efforts to save it having proved fruitless, did the next best thing: he gathered up the pieces, cemented together what he could salvage, and placed it above the new road, in the hope that it would cast a fragment, at least, of its former monumental power. Not even he—and certainly not Wordsworth—could have guessed at what speeds we now whirl beneath it.

2

Bainriggs and White Moss[1]

The vagrants who camped in the White Moss slate quarry, the waggoners, the pedlars, the soldiers, and the tourists in search of the picturesque all travelled from Rydal to Grasmere by going up the road just beyond the quarry, there being no level road through Bainriggs in the early nineteenth century. Some of the travellers became the subjects of Wordsworth's poems—Benjamin the Waggoner, the mother and boys of 'The Beggars', even the tourists:

[1] Map on p. 204.

'GRASMERE'. In Wordsworth's time, the main road passed through this section of Grasmere, called Town End. The slate slabs on the right formed part of the fence in front of Dove Cottage. Helm Crag is in the centre.

ON SEEING SOME TOURISTS OF THE LAKES
PASS BY READING

A PRACTICE VERY COMMON

What waste in the labour of Chariot and Steed!
For this came ye hither? is this your delight?
There are twenty-four letters and these ye can read;
But Nature's ten thousand are Blanks in your sight.
Then throw by your Books, and the study begin;
Or sleep, and be blameless, and wake at your Inn!

Wordsworth, an ardent tourist himself, did not disapprove of
tourists in general—only those who refused to look. Hence perhaps
his frequent dramatic technique of halting travellers—of forcing
them to stop and see something they are about to pass by without
noticing. Part way up the hill past the quarry is a large rock or crag
[A] full of interest to Wordsworth. On one occasion the poet saw the
rock covered with ice: 'The monument of ice here spoken of I
observed while ascending the middle road of the three ways that
[now, in 1843] lead from Rydal to Grasmere. It was on my right
hand, and my eyes were upon it when it fell, as told in these lines'
(I.F.). The traveller—who is told to throw by his books in the
above verses—is here called upon to halt, but then to read aloud, to
hear of the connection between this rock and nature, fancy, and
Fortune.

INSCRIBED UPON A ROCK

Pause, Traveller! whosoe'er thou be
Whom chance may lead to this retreat,
Where silence yields reluctantly
Even to the fleecy straggler's bleat;

Give voice to what my hand shall trace,
And fear not lest an idle sound
Of words unsuited to the place
Disturb its solitude profound.

I saw this Rock, while vernal air
Blew softly o'er the russet heath,

Uphold a Monument as fair
As church or abbey furnisheth.

Unsullied did it meet the day,
Like marble, white, like ether, pure;
As if, beneath, some hero lay,
Honoured with costliest sepulture.

My fancy kindled as I gazed;
And, ever as the sun shone forth,
The flattered structure glistened, blazed,
And seemed the proudest thing on earth.

But frost had reared the gorgeous Pile
Unsound as those which Fortune builds—
To undermine with secret guile,
Sapped by the very beam that gilds.

And, while I gazed, with sudden shock
Fell the whole Fabric to the ground;
And naked left this dripping Rock,
With shapeless ruin spread around!

The rock, which the Wordsworths called Glow-worm Rock 'from the number of glow-worms we have often seen hanging on it' (I.F.), is mentioned in Dorothy's journal, in April 1802, when she, William, and Coleridge 'all stood to look at Glowworm Rock—a primrose that grew there, and just looked out on the Road from its own sheltered bower'. Years later Wordsworth wrote 'The Primrose of the Rock', which begins,

A Rock there is whose homely front
   The passing traveller slights;
Yet there the glow-worms hang their lamps,
   Like stars, at various heights;
And one coy Primrose to that Rock
   The vernal breeze invites.

Over fifteen years later, 'The Pilgrim's Dream, or The Star and the Glow-worm' was suggested at this spot. 'I distinctly recollect the evening on which these verses were suggested in 1818', he told Miss Fenwick. 'I was on the road between Rydal and Grasmere where glow-worms abound. A star was shining above the ridge of Loughrigg Fell just opposite.'

The naming of rocks seems to be a part of Wordsworth's passion for seeing rocks as living things: 'Close clings to earth the living rock, | Though threatening still to fall', he writes of Glow-worm Rock. In the poem 'To Joanna', Joanna's Rock is named after the third Hutchinson sister; the narrator carves her name 'deep in the living stone'. The other Hutchinson sisters had their rocks, too: Sara's Rock and Sara's Crag were other names for the Rock of Names, and Mary Point and Sara Point [B] were the 'two heath-clad Rocks' in Bainriggs Wood. Mary arrived for a visit to Dove Cottage in early April 1800, four months after William and Dorothy had moved in, and in August Dorothy's journal refers to 'Mary Point'. Sara came later, in November, and sometime after that the other point was named for her. But it was not until much later—1845, near the end of his poetic career—that Wordsworth wrote a poem about the spot. His wife Mary was still alive, but Sara had died in 1835. The poem looks back to the Dove Cottage days, when the 'two adventurous Sisters' climbed the hills, then to the present when 'Death's cold hand' has intervened, and on to the future survival of their 'pure joy in nature'.

> Forth from a jutting ridge, around whose base
> Winds our deep Vale, two heath-clad Rocks ascend
> In fellowship, the loftiest of the pair
> Rising to no ambitious height; yet both,
> O'er lake and stream, mountain and flowery mead,
> Unfolding prospects fair as human eyes
> Ever beheld. Up-led with mutual help,
> To one or other brow of those twin Peaks
> Were two adventurous Sisters wont to climb,
> And took no note of the hour while thence they gazed,
> The blooming heath their couch, gazed, side by side,
> In speechless admiration. I, a witness
> And frequent sharer of their calm delight
> With thankful heart, to either Eminence
> Gave the baptismal name each Sister bore.
> Now are they parted, far as Death's cold hand
> Hath power to part the Spirits of those who love

As they did love. Ye kindred Pinnacles—
That, while the generations of mankind
Follow each other to their hiding-place
In time's abyss, are privileged to endure
Beautiful in yourselves, and richly graced
With like command of beauty—grant your aid
For MARY's humble, SARAH's silent claim,
That their pure joy in nature may survive
From age to age in blended memory.

The 'privileged' endurance of Sara Point after her death makes landscape for the Wordsworths part of a living memory, 'that bond betwixt the living and the dead', as Dorothy said of their trips from Rydal to Grasmere, where the poet's two children lay in the churchyard. The named landscape also links people present with those absent. Sara was not at Dove Cottage as often as Mary, but the many spots named for her must have made her in some sense a constant presence. Another vantage point was named after her; it is nearer Dove Cottage, and, unlike Sara Point, still offers a beautiful and extensive view. In late October 1802 Dorothy and Mary walked along the road and paused at a gate [C]: 'I was much affected when I stood upon the 2nd bar of Sara's Gate', Dorothy wrote. 'The lake was perfectly still, the Sun shone on Hill and vale, the distant Birch trees looked like large golden Flowers. Nothing else in colour was distinct and separate but all the beautiful colours seemed to be melted into one another, and joined together in one mass so that there were no differences though an endless variety when one tried to find it out. The Fields were of one sober yellow brown.' Long before the Wordsworths arrived at Grasmere this gate had another name—the Wishing Gate—which survives today. Wordsworth loved traditions as much as family names; in this instance the tradition gave rise to a poem partly in an eighteenth-century style, since the poet is meditating on themes of hoping and wishing that fascinated Pope, Gray, and Johnson. In the end, however, the spirit of this particular place leads the poet to a new view of wishing which celebrates the superstitions of the heart.

THE WISHING-GATE

In the vale of Grasmere, by the side of the old highway leading to Ambleside, is a gate, which, time out of mind, has been called the Wishing-gate, from a belief that wishes formed or indulged there have a favourable issue.

Hope rules a land for ever green:
All powers that serve the bright-eyed Queen
   Are confident and gay;
Clouds at her bidding disappear;
Points she to aught?—the bliss draws near,
   And Fancy smooths the way.

Not such the land of Wishes—there
Dwell fruitless day-dreams, lawless prayer,
   And thoughts with things at strife;
Yet how forlorn, should *ye* depart,
Ye superstitions of the *heart*,
   How poor, were human life!

When magic lore abjured its might,
Ye did not forfeit one dear right,
   One tender claim abate;
Witness this symbol of your sway,
Surviving near the public way,
   The rustic Wishing-gate!

Enquire not if the faery race
Shed kindly influence on the place,
   Ere northward they retired;
If here a warrior left a spell,
Panting for glory as he fell;
   Or here a saint expired.

Enough that all around is fair,
Composed with Nature's finest care,
   And in her fondest love—
Peace to embosom and content—
To overawe the turbulent,
   The selfish to reprove.

Yea! even the Stranger from afar,
Reclining on this moss grown bar,

Unknowing, and unknown,
The infection of the ground partakes,
Longing for his Beloved—who makes
    All happiness her own.

Then why should conscious Spirits fear
The mystic stirrings that are here,
    The ancient faith disclaim?
The local Genius ne'er befriends
Desires whose course in folly ends,
    Whose just reward is shame.

Smile if thou wilt, but not in scorn,
If some, by ceaseless pains outworn,
    Here crave an easier lot;
If some have thirsted to renew
A broken vow, or bind a true,
    With firmer, holier knot.

And not in vain, when thoughts are cast
Upon the irrevocable past,
    Some Penitent sincere
May for a worthier future sigh,
While trickles from his downcast eye
    No unavailing tear.

The Worldling, pining to be freed
From turmoil, who would turn or speed
    The current of his fate,
Might stop before this favoured scene,
At Nature's call, nor blush to lean
    Upon the Wishing-gate.

The Sage, who feels how blind, how weak
Is man, though loth such help to *seek*,
    Yet, passing, here might pause,
And thirst for insight to allay
Misgiving, while the crimson day
    In quietness withdraws;

Or when the church-clock's knell profound
To Time's first step across the bound
  Of midnight makes reply;
Time pressing on with starry crest,
To filial sleep upon the breast
  Of dread eternity.

At a later time, Wordsworth wrote a companion poem, 'The Wishing-Gate Destroyed', also accompanied by a note of explanation: 'Having been told, upon what I thought good authority that this gate had been destroyed, and the opening, where it hung, walled up, I gave vent immediately to my feelings in these stanzas. But going to the place some time after, I found, with much delight, my old favourite unmolested.'

Just across the road from the Wishing Gate was John's Grove [D], named for William and Dorothy's brother, the first of their many visitors at Dove Cottage. They had been in the cottage only about a month when John arrived at the end of January 1800. Since the family had been split up and John had become a seaman, they did not know him well, but during his nine-month stay at Dove Cottage the brothers and sister formed a close and affectionate bond. He was, William said, 'a Poet in everything but words'. Although a successful naval man with prospects of great wealth (he was promoted to Captain while at Dove Cottage), John's wish was to serve William, who, he felt, was destined to leave something far greater for posterity. He hoped to make his fortune early in life, leave the sea, and settle in Grasmere, perhaps married to one of the Hutchinson sisters. That was not to be; when he left Grasmere on 29 September, he never returned.

In those nine months, however, he came to love the fireside at Dove Cottage, the other visitors—like Coleridge and the Hutchinsons—who came to it, and the walks around Grasmere vale. William associated him with the fir grove in Ladywood:

my favourite grove,
Tossing in sunshine its dark boughs aloft,
As if to make the strong wind visible,
Wakes in me agitations like its own,
A spirit friendly to the Poet's task . . .

              (*The Prelude*, vii. 44–8)

The story of how this grove came to be named after John is told in one of the 'Poems on the Naming of Places'. 'The grove still exists,' Wordsworth told Miss Fenwick, 'but the plantation has been walled in, and is not so accessible as when my brother John wore the path in the manner here described. The grove was a favourite haunt with us all while we lived at Town-End.'

> When, to the attractions of the busy world
> Preferring studious leisure, I had chosen
> A habitation in this peaceful Vale,
> Sharp season followed of continual storm
> In deepest winter; and, from week to week,
> Pathway, and lane, and public road, were clogged
> With frequent showers of snow. Upon a hill,
> At a short distance from my cottage, stands
> A stately Fir-grove, whither I was wont
> To hasten, for I found, beneath the roof
> Of that perennial shade, a cloistral place
> Of refuge, with an unincumbered floor.
> Here, in safe covert, on the shallow snow,
> And, sometimes, on a speck of visible earth,
> The redbreast near me hopped; nor was I loth
> To sympathize with vulgar coppice birds
> That, for protection from the nipping blast,
> Hither repaired.—A single beech-tree grew
> Within this grove of firs! and, on the fork
> Of that one beech, appeared a thrush's nest;
> A last year's nest, conspicuously built
> At such small elevation from the ground
> As gave sure sign that they, who in that house
> Of nature and of love had made their home
> Amid the fir-trees, all the summer long
> Dwelt in a tranquil spot. And oftentimes
> A few sheep, stragglers from some mountain-flock,
> Would watch my motions with suspicious stare,
> From the remotest outskirts of the grove,—
> Some nook where they had made their final stand,
> Huddling together from two fears—the fear
> Of me and of the storm. Full many an hour
> Here did I lose. But in this grove the trees
> Had been so thickly planted, and had thriven

In such perplexed and intricate array,
That vainly did I seek, beneath their stems,
A length of open space, where to and fro
My feet might move without concern or care;
And, baffled thus, though earth from day to day
Was fettered, and the air by storm disturbed,
I ceased the shelter to frequent,—and prized,
Less than I wished to prize, that calm recess.

The snows dissolved, and genial Spring returned
To clothe the fields with verdure. Other haunts
Meanwhile were mine; till one bright April day,
By chance retiring from the glare of noon
To this forsaken covert, there I found
A hoary pathway traced between the trees,
And winding on with such an easy line
Along a natural opening, that I stood
Much wondering how I could have sought in vain
For what was now so obvious. To abide,
For an allotted interval of ease,
Under my cottage-roof, had gladly come
From the wild sea a cherished Visitant;
And with the sight of this same path—begun,
Begun and ended, in the shady grove,
Pleasant conviction flashed upon my mind
That, to this opportune recess allured,
He had surveyed it with a finer eye,
A heart more wakeful; and had worn the track
By pacing here, unwearied and alone,
In that habitual restlessness of foot
That haunts the Sailor measuring o'er and o'er
His short domain upon the vessel's deck,
While she pursues her course through the dreary sea.

When thou hadst quitted Esthwaite's pleasant shore,
And taken thy first leave of those green hills
And rocks that were the play-ground of thy youth,
Year followed year, my Brother! and we two,
Conversing not, knew little in what mould
Each other's mind was fashioned; and at length,
When once again we met in Grasmere Vale,

Between us there was little other bond
Than common feelings of fraternal love.
But thou, a School-boy, to the sea hadst carried
Undying recollections; Nature there
Was with thee; she, who loved us both, she still
Was with thee; and even so didst thou become
A *silent* Poet; from the solitude
Of the vast sea didst bring a watchful heart
Still couchant, an inevitable ear,
And an eye practised like a blind man's touch.
—Back to the joyless Ocean thou art gone;
Nor from this vestige of thy musing hours
Could I withhold thy honoured name,—and now
I love the fir-grove with a perfect love.
Thither do I withdraw when cloudless suns
Shine hot, or wind blows troublesome and strong;
And there I sit at evening, when the steep
Of Silver-how, and Grasmere's peaceful lake,
And one green island, gleam between the stems
Of the dark firs, a visionary scene!
And while I gaze upon the spectacle
Of clouded splendour, on this dream-like sight
Of solemn loveliness, I think on thee,
My Brother, and on all which thou hast lost.
Nor seldom, if I rightly guess, while Thou,
Muttering the verses which I muttered first
Among the mountains, through the midnight watch
Art pacing thoughtfully the vessel's deck
In some far region, here, while o'er my head,
At every impulse of the moving breeze,
The fir-grove murmurs with a sea-like sound,
Alone I tread this path;—for aught I know,
Timing my steps to thine; and, with a store
Of undistinguishable sympathies,
Mingling most earnest wishes for the day
When we, and others whom we love, shall meet
A second time, in Grasmere's happy Vale.

NOTE.—This wish was not granted; the lamented Person not long after perished by
shipwreck, in discharge of his duty as Commander of the Honourable East India Company's
Vessel, the Earl of Abergavenny. [W.W.]

On 29 April 1802—'a beautiful morning'—Dorothy recorded a walk with William: 'We . . . went to John's Grove, sat a while at first. Afterwards William lay, and I lay in the trench under the fence—he with his eyes shut and listening to the waterfalls and the Birds. There was no one waterfall above another—it was a sound of waters in the air—the voice of the air.' A few days later William began 'The Leech Gatherer', later published as 'Resolution and Independence'. The first stanza perhaps grew out of 'the voice of the air' that they heard in John's Grove.

> There was a roaring in the wind all night;
> The rain came heavily and fell in floods;
> But now the sun is rising calm and bright;
> The birds are singing in the distant woods;
> Over his own sweet voice the Stock-dove broods;
> The Jay makes answer as the Magpie chatters;
> And all the air is filled with pleasant noise of waters.

The poet's encounter with the old man gathering leeches was based on what a beggar had told them a year and a half earlier.[2] 'This old man I met a few hundred yards from my cottage at Town-End, Grasmere; and the account of him is taken from his own mouth.' The old man was not actually gathering leeches, though he had done it earlier in his life; now he was begging. Furthermore, he was not quite the character described in the poem. Wordsworth told Henry Crabb Robinson that he met the leech-gatherer 'near Grasmere, except that he gave to his poetic character powers of mind which his original did not possess'. Wordsworth met the man after he and Dorothy had accompanied a friend part of the way to Keswick and were returning home. Dorothy entered the meeting in her journal under 3 October 1803:

When Wm and I returned from accompanying Jones we met an old man almost double, he had on a coat thrown over his shoulders above his waistcoat and coat. Under this he carried a bundle and had an apron on and a night cap. His face was interesting. He had dark eyes and a long nose. John who afterwards met him at Wythburn took him for a Jew. He was of Scotch parents but had been born in the army. He had had a wife 'and a good woman and it pleased God to bless us with ten children'. All these

---

[2] Leeches were used for drawing blood, a common medical practice at the time.

were dead but one of whom he had not heard for many years, a sailor. His trade was to gather leeches, but now leeches are scarce and he had not strength for it. He lived by begging and was making his way to Carlisle where he should buy a few godly books to sell. He said leeches were very scarce partly owing to this dry season, but many years they have been scarce—he supposed it owing to their being much sought after, that they did not breed fast, and were of slow growth. Leeches were formerly 2/6 [per] 100; they are now 30/. He had been hurt in driving a cart, his leg broke his body driven over his skull fractured. He felt no pain till he recovered from his first insensibility. It was then late in the evening, when the light was just going away.

Sara Hutchinson was displeased by part of an early draft of the poem, which prompted Wordsworth to write an impassioned and fascinating defence of it in a letter. He pointed to the 'naked simplicity' of the old man and the 'feeling of spirituality or supernaturalness'. 'I then describe him,' the poet continued, 'whether ill or well is not for me to judge with perfect confidence, but this I can *confidently* affirm, that, though I believe God has given me a strong imagination, I cannot conceive a figure more impressive than that of an old Man like this, the survivor of a Wife and ten children, travelling alone among the mountains and all lonely places, carrying with him his own fortitude, and the necessities which an unjust state of society has entailed upon him. . . . Good God! Such a figure in such a place, a pious self-respecting, miserably infirm . . . Old Man telling such a tale!' (*Letters*, 14 June 1802).

Wordsworth is clearly thinking here of the man he met on the road ('the survivor of a Wife and ten children'), and that beggar had clearly suggested the leech-gatherer on the lonely moor: both were from Scotland; both were old, feeble, bent double, and 'had many hardships to endure'; both talked of the scarcity of leeches. But the leech-gatherer of the poem is a product of Wordsworth's 'strong imagination', prompted by his memory of the beggar: he is resolute and independent, not yet reduced to beggary but gathering leeches in a pond on the lonely moor—a character, perhaps, except for his powers of mind, like the beggar had once been, before Wordsworth met him. The poem, it is safe to say, would not have been written if William and Dorothy had not met the beggar on the road, but its dramatic action is altogether different from the event described in Dorothy's journal and its imaginative truth more powerful than the recorded facts.

Wordsworth's imagination transformed, not translated, an old beggar's tale into a poem about a leech-gatherer. But the imagination, Wordsworth would insist, is not only for making poems; it is also for bringing alive the world that one sees—for making an ordinary gate into a wishing gate or into Sara's Gate, and for making stone into living rock.

3

Greenhead Gill [1]

Wordsworth sometimes wrote at the same time of travellers and shepherds, two groups—distinct though they are—which frequent the mountains of the Lake District. In 'Michael' he tempts the first—those who follow 'the public way'—to hear about the second, 'a Shepherd, Michael was his name; | An old man, stout of heart, and strong of limb'. Can any foot traveller in the Grasmere area who is also an admirer of Wordsworth's poetry fail to take personally the 'you' in the opening lines of the poem?

> If from the public way you turn your steps
> Up the tumultuous brook of Green-head Ghyll,
> You will suppose that with an upright path
> Your feet must struggle; in such bold ascent
> The pastoral mountains front you, face to face.
> But, courage! for around that boisterous brook
> The mountains have all opened out themselves,
> And made a hidden valley of their own.
> No habitation can be seen; but they

[1] Map on p. 208.

'GRASMERE FROM TAIL END', or what is now called Dale End, on the west side of the lake. The gap is Dunmail Raise, with Helm Crag and Seat Sandal to the left and Seat Sandal to the right. The high knob on the ridge to the right of Seat Sandal is Stone Arthur ('There is an Eminence') and below it is the valley of Greenhead Gill ('Michael').

> Who journey thither find themselves alone
> With a few sheep, with rocks and stones, and kites
> That overhead are sailing in the sky.
> It is in truth an utter solitude;
> Nor should I have made mention of this Dell
> But for one object which you might pass by,
> Might see and notice not. Beside the brook
> Appears a straggling heap of unhewn stones!

Beginnings are sometimes deceiving, though. Looking at that boisterous brook as it runs by the Swan Inn, you may think that following it would be a hard, uphill struggle, but in truth it is an easy walk, since around an unexpected bend the mountains open up into a hidden valley. Likewise this poem seems at first to invite travellers from the public way to stop and listen, but it does not insist on halting travellers. There is no Ancient Mariner grabbing us, and no 'Pause, Traveller!' or 'Nay, Traveller! rest'. *If* you turn your steps up Greenhead Gill, you will find—well, not much: 'an utter solitude', and 'one object which you might pass by, | Might see and notice not'.

But if you are interested in stories 'unenriched with strange events', the poet has one 'not unfit . . . for the fireside, | Or for the summer shade'. It is not for everyone; it is a 'domestic tale', 'homely and rude', but he will tell it

> For the delight of a few natural hearts;
> And, with yet fonder feeling, for the sake
> Of youthful Poets, who among these hills
> Will be my second self when I am gone.

A fit audience, though few, will do for Wordsworth, as for Milton. Yet 'Michael' has proved to be one of Wordsworth's most popular poems, speaking with apparent simplicity of a few elemental affections—love, hope, and sorrow. There are more than a few natural hearts which are moved by Michael's story and take delight in it.

The first thing that we know about the composition of this poem is, appropriately, that Wordsworth walked up Greenhead Gill. Here is Dorothy's journal for 11 October 1800:

After Dinner we walked up Greenhead Gill in search of a sheepfold. . . . The colours of the mountains soft and rich, with orange fern—the Cattle pasturing upon the hill-tops Kites sailing in the sky above our heads—Sheep bleating and in lines and chains and patterns scattered over the mountains. They come down and feed on the little green islands in the beds of the torrents and so may be swept away.[2] The Sheepfold is falling away it is built nearly in the form of a heart unequally divided. Look down the brook and see the drops rise upwards and sparkle in the air, at the little falls the higher sparkles the tallest. We walked along the turf of the mountain till we came to a Cattle track—made by the cattle which come upon the hills. We drank tea at Mr Simpson's[3] returned at about nine—a fine mild night.

Wordsworth undertook this poem for the second volume of *Lyrical Ballads*, and it gave him a good deal of trouble, as evidenced by a few other entries in Dorothy's journal:

15 Oct.:   Wm again composed at the sheep-fold after dinner.
18 Oct.:   William worked all the morning at the Sheep-fold but in vain.
20 Oct.:   William worked in the morning at the sheep-fold.
21 Oct.:   Wm had been unsuccessful in the morning at the sheep-fold.
22 Oct.:   Wm composed without much success at the Sheepfold.

We are not to understand that he went up the boisterous brook of Greenhead Gill every time he wanted to write 'Michael'. He was in fact writing a poem called 'The Sheepfold'; the place of writing is unspecified. It was about Michael but it was rhymed, unlike the blank verse poem that we know. Only a short fragment of this early poem remains because on 9 November, according to Dorothy's journal, 'W. burnt the sheep fold', meaning again the poem, not the rocks. Two days later he was 'working at the sheep-fold' again, with more success this time since, on 9 December, 'Wm finished his poem today'. Shortly thereafter, the writing finally done, the new

---

[2] This very thing happens in a passage originally written for 'Michael' but included in the 1805 *Prelude* (viii. 222–311). A lost lamb has jumped on an island to feed, the boy finds him and jumps to the island, the lamb springs to the further shore but misses and is borne headlong down the stream, and the boy is stranded on the island, fearing to jump either way, until his father rescues him.

[3] The vicar of Wythburn, who lived at High Broadrain.

edition of *Lyrical Ballads* appeared, dated 1800 but not in fact published until January 1801.

Years later Wordsworth told Miss Fenwick that 'the Sheepfold, on which so much of the poem turns, remains, or rather the ruins of it'. Whether it still remains is open to doubt. There are ruined walls [A] up the valley in a spot where Michael's sheep-fold might well have been, but there has clearly been other activity there. The exact location of Michael's sheep-fold may no longer be identifiable with any certainty, but that this boisterous brook, hidden valley, and utter solitude remain as they were when William and Dorothy looked for the sheep-fold in 1800, there can be no doubt. Those with natural hearts capable of being moved by 'Michael' will be amply rewarded if they journey thither in search of a straggling heap of unhewn stones. 'Great changes have been wrought | In all the neighbourhood', but the valley remains where, in the poem, the boy Luke learned to use his shepherd's staff, 'Something between a hindrance and a help', where the eighteen-year-old Luke and his eighty-four-year-old father, Michael, made their covenant of love by the heap of stones, and where Michael, his son lost to him, came and sat.

> . . . many and many a day he thither went,
> And never lifted up a single stone.
>
> There, by the Sheep-fold, sometimes was he seen
> Sitting alone, or with his faithful Dog,
> Then old, beside him, lying at his feet.
> The length of full seven years, from time to time,
> He at the building of this Sheep-fold wrought,
> And left the work unfinished when he died.

The story of Luke's leaving his parents to try to redeem their estate was based on a story that Wordsworth had heard from Ann Tyson during his school-days. She had lived and worked at Rydal and knew much about the neighbourhood; Wordsworth no doubt had it from her that Luke's family had lived in what is now Dove Cottage. 'The character and circumstances of Luke', Wordsworth said, 'were taken from a family to whom had belonged, many years before, the house we lived in at Town-End, along with some fields and woodlands on the eastern shore of Grasmere' (I.F.). Their house in the poem, however, was not Dove Cottage but 'another on the same side of the valley more to the north' (I.F.).

> Their cottage on a plot of rising ground
> Stood single, with large prospect, north and south,
> High into Easedale, up to Dunmail-Raise,
> And westward to the village near the lake;
> And from this constant light, so regular,
> And so far seen, the House itself, by all
> Who dwelt within the limits of the vale,
> Both old and young, was named THE EVENING STAR.

Wordsworth clearly had in mind a particular spot closer to Greenhead Gill. Professor Knight said at the end of the last century that the cottage stood where the coach-house and stables of The Hollens now stand; Mrs Rawnsley thought the 'Evening Star' was High Broadrain; and the owners of Michael's Nook, just north of Greenhead Gill, claim that it stood where their fashionable country hotel now stands. But the line, 'Upon the forest-side in Grasmere Vale', as de Selincourt points out, suggests that it stood south of Greenhead Gill, between it and The Hollens, at what is still called Forest Side. That it should stand in this vicinity rather than at Town End is important because the light from the cottage, as the family worked industriously into the night, becomes the public manifestation of their private ways:

> This light was famous in its neighbourhood,
> And was a public symbol of the life
> That thrifty Pair had lived.

The traveller turns 'from the public way', the light is 'a public symbol', and Luke leaves by 'the public way' to reach the dissolute city, but the heap of stones is in a secluded and private spot, and this tale for natural hearts is of love and private grief.

MICHAEL

A PASTORAL POEM

> If from the public way you turn your steps
> Up the tumultuous brook of Green-head Ghyll,

You will suppose that with an upright path
Your feet must struggle; in such bold ascent
The pastoral mountains front you, face to face.
But, courage! for around that boisterous brook
The mountains have all opened out themselves,
And made a hidden valley of their own.
No habitation can be seen; but they
Who journey thither find themselves alone
With a few sheep, with rocks and stones, and kites
That overhead are sailing in the sky.
It is in truth an utter solitude;
Nor should I have made mention of this Dell
But for one object which you might pass by,
Might see and notice not. Beside the brook
Appears a straggling heap of unhewn stones!
And to that simple object appertains
A story—unenriched with strange events,
Yet not unfit, I deem, for the fireside,
Or for the summer shade. It was the first
Of those domestic tales that spake to me
Of Shepherds, dwellers in the valleys, men
Whom I already loved;—not verily
For their own sakes, but for the fields and hills
Where was their occupation and abode.
And hence this Tale, while I was yet a Boy
Careless of books, yet having felt the power
Of Nature, by the gentle agency
Of natural objects, led me on to feel
For passions that were not my own, and think
(At random and imperfectly indeed)
On man, the heart of man, and human life.
Therefore, although it be a history
Homely and rude, I will relate the same
For the delight of a few natural hearts;
And, with yet fonder feeling, for the sake
Of youthful Poets, who among these hills
Will be my second self when I am gone.

    Upon the forest-side in Grasmere Vale
There dwelt a Shepherd, Michael was his name;
An old man, stout of heart, and strong of limb.

His bodily frame had been from youth to age
Of an unusual strength: his mind was keen,
Intense, and frugal, apt for all affairs,
And in his shepherd's calling he was prompt
And watchful more than ordinary men.
Hence had he learned the meaning of all winds,
Of blasts of every tone; and oftentimes,
When others heeded not, He heard the South
Make subterraneous music, like the noise
Of bagpipers on distant Highland hills.
The Shepherd, at such warning, of his flock
Bethought him, and he to himself would say,
"The winds are now devising work for me!"
And, truly, at all times, the storm, that drives
The traveller to a shelter, summoned him
Up to the mountains: he had been alone
Amid the heart of many thousand mists,
That came to him, and left him, on the heights.
So lived he till his eightieth year was past.
And grossly that man errs, who should suppose
That the green valleys, and the streams and rocks,
Were things indifferent to the Shepherd's thoughts.
Fields, where with cheerful spirits he had breathed
The common air; hills, which with vigorous step
He had so often climbed; which had impressed
So many incidents upon his mind
Of hardship, skill or courage, joy or fear;
Which, like a book, preserved the memory
Of the dumb animals, whom he had saved,
Had fed or sheltered, linking to such acts
The certainty of honourable gain;
Those fields, those hills—what could they less? had laid
Strong hold on his affections, were to him
A pleasurable feeling of blind love,
The pleasure which there is in life itself.

His days had not been passed in singleness.
His Helpmate was a comely matron, old—
Though younger than himself full twenty years.
She was a woman of a stirring life,
Whose heart was in her house: two wheels she had

Of antique form; this large, for spinning wool;
That small, for flax; and if one wheel had rest,
It was because the other was at work.
The Pair had but one inmate in their house,
An only Child, who had been born to them
When Michael, telling o'er his years, began
To deem that he was old,—in shepherd's phrase,
With one foot in the grave. This only Son,
With two brave sheep-dogs tried in many a storm,
The one of an inestimable worth,
Made all their household. I may truly say,
That they were as a proverb in the vale
For endless industry. When day was gone,
And from their occupations out of doors
The Son and Father were come home, even then,
Their labour did not cease; unless when all
Turned to the cleanly supper-board, and there,
Each with a mess of pottage and skimmed milk,
Sat round the basket piled with oaten cakes,
And their plain home-made cheese. Yet when the meal
Was ended, Luke (for so the Son was named)
And his old Father both betook themselves
To such convenient work as might employ
Their hands by the fire-side; perhaps to card
Wool for the Housewife's spindle, or repair
Some injury done to sickle, flail, or scythe,
Or other implement of house or field.

  Down from the ceiling, by the chimney's edge,
That in our ancient uncouth country style
With huge and black projection overbrowed
Large space beneath, as duly as the light
Of day grew dim the Housewife hung a lamp;
An aged utensil, which had performed
Service beyond all others of its kind.
Early at evening did it burn—and late,
Surviving comrade of uncounted hours,
Which, going by from year to year, had found,
And left the couple neither gay perhaps
Nor cheerful, yet with objects and with hopes,
Living a life of eager industry.

And now, when Luke had reached his eighteenth year,
There by the light of this old lamp they sate,
Father and Son, while far into the night
The Housewife plied her own peculiar work,
Making the cottage through the silent hours
Murmur as with the sound of summer flies.
This light was famous in its neighbourhood,
And was a public symbol of the life
That thrifty Pair had lived. For, as it chanced,
Their cottage on a plot of rising ground
Stood single, with large prospect, north and south,
High into Easedale, up to Dunmail-Raise,
And westward to the village near the lake;
And from this constant light, so regular,
And so far seen, the House itself, by all
Who dwelt within the limits of the vale,
Both old and young, was named THE EVENING STAR.

   Thus living on through such a length of years,
The Shepherd, if he loved himself, must needs
Have loved his Helpmate; but to Michael's heart
This son of his old age was yet more dear—
Less from instinctive tenderness, the same
Fond spirit that blindly works in the blood of all—
Than that a child, more than all other gifts
That earth can offer to declining man,
Brings hope with it, and forward-looking thoughts,
And stirrings of inquietude, when they
By tendency of nature needs must fail.
Exceeding was the love he bare to him,
His heart and his heart's joy! For often-times
Old Michael, while he was a babe in arms,
Had done him female service, not alone
For pastime and delight, as is the use
Of fathers, but with patient mind enforced
To acts of tenderness; and he had rocked
His cradle, as with a woman's gentle hand.

   And in a later time, ere yet the Boy
Had put on boy's attire, did Michael love,
Albeit of a stern unbending mind,

To have the Young-one in his sight, when he
Wrought in the field, or on his shepherd's stool
Sate with a fettered sheep before him stretched
Under the large old oak, that near his door
Stood single, and, from matchless depth of shade,
Chosen for the Shearer's covert from the sun,
Thence in our rustic dialect was called
The CLIPPING TREE,[1] a name which yet it bears.
There, while they two were sitting in the shade,
With others round them, earnest all and blithe,
Would Michael exercise his heart with looks
Of fond correction and reproof bestowed
Upon the Child, if he disturbed the sheep
By catching at their legs, or with his shouts
Scared them, while they lay still beneath the shears.

    And when by Heaven's good grace the boy grew up
A healthy Lad, and carried in his cheek
Two steady roses that were five years old;
Then Michael from a winter coppice cut
With his own hand a sapling, which he hooped
With iron, making it throughout in all
Due requisites a perfect shepherd's staff,
And gave it to the Boy; wherewith equipt
He as a watchman oftentimes was placed
At gate or gap, to stem or turn the flock;
And, to his office prematurely called,
There stood the urchin, as you will divine,
Something between a hindrance and a help;
And for this cause not always, I believe,
Receiving from his Father hire of praise;
Though nought was left undone which staff, or voice,
Or looks, or threatening gestures, could perform.

    But soon as Luke, full ten years old, could stand
Against the mountain blasts; and to the heights,
Not fearing toil, nor length of weary ways,
He with his Father daily went, and they

[1] Clipping is the word used in the North of England for shearing. [W. W.'s note]

Were as companions, why should I relate
That objects which the Shepherd loved before
Were dearer now? that from the Boy there came
Feelings and emanations—things which were
Light to the sun and music to the wind;
And that the old Man's heart seemed born again?

    Thus in his Father's sight the Boy grew up:
And now, when he had reached his eighteenth year,
He was his comfort and his daily hope.

    While in this sort the simple household lived
From day to day, to Michael's ear there came
Distressful tidings. Long before the time
Of which I speak, the Shepherd had been bound
In surety for his brother's son, a man
Of an industrious life, and ample means;
But unforeseen misfortunes suddenly
Had prest upon him; and old Michael now
Was summoned to discharge the forfeiture,
A grievous penalty, but little less
Than half his substance. This unlooked-for claim,
At the first hearing, for a moment took
More hope out of his life than he supposed
That any old man ever could have lost.
As soon as he had armed himself with strength
To look his trouble in the face, it seemed
The Shepherd's sole resource to sell at once
A portion of his patrimonial fields.
Such was his first resolve; he thought again,
And his heart failed him. 'Isabel,' said he,
Two evenings after he had heard the news,
'I have been toiling more than seventy years,
And in the open sunshine of God's love
Have we all lived; yet if these fields of ours
Should pass into a stranger's hand, I think
That I could not lie quiet in my grave.
Our lot is a hard lot; the sun himself
Has scarcely been more diligent than I;
And I have lived to be a fool at last
To my own family. An evil man

That was, and made an evil choice, if he
Were false to us; and, if he were not false,
There are ten thousand to whom loss like this
Had been no sorrow. I forgive him;—but
'Twere better to be dumb than to talk thus.

   'When I began, my purpose was to speak
Of remedies and of a cheerful hope.
Our Luke shall leave us, Isabel; the land
Shall not go from us, and it shall be free;
He shall possess it, free as is the wind
That passes over it. We have, thou know'st,
Another kinsman—he will be our friend
In this distress. He is a prosperous man,
Thriving in trade—and Luke to him shall go,
And with his kinsman's help and his own thrift
He quickly will repair this loss, and then
He may return to us. If here he stay,
What can be done? Where every one is poor,
What can be gained?'
                At this the old Man paused,
And Isabel sat silent, for her mind
Was busy, looking back into past times.
There's Richard Bateman, thought she to herself,
He was a parish-boy—at the church-door
They made a gathering for him, shillings, pence,
And halfpennies, wherewith the neighbours bought
A basket, which they filled with pedlar's wares;
And, with this basket on his arm, the lad
Went up to London, found a master there,
Who, out of many, chose the trusty boy
To go and overlook his merchandise
Beyond the seas; where he grew wondrous rich,
And left estates and monies to the poor,
And, at his birth-place, built a chapel floored
With marble, which he sent from foreign lands.
These thoughts, and many others of like sort,
Passed quickly through the mind of Isabel,
And her face brightened. The old Man was glad,
And thus resumed:—'Well, Isabel! this scheme
These two days has been meat and drink to me.

Far more than we have lost is left us yet.
—We have enough—I wish indeed that I
Were younger;—but this hope is a good hope.
Make ready Luke's best garments, of the best
Buy for him more, and let us send him forth
To-morrow, or the next day, or to-night:
—If he *could* go, the Boy should go to-night.'

Here Michael ceased, and to the fields went forth
With a light heart. The Housewife for five days
Was restless morn and night, and all day long
Wrought on with her best fingers to prepare
Things needful for the journey of her son.
But Isabel was glad when Sunday came
To stop her in her work: for, when she lay
By Michael's side, she through the last two nights
Heard him, how he was troubled in his sleep:
And when they rose at morning she could see
That all his hopes were gone. That day at noon
She said to Luke, while they two by themselves
Were sitting at the door, 'Thou must not go:
We have no other Child but thee to lose,
None to remember—do not go away,
For if thou leave thy Father he will die.'
The Youth made answer with a jocund voice;
And Isabel, when she had told her fears,
Recovered heart. That evening her best fare
Did she bring forth, and all together sat
Like happy people round a Christmas fire.

With daylight Isabel resumed her work;
And all the ensuing week the house appeared
As cheerful as a grove in Spring: at length
The expected letter from their kinsman came,
With kind assurances that he would do
His utmost for the welfare of the Boy;
To which, requests were added, that forthwith
He might be sent to him. Ten times or more
The letter was read over; Isabel
Went forth to show it to the neighbours round;
Nor was there at that time on English land

A prouder heart than Luke's. When Isabel
Had to her house returned, the old Man said,
'He shall depart to-morrow.' To this word
The Housewife answered, talking much of things
Which, if at such short notice he should go,
Would surely be forgotten. But at length
She gave consent, and Michael was at ease.

   Near the tumultuous brook of Green-head Ghyll,
In that deep valley, Michael had designed
To build a Sheep-fold; and, before he heard
The tidings of his melancholy loss,
For this same purpose he had gathered up
A heap of stones, which by the streamlet's edge
Lay thrown together, ready for the work.
With Luke that evening thitherward he walked:
And soon as they had reached the place he stopped,
And thus the old Man spake to him:—'My son,
To-morrow thou wilt leave me: with full heart
I look upon thee, for thou art the same
That wert a promise to me ere thy birth,
And all thy life hast been my daily joy.
I will relate to thee some little part
Of our two histories; 'twill do thee good
When thou art from me, even if I should touch
On things thou canst not know of.—After thou
First cam'st into the world—as oft befalls
To new-born infants—thou didst sleep away
Two days, and blessings from thy Father's tongue
Then fell upon thee. Day by day passed on,
And still I loved thee with increasing love.
Never to living ear came sweeter sounds
Than when I heard thee by our own fire-side
First uttering, without words, a natural tune;
While thou, a feeding babe, didst in thy joy
Sing at thy Mother's breast. Month followed month,
And in the open fields my life was passed
And on the mountains; else I think that thou
Hadst been brought up upon thy Father's knees.
But we were playmates, Luke: among these hills,
As well thou knowest, in us the old and young

Have played together, nor with me didst thou
Lack any pleasure which a boy can know.'
Luke had a manly heart; but at these words
He sobbed aloud. The old Man grasped his hand,
And said, 'Nay, do not take it so—I see
That these are things of which I need not speak.
—Even to the utmost I have been to thee
A kind and a good Father: and herein
I but repay a gift which I myself
Received at others' hands; for, though now old
Beyond the common life of man, I still
Remember them who loved me in my youth.
Both of them sleep together: here they lived,
As all their Forefathers had done; and when
At length their time was come, they were not loth
To give their bodies to the family mould.
I wished that thou should'st live the life they lived,
But 'tis a long time to look back, my Son,
And see so little gain from threescore years.
These fields were burthened when they came to me;
Till I was forty years of age, not more
Than half of my inheritance was mine.
I toiled and toiled; God blessed me in my work,
And till these three weeks past the land was free.
—It looks as if it never could endure
Another Master. Heaven forgive me, Luke,
If I judge ill for thee, but it seems good
That thou shouldst go.'
              At this the old man paused;
Then, pointing to the stones near which they stood,
Thus, after a short silence, he resumed:
'This was a work for us; and now, my Son,
It is a work for me. But, lay one stone—
Here, lay it for me, Luke, with thine own hands.
Nay, Boy, be of good hope;—we both may live
To see a better day. At eighty-four
I still am strong and hale;—do thou thy part;
I will do mine.—I will begin again
With many tasks that were resigned to thee:
Up to the heights, and in among the storms,
Will I without thee go again, and do

All works which I was wont to do alone,
Before I knew thy face.—Heaven bless thee, Boy!
Thy heart these two weeks has been beating fast
With many hopes; it should be so—yes—yes—
I knew that thou couldst never have a wish
To leave me, Luke: thou hast been bound to me
Only by links of love: when thou art gone,
What will be left to us!—But I forget
My purposes. Lay now the corner-stone,
As I requested; and hereafter, Luke,
When thou art gone away, should evil men
Be thy companions, think of me, my Son,
And of this moment; hither turn thy thoughts,
And God will strengthen thee: amid all fear
And all temptation, Luke, I pray that thou
May'st bear in mind the life thy Fathers lived,
Who, being innocent, did for that cause
Bestir them in good deeds. Now, farc thee well—
When thou return'st, thou in this place wilt see
A work which is not here: a covenant
'Twill be between us; but, whatever fate
Befall thee, I shall love thee to the last,
And bear thy memory with me to the grave.'

The Shepherd ended here; and Luke stooped down,
And, as his Father had requested, laid
The first stone of the Sheep-fold. At the sight
The old Man's grief broke from him; to his heart
He pressed his Son, he kissèd him and wept;
And to the house together they returned.
—Hushed was that House in peace, or seeming peace,
Ere the night fell:—with morrow's dawn the Boy
Began his journey, and when he had reached
The public way, he put on a bold face;
And all the neighbours, as he passed their doors,
Came forth with wishes and with farewell prayers,
That followed him till he was out of sight.

A good report did from their Kinsman come,
Of Luke and his well-doing: and the Boy
Wrote loving letters, full of wondrous news,

Which, as the Housewife phrased it, were throughout
'The prettiest letters that were ever seen.'
Both parents read them with rejoicing hearts.
So, many months passed on: and once again
The Shepherd went about his daily work
With confident and cheerful thoughts; and now
Sometimes when he could find a leisure hour
He to that valley took his way, and there
Wrought at the Sheep-fold. Meantime Luke began
To slacken in his duty; and, at length,
He in the dissolute city gave himself
To evil courses: ignominy and shame
Fell on him, so that he was driven at last
To seek a hiding-place beyond the seas.

   There is a comfort in the strength of love;
'Twill make a thing endurable, which else
Would overset the brain, or break the heart:
I have conversed with more than one who well
Remember the old Man, and what he was
Years after he had heard this heavy news.
His bodily frame had been from youth to age
Of an unusual strength. Among the rocks
He went, and still looked up to sun and cloud,
And listened to the wind; and, as before,
Performed all kinds of labour for his sheep,
And for the land, his small inheritance.
And to that hollow dell from time to time
Did he repair, to build the Fold of which
His flock had need. 'Tis not forgotten yet
The pity which was then in every heart
For the old Man—and 'tis believed by all
That many and many a day he thither went,
And never lifted up a single stone.

   There by the Sheep-fold, sometimes was he seen
Sitting alone, or with his faithful Dog,
Then old, beside him, lying at his feet.
The length of full seven years, from time to time,
He at the building of this Sheep-fold wrought,
And left the work unfinished when he died.

Three years, or little more, did Isabel
Survive her Husband: at her death the estate
Was sold, and went into a stranger's hand.
The Cottage which was named the EVENING STAR
Is gone—the ploughshare has been through the ground
On which it stood; great changes have been wrought
In all the neighbourhood:—yet the oak is left
That grew beside their door; and the remains
Of the unfinished Sheep-fold may be seen
Beside the boisterous brook of Green-head Ghyll.

4

Helvellyn[1]

'The brow of old Helvellyn' looms over Thirlmere and Grasmere, an ancient presence which endures tourists, climbers, foresters, miners, and sheep, and outlives them all. 'Old' is almost a Homeric epithet for Helvellyn in Wordsworth's poems: the mists and clouds, travellers and shepherds, come and go, while its presence and power endure. But its presence and power change, depending on who is looking, and when. Often enough to a traveller, the ascent of Helvellyn is a tiring climb, busy with people, and has a way of altering unhappily our perspective of human life:

Enough of climbing toil!—Ambition treads
Here, as 'mid busier scenes, ground steep and rough,
Or slippery even to peril! and each step,
As we for most uncertain recompence
Mount toward the empire of the fickle clouds,
Each weary step, dwarfing the world below,
Induces, for its old familiar sights,
Unacceptable feelings of contempt,

[1] Map on p. 211.

'RED TARN'. Striding Edge, the scene of Gough's disaster ('Fidelity'), is on the left, Swirral Edge on the right, and the summit of Helvellyn in the distance.

> With wonder mixed—that Man could e'er be tied,
> In anxious bondage, to such nice array
> And formal fellowship of petty things!

(PW, iv. 96)

So wrote Wordsworth in 1817 after he had climbed Helvellyn twice within three weeks, the first time returning from Ullswater with his sister and the second time going from Rydal Mount with his wife.

To dwarf familiar sights, however, is only one of Helvellyn's powers. When Wordsworth came to write in his autobiographical poem of an important shift of affection in his life—'Love of Nature Leading to Love of Man'—he began with Helvellyn as an emblem of solitary nature and with the annual fair in Grasmere as an emblem of society.

> What sounds are those, Helvellyn, which are heard
> Up to thy summit? Through the depth of air
> Ascending, as if distance had the power
> To make the sounds more audible: what Crowd
> Is yon, assembled in the gay green Field?
> Crowd seems it, solitary Hill! to thee,
> Though but a little Family of Men,
> Twice twenty, with their Children and their Wives,
> And here and there a Stranger interspers'd.
> It is a summer festival, a Fair,
> Such as, on this side now, and now on that,
> Repeated through his tributary Vales,
> Helvellyn, in the silence of his rest,
> Sees annually, if storms be not abroad,
> And mists have left him an unshrouded head.

(1805 Prelude, viii. 1–15)

Helvellyn—towering above the secluded glens, silent, often obscured by clouds or mists—can be more than a hard climb. For Wordsworth it was among the grandest of those sublime forms which profoundly affected his inner life. The sublime, however, does not exist in isolation; it requires an active, participating observer.

> Minds that have nothing to confer
> Find little to perceive.

(PW, ii. 35)

The mountain bountifully rewarded Wordsworth's perceptions
and those of his sister, wife, and friends, such as a Miss Blackett,
who in 1816 was staying nearby in Fox Ghyll. Some years later,
Wordsworth recounted their descent: 'We were tempted to remain
too long upon the mountain; and I, imprudently, with the hope of
shortening the way, led her among the crags and down a steep slope,
which entangled us in difficulties that were met by her with much
spirit and courage' (I.F.). His poem about the occasion, however,
has nothing to do with the spirited descent, and everything to do
with the sublime experience, the potent spell, of Helvellyn working
on Miss Blackett, making her feel 'the power of hills'.

> Inmate of a mountain-dwelling,
> Thou hast clomb aloft, and gazed
> From the watch-towers of Helvellyn;
> Awed, delighted, and amazed!
>   . . .
> For the power of hills is on thee,
> As was witnessed through thine eye
> Then, when old Helvellyn won thee
> To confess their majesty!

('To — on Her First Ascent to the Summit of Helvellyn')

Long before he moved to Grasmere, Helvellyn had been a
presence in Wordsworth's life. In one of his earliest prose
fragments, an Ossianic bard proclaims, 'Spirit of these Mountains I
see thee throned on Helvellyn, but thy feet and head are wrapped
in mist.' His old dame at Hawkshead, Ann Tyson, had lived near
Helvellyn and told him stories of it, one of them about a shepherd
and his son who ranged the mountains looking for a lost sheep:

> All over their own pastures and beyond,
> And now, at sun-rise sallying out again
> Renew'd their search begun where from Dove Crag,
> Ill home for bird so gentle, they look'd down
> On Deep-dale Head, and Brothers-water, named
> From those two Brothers that were drown'd therein,
> Thence, northward, having pass'd by Arthur's Seat,
> To Fairfield's highest summit; on the right
> Leaving St. Sunday's Pike, to Grisdale Tarn
> They shot, and over that cloud-loving Hill,

> Seat Sandal, a fond lover of the clouds;
> Thence up Helvellyn, a superior Mount
> With prospect underneath of Striding-Edge,
> And Grisdale's houseless Vale, along the brink
> Of Russet Cove, and those two other Coves,
> Huge skeletons of crags, which from the trunk
> Of old Helvellyn spread their arms abroad,
> And make a stormy harbour for the winds.[2]

(1805 *Prelude*, viii. 228–44)

This passage, and the entire tale of the lost sheep, was originally written for the poem 'Michael' but not used until the 1805 *Prelude*. Another passage, written for 'Michael' but not used in any published poem, tells of the old shepherd and his son on top of Helvellyn, looking down on Thirlmere and taking a drink at what is now called Brownrigg Well [E], or Whelpside Gill Spring.

> So to Helvellyn's eastern[3] side they went
> Down looking on that hollow, where the pool
> Of Thirlmere flashes like a Warriour's shield
> His light high up among the gloomy rocks
> With gift of now and then a straggling gleam
> To Armath's[4] pleasant fields. And now they came
> To that high spring which bears the human name
> Of one unknown by others, aptly called
> The fountain of the mists. The Father stoop'd
> To drink of the clear water, laid himself
> Flat on the ground even as a Boy might do,
> To drink of the cold well; when in like sort
> His son had drunk, the old Man said to him
> That now he might be proud, for he that day
> Had slak'd his thirst out of a famous well
> The highest fountain known on British Land.

(*PW*, ii. 483–4)

[2] 'Russet Cove' is Ruthwaite (pronounced 'Ruthet') Cove. The 'two other coves' are Nethermost Cove and Cock Cove.
[3] The manuscript clearly says 'eastern', but the well, Thirlmere, and Armboth are west of the summit.
[4] Armboth Fell is opposite Helvellyn on the west side of Thirlmere; Armboth Farm was on the north-west side of the lake.

The mountain, though it towered far above Grasmere Fair, had its human connections through the shepherd's daily work, the weariness or awe of its visitors, and sometimes through events or associations of tragedy and sorrow. One such—the death of Charles Gough, an angler, from falling off Striding Edge [D] above Red Tarn in April 1805—is recounted by Wordsworth in his *Guide:*

This desolate spot was formerly haunted by eagles, that built in the precipice which forms its western barrier. These birds used to wheel and hover round the head of the solitary angler. It also derives a melancholy interest from the fate of a young man, a stranger, who perished some years ago, by falling down the rocks in his attempt to cross over to Grasmere. His remains were discovered by means of a faithful dog that had lingered here for the space of three months, self-supported, and probably retaining to the last an attachment to the skeleton of its master.

A month after this accident was discovered, Wordsworth climbed Helvellyn with Walter Scott and the chemist Humphry Davy. The climb itself was a jovial one, at least for the poets—'What a happy day we had together there! I often think of it with delight', Wordsworth wrote to Scott—and he later described it to Miss Fenwick: 'We had ascended from Patterdale,[5] and I could not but admire the vigour with which Scott scrambled along that horn of the mountain called "Striding Edge". Our progress was necessarily slow,'—Scott was lame—'and was beguiled by Scott's telling many stories and amusing anecdotes, as was his custom.' The important story of the day, however, was one that Wordsworth told Scott: the tale of Charles Gough and his faithful dog. Within the next few months, Wordsworth wrote a poem about the incident.

FIDELITY

A barking sound the Shepherd hears,
A cry as of a dog or fox;
He halts—and searches with his eyes
Among the scattered rocks:
And now at distance can discern
A stirring in a brake of fern;

[5] For their comic behaviour there, and their problem of getting to bed, see the anecdote on p. 130.

And instantly a dog is seen,
Glancing through that covert green.

The Dog is not of mountain breed;
Its motions, too, are wild and shy;
With something, as the Shepherd thinks,
Unusual in its cry:
Nor is there any one in sight
All round, in hollow or on height;
Nor shout, nor whistle strikes his ear;
What is the creature doing here?

It was a cove, a huge recess,
That keeps, till June, December's snow;
A lofty precipice in front,
A silent tarn below!
Far in the bosom of Helvellyn,
Remote from public road or dwelling,
Pathway, or cultivated land;
From trace of human foot or hand.

There sometimes doth a leaping fish
Send through the tarn a lonely cheer;
The crags repeat the raven's croak,
In symphony austere;
Thither the rainbow comes—the cloud—
And mists that spread the flying shroud;
And sunbeams; and the sounding blast,
That, if it could, would hurry past;
But that enormous barrier holds it fast.

Not free from boding thoughts, a while
The Shepherd stood; then makes his way
O'er rocks and stones, following the Dog
As quickly as he may;
Nor far had gone before he found
A human skeleton on the ground;
The appalled Discoverer with a sigh
Looks round, to learn the history.

From those abrupt and perilous rocks
The Man had fallen, that place of fear!
At length upon the Shepherd's mind
It breaks, and all is clear:
He instantly recalled the name,
And who he was, and whence he came;
Remembered, too, the very day
On which the Traveller passed this way.

But hear a wonder, for whose sake
This lamentable tale I tell!
A lasting monument of words
This wonder merits well.
The Dog, which still was hovering nigh,
Repeating the same timid cry,
This Dog, had been through three months' space
A dweller in that savage place.

Yes, proof was plain that, since the day
When this ill-fated Traveller died,
The Dog had watched about the spot,
Or by his master's side:
How nourished here through such long time
He knows who gave that love sublime;
And gave that strength of feeling, great
Above all human estimate!

At about the same time, and not knowing that Wordsworth was writing this poem, Scott wrote 'Helvellyn', also about Gough and his dog.

Some thirty years later, when Wordsworth was touring Italy, the sight of the Apennines triggered a recollection of his local mountains and his thoughts flew back to them.

The local Genius hurries me aloft,
Transported over that cloud-wooing hill,
Seat Sandal, a fond suitor of the clouds,
With dream-like smoothness, to Helvellyn's top,
There to alight upon crisp moss and range,
Obtaining ampler boon, at every step,
Of visual sovereignty—hills multitudinous,

(Not Apennine can boast of fairer) hills
Pride of two nations, wood and lake and plains,
And prospect right below of deep coves shaped
By skeleton arms, that, from the mountain's trunk
Extended, clasp the winds, with mutual moan
Struggling for liberty, while undismayed
The shepherd struggles with them.

In particular, he thought of Sir Walter Scott, now dead for five years, who had, shortly before his death, travelled to Italy in search of health.

'The Wizard of the North,' with anxious hope
Brought to this genial climate, when disease
Preyed upon body and mind—yet not the less
Had his sunk eye kindled at those dear words
That spake of bards and minstrels; and his spirit
Had flown with mine to old Helvellyn's brow,
Where once together, in his day of strength,
We stood rejoicing, as if earth were free
From sorrow, like the sky above our heads.

('Musings Near Aquapendente', lines 34–47, 57–65)

But there was one sorrow which Wordsworth often associated with the route to Hellvellyn—the death of his brother John, 'the silent poet', in the wreck of his ship, the *Earl of Abergavenny*. The last time William and Dorothy saw John in Grasmere was when they parted on 29 September 1800 at Grisedale Tarn [B]. He had been staying with them at Dove Cottage but had to return to his ship; there must have been some excitement as well as sorrow in the parting, for John had recently been named Captain. 'O dear John Wordsworth!' Coleridge wrote in his notebook, 'What joy at Grasmere when you were made Captain of the Abergavenny!' John sailed the East India trade route for nearly four and a half years, until February 1805, when the ship went down at sea and its captain, along with many of its passengers and crew, was drowned. A few months later Dorothy wrote to a friend,

My Brother [William] is at Patterdale, he took his fishing-rod over the mountains, there being a pass from Grasmere thither. My Sister and I´ accompanied him to the top of it, and parted from him near a Tarn

[Grisedale Tarn] under a part of Helvellyn—he had gone up on Saturday with a neighbour of ours to fish there, but he quitted his companion, and poured out his heart in some beautiful verses to the memory of our lost Brother, who used to go sometimes alone to that same Tarn; for the pleasure of angling in part, but still more, for his love of solitude and of the mountains. Near that very Tarn William and I bade him farewell the last time he was at Grasmere, when he went from us to take the command of the ship. We were in view of the head of Ulswater, and stood till we could see him no longer, watching him as he *hurried* down the stony mountain. Oh! my dear Friend, you will not wonder that we love that place. I have been twice to it since his death. The first time was agony, but it is now a different feeling—poor William was overcome on Saturday—and with floods of tears wrote those verses—

(*Letters*, 11 June 1805)

The verses—'Elegiac Verses, In Memory of My Brother, John Wordsworth'—focus on this place of parting ('Here did we stop; and here looked round'), which Wordsworth later described exactly: 'The point is 2 or 3 yards below the outlet of Grisdale Tarn on a foot-road by which a horse may pass to Patterdale, a ridge of Helvellyn on the left, and the summit of Fairfield on the right' (I.F.). The poem consecrates the 'precious Spot', as it is called in an unused manuscript line, concluding with a wish that there be a monumental stone, linking the poet, his dead brother, the traveller, the shepherd, and the mighty rocks—and also linking past, present, and future. The idea of the last stanza, about our life in the face of death, was rooted for Wordsworth in this particular spot.

> —Brother and friend, if verse of mine
> Have power to make thy virtues known,
> Here let a monumental Stone
> Stand—sacred as a Shrine;
> And to the few who pass this way,
> Traveller or Shepherd, let it say,
> Long as these mighty rocks endure,—
> Oh do not Thou too fondly brood,
> Although deserving of all good,
> On any earthly hope, however pure!

In the 1880s, the Reverend H. D. Rawnsley and other Wordsworthians heeded the poet's injunction and had eight lines of the poem incised on a large rock facing Ullswater, not far below the outlet of Grisedale Tarn. It seems a fitting gesture: carved in native volcanic rock, Wordsworth's lines have become part of old Helvellyn.

5

Keswick[1]

For its size, Keswick probably has more literary associations than any town in the country. The Poet Laureate, Robert Southey, lived there for forty years, having been urged to come by Coleridge, with whom he shared a house. Shelley came, newly wed to Harriet Westbrook, and stayed for four months, though he quickly recognized that Southey, whom he sought out, was no longer radical enough to suit his high standards. Wordsworth came too as a traveller and stayed for a shorter time—six weeks or so—but there were schemes to get him back as a permanent resident. In addition, there was William Brownrigg of Ormathwaite, a chemist, author, and friend of Joseph Priestley and Benjamin Franklin (who visited him there); Jonathan Otley, a geologist and author of *A Concise Description of the English Lakes* (1823); the mystic William Smith, philosopher and journalist; and the indefatigable Canon H. D. Rawnsley, author, Vicar of the Crosthwaite Church and co-founder of the National Trust in 1895.

When Wordsworth stayed at Keswick, his poetic genius was unknown, although two people—his sister Dorothy and Raisley Calvert, a friend and resident of Keswick—recognized his promise. After having left Cambridge, Wordsworth went to Keswick to visit his friend from Hawkshead school, William Calvert, and Calvert's younger brother Raisley. The Calverts were an old family of Cumberland yeoman farmers and their father had been the steward

[1] Map on p. 214.

'SKIDDAW'. This view of Keswick shows Crosthwaite Church on the left, below Bassenthwaite Lake; Greta Hall, the prominent building to the right of the Church; and Moot Hall, with the tower, further to the right. Applethwaite is at the bottom of the steep valley below the peaks on the right.

of the Duke of Norfolk. William Calvert owned Windy Brow [F] on Latrigg and built the house nearby at Greta Bank. The Calverts apparently offered the use of Windy Brow to William and Dorothy. The brother and sister had seen each other seldom, and never for long enough, since their Cockermouth days. When they were finally reunited in Halifax in early 1794, they decided to make what was to be the first of their many tours together, going by coach to Kendal, then by foot to the Calvert farmhouse near Keswick, where they stayed for six weeks (instead of a few days, as they intended), William writing and revising and Dorothy making a copy of his Salisbury Plain poem. And, of course, they took pleasure in their favourite pastime—walking. Dorothy's unpleasant aunt Crackenthorpe wrote a severe letter condemning her stay at Windy Brow and especially her horrid 'rambling about the country on foot', but Dorothy sent back a spirited reply; she clearly had no intention of changing her ways.

Raisley Calvert proved to have an important effect on Wordsworth's life, though before this time Wordsworth had scarcely known him. After he and Dorothy parted, Wordsworth spent most of the summer with Calvert. By the end of the summer, it became evident that Calvert was dying of consumption. Wordsworth stayed with him, helping and keeping him company, until his death in January 1795. Calvert knew of Wordsworth's unpromising financial circumstances, his distaste for the professions that his guardians wished for him, and his need for enough financial independence to write. It was in Calvert's power to help, which he did by bequeathing £900 to Wordsworth—an act of generosity that freed Wordsworth to be a poet. Later, he described the gift in this way: 'I the second Son was sent to College with a view to the profession of the Church or Law: Into one of which I should have been forced by necessity had not a friend left me £900; ... the act was done entirely from a confidence on his part that I had powers and attainments which might be of use to mankind.' He paid tribute to Calvert in a sonnet ('To the Memory of Raisley Calvert') and in the following lines from *The Prelude*:

> A Youth (he bore
> The name of Calvert; it shall live, if words
> Of mine can give it life,) without respect

To prejudice or custom, having hope
That I had some endowments by which good
Might be promoted, in his last decay
From his own Family withdrawing part
Of no redundant Patrimony, did
By a Bequest sufficient for my needs
Enable me to pause for choice, and walk
At large and unrestrain'd, nor damp'd too soon
By mortal cares. Himself no Poet, yet
Far less a common Spirit of the world,
He deem'd that my pursuits and labors lay
Apart from all that leads to wealth, or even
Perhaps to necessary maintenance,
Without some hazard to the finer sense;
He clear'd a passage for me, and the stream
Flow'd in the bent of Nature.

(1805 *Prelude*, xiii. 349–67)

Much of the time during Calvert's illness was spent in Keswick, but there was no time for Wordsworth to take pleasure in the scenery or work on his poetry, which had characterized his earlier stay there with Dorothy. He wrote to a friend, 'I begin to wish much to be in town [London]; cataracts and mountains, are good occasional society, but they will not do for constant companions'— understandable enough in the circumstances, but it *sounds* un-Wordsworthian. He did add, though, 'This is a country for poetry it is true; but the muse is not to be won but by the sacrifice of time, and time I have not to spare.'

Five years later, Wordsworth returned to the Lakes, 'a country for poetry', with Dorothy to make their home together in Grasmere. Within several more months their extraordinary friend Coleridge followed them and found a place for himself and his family in Keswick at a newly built house called Greta Hall [A]. He moved into Greta Hall in July 1800, and made it his home for over three years, until he left for Malta. It was a two-family house, and the Coleridges shared it for a while at the outset with its builder, William Jackson, 'a truly good and affectionate man', Coleridge said, who had earned his money as 'a common carrier'—he was probably the employer of Benjamin the Waggoner—'severely frugal, yet almost carelessly generous', and possessed of a 'love of knowledge' and a library of five hundred volumes. He refused to accept any rent from the Coleridges for the first six months on the grounds that the building was not entirely finished. Coleridge was grateful for the generosity as well as for the beauty of the place. As any reader of his journals will know, he had an eye for natural beauty unsurpassed even by Wordsworth's; Greta Hall and the surrounding country were full of delights for him. His study, he wrote, commanded 'six distinct Landscapes—the two Lakes, the Vale, River & mountains, & mists, & Clouds, & sunshine make endless combinations, as if heaven & Earth were for ever talking to each other'.

After frequent invitations, Coleridge eventually persuaded his brother-in-law Southey to come for a visit. Southey had no great interest in the Lakes, but on the death of his only daughter he agreed to the visit in hopes that he and his wife would find some consolation. They moved into the other half of the house, and before long Greta Hall was home. After Coleridge's departure, Mrs Coleridge and the children, plus other Southey relatives, became part of Southey's household. With seven children of his own, Southey eventually filled the entire house and kept it until his death in 1843. Wordsworth was, of course, a frequent visitor, especially when Coleridge was there—less often later, for he and Southey were never close friends, though each admired and respected the other. Near the end of their lives, though they lived less than twenty miles apart, Wordsworth said, 'I . . . hardly see him for years together.' When Southey died in 1843, Wordsworth, seventy-four years old, was not invited to the funeral, but he went anyway, accompanied by his son-in-law Edward Quillinan, to pay his respects by the graveside at Crosthwaite Church [B] on a stormy March day. Shortly afterwards, Wordsworth was asked to write an inscription for a monument inside the church. It proved a difficult task for the old poet: writing any poetry was difficult enough at this time, but an inscription in marble for the Poet Laureate required special care. His lines are now in the church, under an effigy said to be the truest likeness ever made of Southey.

INSCRIPTION

FOR A MONUMENT IN CROSTHWAITE CHURCH, IN THE VALE OF KESWICK

Ye vales and hills whose beauty hither drew
The poet's steps, and fixed him here, on you
His eyes have closed! And ye, lov'd books, no more
Shall Southey feed upon your precious lore,
To works that ne'er shall forfeit their renown,
Adding immortal labours of his own—
Whether he traced historic truth, with zeal
For the State's guidance, or the Church's weal,
Or Fancy, disciplined by studious art,
Inform'd his pen, or wisdom of the heart,
Or judgments sanctioned in the Patriot's mind
By reverence for the rights of all mankind.
Wide were his aims, yet in no human breast
Could private feelings meet for holier rest.
His joys, his griefs, have vanished like a cloud
From Skiddaw's top; but he to heaven was vowed
Through his industrious life, and Christian faith
Calmed in his soul the fear of change and death.

Wordsworth took the advice of friends and revised carefully before allowing the lines to be written in marble. Even so, he changed his mind about the next to last line; a close look at the monument reveals where it has been erased and re-incised, and in the published version, printed above, it is changed again.

In 1807 Wordsworth agreed to move to Greta Hall. Dorothy relates the circumstances in a letter to a friend:

Coleridge had an idea that S[outhey] intended leaving Keswick in the Autumn, in which case, he wished to have the house; and we consented to take it though *very very* reluctantly—Mary and I having many objections to Keswick; and a hundred more to taking Mrs. C.'s place in that house. But in consideration of Coleridge's inclinations, the convenience of having his books already there, and for the sake of Mrs. Wilson [the housekeeper] and Hartley [Coleridge's son], we had consented; but, as Mrs. C.'s letter informs C. that Southey has no thought of leaving Keswick it is out of the question, and we are all right glad in our hearts to be released.

(16 February 1807)

After having left in 1803, Coleridge made only short visits back to his family in Greta Hall, and he never returned after 1812. The scheme for the Wordsworths and Coleridges to live in Greta Hall was just one of several unsuccessful attempts to bring the two poets and their families together, but there were insuperable difficulties, such as Coleridge's estrangement from his wife and difficulties between Mrs Coleridge and the Wordsworths. Early in 1803, before the Southeys arrived, Sir George and Lady Beaumont stayed in the other half of Greta Hall. They were already devoted and highly intelligent admirers of Wordsworth's poetry and wanted to make it easier for the poets to be together. Before even meeting Wordsworth, Sir George bought some property at Applethwaite [C], near Keswick, to present to Wordsworth. It had several buildings on it, and Wordsworth was to fix up and add to one of them to make it liveable for his family. Sir George and Wordsworth met, but it was not until after Sir George's departure that the gift was presented, through Coleridge.

There were problems, however, and even in his letter of thanks to Sir George, Wordsworth had to say that the scheme was not likely to work: 'It is a most delightful situation, and few things would give me greater pleasure than to realize the plan which you had in view for me of building a house there. But I am afraid, I am sorry to say, that the chances are very much against this, partly on account of the state of my own affairs, and still more from the improbability of Mr Coleridge's continuing in the Country.' Since Sir George would not hear of taking it back, Wordsworth kept the property and added to it by purchases in 1813 and 1848. This sonnet honours the gift and the place.

AT APPLETHWAITE, NEAR KESWICK

Beaumont! it was thy wish that I should rear
A seemly Cottage in this sunny Dell,
On favoured ground, thy gift, where I might dwell
In neighbourhood with One to me most dear,
That undivided we from year to year
Might work in our high Calling—a bright hope
To which our fancies, mingling, gave free scope
Till checked by some necessities severe.

And should these slacken, honoured BEAUMONT! still
Even then we may perhaps in vain implore
Leave of our fate thy wishes to fulfil.
Whether this boon be granted us or not,
Old Skiddaw will look down upon the Spot
With pride, the Muses love it evermore.

Wordsworth did love the land on Applethwaite Gill. He kept a drawing Sir George had made of it over his mantle at Dove Cottage, and when someone tried to buy the land from him he refused because of the 'many sacred and personal recollections, . . . a *sacred* feeling' attached to it. His description of Applethwaite in *Select Views* (an early version of his *Guide*) reflects these feelings and his regret over the building of a cotton-mill in 1806.

This is a hamlet of six or seven houses, hidden in a small recess at the foot of Skiddaw, and adorned by a little Brook, which, having descended from a great height in a silver line down the steep blue side of the Mountain, trickles past the doors of the Cottages. This concealed spot is very interesting as you approach from the bottom, with your face towards the green and blue mass of Skiddaw; and is not less pleasing when, having advanced by a gentle slope for some space, you turn your head and look out from this chink or fissure, which is sprinkled with little orchards and trees, and behold the whole splendour of the upper and middle part of the Vale of Keswick, with its Lakes and Mountains spread before your eyes. A small Spinning-mill has lately been erected here, and some of the old Cottages, with their picturesque appendages, are fallen into decay. This is to be regretted; for, these blemishes excepted, the scene is a rare and almost singular combination of minute and sequestered beauty, with splendid and extensive prospects.

As it happened, Wordsworth never owned his own home, but he had building property in three places, Patterdale, Applethwaite, and Rydal. For them, and elsewhere, he had more than enough plans: 'The *temptation* [to build] I like, and I should content myself with the pleasure it gives me, through my whole life (I have at least built five hundred houses, in five hundred different places, with garden, ground, etc.) . . .' But the planning was more attractive than the execution. Dove Cottage, Allan Bank, the Rectory, and finally Rydal Mount—all of them rented—were home.

ii. Home at the Lake Country

6

Cockermouth[1]

Cockermouth stands at the junction of two rivers, the Derwent [B] and the Cocker, and Wordsworth was born there, loving rivers. The Derwent, the Cocker, the Duddon, the Rothay, the Yarrow nourished his life and his poetry, giving to him and drawing from him. A river was for him, as it has been for many others, a fit emblem of life, rising from obscure, often untraceable origins, and flowing toward a vast ocean which is its end as a separate thing and its mysterious merging into something grander. But more particularly, he associated the river with his own life as a poet, with its manifold possibilities and its doublings-back, its hesitations, apparent waywardness, and inevitable, if unknown, end.

After he had been away from the River Derwent for many years, he felt the frustration of not finding his poetic calling, of wandering and hesitating without getting on to the great work which he thought he could produce. His life was too full, in his words, of vacant musing, deliberate holiday, and vain perplexity. At such a time he measured himself against the river of his childhood.

> —Was it for this
> That one, the fairest of all Rivers, lov'd
> To blend his murmurs with my Nurse's song,
> And from his alder shades and rocky falls,
> And from his fords and shallows, sent a voice
> That flow'd along my dreams? For this, didst Thou,
> O Derwent! travelling over the green Plains
> Near my 'sweet Birthplace', didst thou, beauteous Stream,
> Make ceaseless music through the night and day

[1] Map on p. 220.

'COCKERMOUTH'. Cockermouth Castle is in the centre, and the old All Saints' Church, before it burned, is to the left of it. Wordsworth's house is on the River Derwent, downstream, to the right of the Castle.

Which with its steady cadence, tempering
Our human waywardness, compos'd my thoughts
To more than infant softness, giving me,
Among the fretful dwellings of mankind,
A knowledge, a dim earnest, of the calm
That Nature breathes among the hills and groves.
When, having left his Mountains, to the Towers
Of Cockermouth that beauteous River came,
Behind my Father's House he pass'd, close by,
Along the margin of our Terrace Walk.
He was a Playmate whom we dearly lov'd.
Oh! many a time have I, a five years' Child,
A naked Boy, in one delightful Rill,
A little Mill-race sever'd from his stream,
Made one long bathing of a summer's day,
Bask'd in the sun, and plunged, and bask'd again
Alternate all a summer's day, or cours'd
Over the sandy fields, leaping through groves
Of yellow grunsel, or when crag and hill,
The woods, and distant Skiddaw's lofty height,
Were bronz'd with a deep radiance, stood alone
Beneath the sky, as if I had been born
On Indian Plains, and from my Mother's hut
Had run abroad in wantonness, to sport,
A naked Savage, in the thunder shower.

(1805 *Prelude*, i. 271–304)

Hearing the Derwent's music, knowing its calm, playing at its side
while a naked, five-year-old boy was proper nourishment for an
aspiring poet: 'Fair seed-time had my soul'. What grew in
Wordsworth was usually rooted in the memory of the past. Even his
worry and self-doubt—'Was it for this . . .?'—takes him back to the
past and, in doing so, produces the blossom. *The Prelude* is a
recollection of things past, at once a great poem and a record of how
the poet and poem came to be.

Wordsworth speaks of the Derwent running 'Behind my father's
house . . . | Along the margin of our terrace walk'. It still does, and
Wordsworth's house [A], handsomely preserved and displayed, is
the most impressive house along Main Street in Cockermouth.
Owned by Sir James Lowther for the use of his agent,

Wordsworth's father, it was the finest house in the entire town at that time, and it looked then very much like it looks today. There Wordsworth was born on 7 April 1770; there he played with his three brothers, Richard, John, and Christopher, and his sister Dorothy; there they enjoyed the warm affection of their mother until she died in 1778:

> Early died
> My honoured Mother, she who was the heart
> And hinge of all our learnings and our loves:
> She left us destitute, and, as we might,
> Trooping together.

(The Prelude, v. 256–60)

Near the time of her death she said 'the only one of her five children about whose future life she was anxious, was William; and he, she said, would be remarkable either for good or for evil'.[2] Five years after her death, the three oldest boys returned to Cockermouth from Hawkshead Grammar School during their Christmas holidays to find their father dying. Before the end of those holidays they stood at his grave next to the church [E] and saw him buried. Richard was fifteen years old, William thirteen, and John eleven. The youngest child, Christopher, aged nine, was at his grandparents' house in Penrith, and Dorothy, aged twelve, was with her relatives in Halifax. After their father's death, Cockermouth was no longer home.

Nine years, however—the time from Wordsworth's birth until he began school at Hawkshead—is a long and important time in childhood. Compared to the next nine years at Hawkshead, we have a relatively scant poetic record of the time and place, though one can hardly complain after reading the splendid lines on the Derwent in *The Prelude*. But there are other lines and poems that speak of these years. From the 'terrace walk' behind the Wordsworths' house one can no longer see, because of more recent buildings, a sight that fascinated Wordsworth—a road going up a hill and off into unknown territory beyond—but it is still visible from the bridge [C] just below the house, as you look upstream, past Cockermouth Castle. The road goes over Watch Hill towards Isel, but for the boy on the terrace it was 'an invitation into space':

[2] Christopher Wordsworth, *Memoirs of William Wordsworth* (1851), i. 9.

Who doth not love to follow with his eye
The windings of a public way? the sight,
Familiar object as it is, hath wrought
On my imagination since the morn
Of childhood, when a disappearing line,
One daily present to my eyes, that crossed
The naked summit of a far-off hill
Beyond the limits that my feet had trod,
Was like an invitation into space
Boundless, or guide into eternity.

(*The Prelude*, xiii. 142–51)

William and his sister Dorothy, who was christened at the same time as William in the old parish church, used to play together on the terrace until they were separated after the death of their mother. Years later, when they were together again at Grasmere, he wrote 'The Sparrow's Nest'. 'At the end of the garden at my Father's house at Cockermouth', he told Miss Fenwick, 'was a high terrace that commanded a fine view of the River Derwent and Cockermouth Castle. This was our favourite playground. The terrace-wall, a low one, was covered with closely-clipt privet and roses, which gave an almost impervious shelter to birds that built their nests there. The latter of these stanzas alludes to one of these nests.' Here, and elsewhere, he uses the name Emmeline for Dorothy.

THE SPARROW'S NEST

Behold, within the leafy shade,
Those bright blue eggs together laid!
On me the chance-discovered sight
Gleamed like a vision of delight.
I started—seeming to espy
The home and sheltered bed,
The Sparrow's dwelling, which, hard by
My Father's house, in wet or dry
My sister Emmeline and I
    Together visited.

She looked at it and seemed to fear it;
Dreading, tho' wishing, to be near it:

> Such heart was in her, being then
> A little Prattler among men.
> The Blessing of my later years
> Was with me when a boy:
> She gave me eyes, she gave me ears;
> And humble cares, and delicate fears;
> A heart, the fountain of sweet tears;
>   And love, and thought, and joy.

If the Derwent nourished his soul, Dorothy deserves credit as well, for the eyes and the ears she gave him contributed to the building-up of what the Pastor in *The Excursion* calls 'the pure soul . . . | With her two faculties of eye and ear' (v, 986–7). Years later, Dorothy described the garden at their first home and her visit to it in 1794:

It is at the outskirts of the Town, the garden bordering on the River Derwent or rather a *Terrace* which overlooks the River, a spot which I remember as vividly as if I had been there but the other day, though I have never seen it in its neatness, as my Father and Mother used to keep it, since I was just six years old, a few months before my Mother's death. I visited the place again at the age of twenty three and all was in ruin, the terrace-walk buried and choked up with the old privot hedge which had formerly been most beautiful, roses and privot intermingled—the same hedge where the sparrows were used to build their nests.

(Letters, 7 August 1805)

Another poem was written in Grasmere about his recollection of Cockermouth, this one triggered by the sight of a butterfly in the garden at Dove Cottage.

TO A BUTTERFLY

> Stay near me—do not take thy flight!
> A little longer stay in sight!
> Much converse do I find in thee,
> Historian of my infancy!
> Float near me; do not yet depart!
> Dead times revive in thee:
> Thou bring'st, gay creature as thou art!
> A solemn image to my heart,
> My father's family!

Oh! pleasant, pleasant were the days,
The time, when, in our childish plays,
My sister Emmeline and I
Together chased the butterfly!
A very hunter did I rush
Upon the prey:—with leaps and springs
I followed on from brake to bush;
But she, God love her! feared to brush
The dust from off its wings.

The nourishment of love and beauty was an important part of these Cockermouth days, but Wordsworth was also a 'naked savage', 'a very hunter', preying and being preyed upon. He told Dorothy that he killed all the white butterflies on the way to school in Cockermouth 'because they were Frenchmen'. He was no 'model' child or 'miracle of scientific lore', not a boy who never quarrelled, was never selfish, and never susceptible to 'natural or supernatural fear, | Unless it leap upon him in a dream.'[3] The combined nourishment of beauty *and* fear is best expressed in a fine sonnet about Cockermouth Castle [D], the ruins of which still stand above the junction of the Rivers Derwent and Cocker. It is an awesome sight when seen, unobstructed by the brewery, from up the Derwent, and it still contains the dungeons where Wordsworth used to play. In this sonnet, however, the poet returns as an old man, looking at his former play spot and fancying that he and the castle, both 'stricken . . . by years', are linked more closely now. The castle corrects him ('fondly' means 'credulously' here) and, still his tutor, reminds him of the 'sterner link' of the earlier years.

ADDRESS FROM THE SPIRIT OF
COCKERMOUTH CASTLE

'Thou look'st upon me, and dost fondly think,
Poet! that, stricken as both are by years,
We, differing once so much, are now Compeers,
Prepared, when each has stood his time, to sink
Into the dust. Erewhile a sterner link

[3] This ironic portrait of a 'model child' in *The Prelude* (v. 299–346) stands in contrast to his description of 'a race of real children' (v. 406–25).

United us; when thou, in boyish play,
Entering my dungeon, didst become a prey
To soul-appalling darkness. Not a blink
Of light was there;—and thus did I, thy Tutor,
Make thy young thoughts acquainted with the grave;
While thou wert chasing the wing'd butterfly
Through my green courts; or climbing, a bold suitor,
Up to the flowers whose golden progeny
Still round my shattered brow in beauty wave.'

Butterflies, flowers, and the grave; soul-appalling darkness and
beauty—such was the nourishment of boyish play within the castle,
high above the River Derwent.

7

Hawkshead[1]

Unlike his sister Dorothy, who was sent to live with their stern
relatives in Penrith after they were orphaned, Wordsworth was
blessed with a happy childhood even after the Cockermouth years.
Although he went to Cockermouth or Penrith for holidays, his true
boyhood home was Hawkshead, a small village noted for its wool
and cloth trade and its excellent grammar school. William and the
other Wordsworth boys were probably fortunate not to be lodged in
the main boarding-house near the school with fifty or more other
boys. They lived instead in the house of Ann Tyson. Childless
herself, she became a mother to them, caring for them and at the
same time leaving William free to roam the countryside from the
time he arrived at the age of nine. 'The Child is father of the Man',
Wordsworth wrote, and Hawkshead figures prominently in his
autobiographical poem, *The Prelude, or Growth of a Poet's Mind*,
for it was in Hawkshead, as well as in Cockermouth, that the boy

[1] Map on p. 225.

Drawn & Engd by W. Banks & Son, Edinr

was 'fostered alike by beauty and by fear'. Books i, ii, and iv of *The Prelude* tell of his school-days, from 1779 to 1787, and of his return in 1788 for the summer vacation after his first year at Cambridge.

The buildings that Wordsworth knew are, for the most part, still standing, though when he returned for a visit in 1799 he noticed 'great change amongst the people since we were last there' and some changes in the architecture. When he was a schoolboy, there had been a large stone in the Market Square from which an 'old Dame' named Nanny Holme sold her goods to the schoolchildren and villagers. But in 1790 it had been broken up to make way for the present 'smart Assembly-room', part of the new Market House [A], now the Town Hall.

> A grey Stone
> Of native rock, left midway in the Square
> Of our small market Village, was the home
> And centre of these joys, and when, return'd
> After long absence, thither I repair'd,
> I found that it was split, and gone to build
> A smart, Assembly-room that perk'd and flar'd
> With wash and rough-cast elbowing the ground
> Which had been ours. But let the fiddle scream,
> And be ye happy! yet, my Friends! I know
> That more than one of you will think with me
> Of those soft starry nights, and that old Dame
> From whom the Stone was nam'd who there had sate
> And watch'd her Table with its huckster's wares
> Assiduous, thro' the length of sixty years.

(1805 *Prelude*, ii. 33–47)

Much 'elbowing' besides this has taken place since Wordsworth's time, but the house [B] where he lived for his first four years in Hawkshead remains a few steps from the Market Square. Just above the square is Hawkshead Church [D]. It was the first thing visible when he came over Claife Heights, returning for his summer vacation:

> . . . now drawing towards home,
> To that sweet Valley where I had been rear'd;
> . . . veering round,
> I saw the snow-white Church upon its hill

> Sit like a thronèd Lady, sending out
> A gracious look all over its domain.

(1805 Prelude, iv. 10–15)

'Snow-white' was accurate then, though not now; until 1875 the stone exterior was covered with mortar and gravel, and white-washed. Inside the church, 'Admonitory texts inscribed the walls' (*The Excursion*, v. 150) in Wordsworth's school-days and today, although they were covered over in the mid-1790s and later restored. Some changes we can be grateful for. Tourists and residents alike are probably better pleased not to be greeted at the churchyard gates by the gory sight of earlier days: 'I recollect frequently seeing, when a boy,' Wordsworth wrote in his *Guide*, 'bunches of unfledged ravens suspended from the churchyard gates of H[awkshead], for which a reward of *so* much a head was given to the adventurous destroyer.' Since ravens were enemies of lambs, schoolboys were encouraged by a small reward to raid the nests. One of Wordsworth's school-fellows left an exciting account of an expedition to the Yewdale Crags in search of ravens' eggs. The boy who climbed down the cliff to get the eggs became frightened and could not move, and the youngest boy, 'Bill Wordsworth', with two others was sent to find help.[2] Wordsworth records another occasion when he went hunting alone in springtime:

> when the Vales
> And woods were warm, was I a plunderer then
> In the high places, on the lonesome peaks
> Where'er, among the mountains and the winds,
> The Mother Bird had built her lodge. Though mean
> My object, and inglorious, yet the end
> Was not ignoble. Oh! when I have hung
> Above the raven's nest, by knots of grass
> And half-inch fissures in the slippery rock
> But ill sustain'd, and almost, as it seem'd,
> Suspended by the blast which blew amain,
> Shouldering the naked crag; Oh! at that time,
> While on the perilous ridge I hung alone,

[2] The story is recounted in T. W. Thompson, *Wordsworth's Hawkshead* (1970), pp. 211–15.

With what strange utterance did the loud dry wind
Blow through my ears! the sky seem'd not a sky
Of earth, and with what motion mov'd the clouds!

(1805 Prelude, i. 335–50)

Below the churchyard Hawkshead Grammar School [E] still stands, where 'noble Sandys, inspir'd with great design, | Reared Hawkshead's happy roof'. So Wordsworth, a fourteen-year-old poet, wrote in a school exercise for the two-hundredth anniversary of its founding by Archbishop Sandys. At this school Wordsworth read the classics, received excellent training in mathematics, borrowed the eighteenth-century poets from the Headmaster, Henry Taylor, and—an ordinary schoolboy—carved his name on the oak desk. Already he had a formidable reputation as a poet: 'How is it, Bill, thee doest write such good verses?' an older school-fellow asked. 'Doest thee invoke Muses?'

Probably in 1783, Ann Tyson and her husband Hugh, a joiner, moved to the hamlet of Colthouse, half a mile from Hawkshead, taking the Wordsworth boys and a few other lodgers with them. Their house, 'our rural dwelling', was most likely what is now called Green End Cottage [F]. Wordsworth was delighted to survey it again after returning from his confined life in Cambridge, where he had felt like the 'boxed' brook in the garden.

The rooms, the court, the garden were not left
Long unsaluted, and the spreading Pine
And broad stone Table underneath its boughs,
Our summer seat in many a festive hour;
And that unruly Child of mountain birth,
The froward Brook, which soon as he was box'd
Within our Garden, found himself at once,
As if by trick insidious and unkind,
Stripp'd of his voice, and left to dimple down
Without an effort and without a will,
A channel pavèd by the hand of man.

(1805 Prelude, iv. 35–45)

The 'court' is by the lane at the rear of the cottage; the garden is where it was, though the pine and stone table are gone; and the boxed brook—so troublesome before Mrs Heelis discovered that

Ann Tyson had lived in Colthouse—is just where the poet says it was: 'Within our garden'.[3] *The Prelude* describes the boys 'by the warm peat-fire | At evening' playing tic-tac-toe and cards, hearing occasionally the sounds from 'Esthwaite's splitting fields of ice' (i. 499–543). And it describes how William during a summer evening would gaze, his imagination kindled, out of the front door to Spring Wood [H] on the hillside.

> There was a Copse
> An upright bank of wood and woody rock
> That opposite our rural Dwelling stood,
> In which a sparkling patch of diamond light
> Was in bright weather duly to be seen
> On summer afternoons, within the wood
> At the same place. 'Twas doubtless nothing more
> Than a black rock, which, wet with constant springs
> Glister'd far seen from out its lurking-place
> As soon as ever the declining sun
> Had smitten it. Beside our Cottage hearth,
> Sitting with open door, a hundred times
> Upon this lustre have I gaz'd, that seem'd
> To have some meaning which I could not find;
> And now it was a burnished shield, I fancied,
> Suspended over a Knight's Tomb, who lay
> Inglorious, buried in the dusky wood;
> An entrance now into some magic cave
> Or Palace for a Fairy of the rock;
> Nor would I, though not certain whence the cause
> Of the effulgence, thither have repair'd
> Without a precious bribe, and day by day
> And month by month I saw the spectacle,
> Nor ever once have visited the spot
> Unto this hour. Thus sometimes were the shapes
> Of wilful fancy grafted upon feelings
> Of the imagination, and they rose
> In worth accordingly.

(1805 *Prelude*, viii. 559–86)

---

[3] Mrs Heelis (née Beatrix Potter) discovered this from some old papers found in a barn she had purchased. She lived nearby, at Hill Top Farm, in Near Sawrey.

Wordsworth seems always to have regarded Ann Tyson with great affection, but when he returned from Cambridge he saw her 'with something of another eye':

> With new delight,
> This chiefly, did I view my grey-hair'd Dame,
> Saw her go forth to Church, or other work
> Of state, equipp'd in monumental trim,
> Short Velvet Cloak (her Bonnet of the like)
> A Mantle such as Spanish Cavaliers
> Wore in old time. Her smooth domestic life,
> Affectionate without uneasiness,
> Her talk, her business pleas'd me, and no less
> Her clear though shallow stream of piety,
> That ran on Sabbath days a fresher course.
> With thoughts unfelt till now, I saw her read
> Her Bible on the Sunday afternoons;
> And lov'd the book, when she had dropp'd asleep,
> And made of it a pillow for her head.

(1805 *Prelude*, iv. 207–21)

Ann Tyson loved to tell tales ('half as long as an ancient romance', Dorothy wrote) and William, no doubt, loved to listen. Hers is 'the matron's tale' of the shepherd and the lost son told in Book viii of the 1805 *Prelude*, and from her came the story of two Hawkshead men, one a Jacobite and the other a Hanoverian Whig, in Book vi of *The Excursion* ('Their stories I had from the dear old Dame with whom, as a schoolboy and afterwards, I lodged for nearly the space of ten years'—I.F.). And she told William the tale of Mary Rigge, 'the fairest maid of Esthwaite's vale', who had been seduced and abandoned by a neighbourhood gentleman, gave birth to his child, named Benoni, and died aged twenty-one. William retold it in a very early (and undistinguished) poem called 'A Ballad' and later in *Peter Bell* (lines 906–15). Mary Rigge had lived at Green End House [G], just across the lane from Green End Cottage. The Wordsworth boys stayed there for two or three weeks with her parents when Ann Tyson was unable to keep them, probably during her husband's fatal illness.

T. W. Thompson, in *Wordsworth's Hawkshead*, has discussed other local characters whom Wordsworth wrote about—models for

the Matthew poems, the packman–Wanderer of *The Excursion*, and
the grandson and grandsire of 'The Two Thieves'. Among them is
an account of the Reverend William Braithwaite, who built a seat
under an ancient yew tree by Esthwaite Water, less than a mile from
Colthouse, just before Waterside [L]. He had been a student at
Hawkshead and St. John's, Cambridge (like Wordsworth, but
fifteen years earlier), had taken Holy Orders but, not receiving a
Living, retired to the Sawrey area, where he lived while
Wordsworth was a schoolboy. There is no evidence that
Wordsworth knew him personally, but he did know the yew tree
and its seat, for 'this spot was my favourite walk in the evenings
during the latter part of my school-time' (I.F.). From this yew tree,
the seat, and the melancholic character, Wordsworth wrote a poem
in 1797, though begun, he said, 'at school in Hawkshead', with this
title: 'Lines Left upon a Seat in a Yew-tree, which stands near the
lake of Esthwaite, on a desolate part of the shore, commanding a
beautiful prospect'. When Wordsworth wrote an unpublished tour
book in 1811 or 1812, he regretted that someone had ruined the
walk by enclosing it with a wall (which is still there): 'In the wall
that bounds this obnoxious enclosure is yet to be seen the remnant
of a decaying Yew tree within which some contemplative Man
erected a seat. . . . The boughs had been trained to bend round the
seat and almost embrace the Person who might occupy the seat
within, allowing only an opening for the beautiful landscape. The
narrow space between the yew tree & the Lake was scattered over
with juniper furze, heath, & wild time. . . .'[4] In 1843 the regret
remained, but the yew tree did not. 'The tree has disappeared, and
the slip of Common on which it stood, that ran parallel to the lake,
and lay open to it, has long been enclosed; so that the road has lost
much of its attraction' (I.F.). And the motor traffic, we might add,
has not helped. But the poem has lost none of its attraction. It has
never required sight of the yew tree or knowledge of the Reverend
Braithwaite to be properly read—indeed, it imagines a 'lonely yew-
tree . . . | Far from all human dwelling', which this was not, and
that the melancholic 'died, this seat his only monument', which the
clergyman had not done when Wordsworth wrote the poem. It

---

[4] Now published in *Prose Works*, ii. 336.

appears, however, that Wordsworth's imagination required the yew tree and seat and the clergyman—or reports of him—to give rise to the poem. For the modern reader the poem yields its pleasures at least as freely as it did in 1798, when it stood as Wordsworth's first poem in *Lyrical Ballads*. The reader-traveller who visits the spot today will find, in spite of the changes, a shore not far different, a distant prospect still beautiful, and a place to heed the poet's injunction: 'Nay, Traveller! rest. . . . how lovely 'tis Thou seest. . . .'

From Colthouse Wordsworth walked to school, sometimes experiencing the 'Fallings from us, vanishings' that he described in his famous comment on the 'Immortality Ode': 'I was unable to think of external things as having external existence, and I communed with all that I saw as something not apart from, but inherent in, my own immaterial nature. Many times while going to school have I grasped at a wall or tree to recall myself from this abyss of idealism to the reality. At that time I was afraid of such processes' (I.F.). Indeed, fear was crucial to his Hawkshead upbringing: it was surely part of the appeal of raiding ravens' nests on the Yewdale Crags and, allied with guilt, was among the emotions felt when snaring woodcocks between Hawkshead and Hawkshead Moor [C]:

> Well I call to mind
> ('Twas at an early age, ere I had seen
> Nine summers) when upon the mountain slope
> The frost and breath of frosty wind had snapp'd
> The last autumnal crocus, 'twas my joy
> To wander half the night among the Cliffs
> And the smooth Hollows, where the woodcocks ran
> Along the open turf. In thought and wish
> That time, my shoulder all with springes hung,
> I was a fell destroyer. On the heights
> Scudding away from snare to snare, I plied
> My anxious visitation, hurrying on,
> Still hurrying, hurrying onward; moon and stars
> Were shining o'er my head; I was alone,
> And seem'd to be a trouble to the peace
> That was among them. Sometimes it befel
> In these night-wanderings, that a strong desire

O'erpower'd my better reason, and the bird
Which was the captive of another's toils
Became my prey; and, when the deed was done
I heard among the solitary hills
Low breathings coming after me, and sounds
Of undistinguishable motion, steps
Almost as silent as the turf they trod.

(1805 *Prelude*, i. 309–32)

Yet on one occasion, shortly after the nine-year-old boy had arrived
at Hawkshead, he experienced something along Esthwaite Water
[K] that might have been terrifying, but was not; it aroused 'no vulgar
fear', though it made a deep impression.

Well do I call to mind the very week
When I was first entrusted to the care
Of that sweet Valley; when its paths, its shores,
And brooks, were like a dream of novelty
To my half-infant thoughts; that very week
While I was roving up and down alone,
Seeking I knew not what, I chanced to cross
One of those open fields, which, shaped like ears,
Make green peninsulas on Esthwaite's Lake:
Twilight was coming on; yet through the gloom,
I saw distinctly on the opposite Shore
A heap of garments, left, as I suppos'd,
By one who there was bathing; long I watch'd,
But no one own'd them; meanwhile the calm Lake
Grew dark, with all the shadows on its breast,
And, now and then, a fish up-leaping, snapp'd
The breathless stillness. The succeeding day,
(Those unclaimed garments telling a plain Tale)
Went there a Company, and, in their Boat
Sounded with grappling irons, and long poles.
At length, the dead Man, 'mid that beauteous scene
Of trees, and hills and water, bolt upright
Rose with his ghastly face; a spectre shape
Of terror even! and yet no vulgar fear,
Young as I was, a Child not nine years old,
Possess'd me; for my inner eye had seen
Such sights before, among the shining streams
Of Fairy Land, the Forests of Romance:

Thence came a spirit hallowing what I saw
With decoration and ideal grace;
A dignity, a smoothness, like the works
Of Grecian Art, and purest Poesy.

(1805 *Prelude*, v. 450–81)

In his later years he described himself as 'one who spent half of
his boyhood in running wild among the Mountains'. He wandered
'half the night among the Cliffs', or he climbed out of bed very early
to cover five miles before school, which began as early as six o'clock,
or seven in the winter:

My morning walks
Were early; oft, before the hours of School
I travell'd round our little Lake, five miles
Of pleasant wandering, happy time! more dear
For this, that one was by my side, a Friend
Then passionately lov'd. . . .

(1805 *Prelude*, ii. 348–53)

The friend was a school-fellow, John Fleming: 'Friendship and
Fleming are the same', he wrote in his juvenile poem, 'The Vale of
Esthwaite'. They often spouted poetry to each other, being like-
minded enthusiasts. Later, during the summer vacation from
Cambridge, Wordsworth often walked alone, composing aloud,
though at the risk of being thought crazy. On such occasions, the
Tyson dog, 'rough terrier of the hills', proved invaluable:

And when, in the public roads at eventide
I saunter'd, like a river murmuring
And talking to itself, at such a season
It was his custom to jog on before;
But, duly, whensoever he had met
A passenger approaching, would he turn
To give me timely notice, and straitway,
Punctual to such admonishment, I hush'd
My voice, composed my gait, and shap'd myself
To give and take a greeting that might save
My name from piteous rumours, such as wait
On men suspected to be craz'd in brain.

(1805 *Prelude*, iv. 109–20)

The school-days were filled to abundance not only with books but with solitary and sociable walks, hunting, fishing, ice-skating, boating, and horse-riding, all recorded in *The Prelude*. And, 'like most of my schoolfellows I was an impassioned nutter' (I.F.). 'Nutting' shows him in this role, off to collect hazels in the Graythwaite woods [P],

> a Figure quaint,
> Tricked out in proud disguise of cast-off weeds,
> Which for that service had been husbanded,
> By exhortation of my frugal Dame—
> Motley accoutrement, of power to smile
> At thorns, and brakes, and brambles,—and, in truth,
> More ragged than need was!

Wordsworth was fortunate indeed to have been a schoolboy in Esthwaite vale, nourished by Ann Tyson's 'frugal, Sabine fare', her love, and her *laissez-faire*. She died in 1796, aged 83, and was buried in the Hawkshead churchyard. This is Wordsworth's tribute to 'my old dame, so motherly and good':

> While my heart
> Can beat I never will forget thy name.
> Heaven's blessing be upon thee where thou liest,
> After thy innocent and busy stir
> In narrow cares, thy little daily growth
> Of calm enjoyments, after eighty years,
> And more than eighty, of untroubled life,
> Childless, yet by the strangers to thy blood
> Honour'd with little less than filial love.
>
> (1805 *Prelude*, iv. 20–8)

He loved the vale while he was a pupil at Hawkshead, prophesying in some school verses that if, in his final hour, 'a single tie | Survive of local sympathy', he will then think back on his 'Dear native regions' (*PW*, i. 2). *The Prelude*, worked on throughout his life and not published until after his death, is a tribute to the liveliness of that 'local sympathy'.

8

Grasmere[1]

While a pupil at Hawkshead, Wordsworth must have passed through Grasmere vale several times. On one of the few recorded visits he looked down on the vale from Hammerscar [Q] on the Red Bank road, near the southern end of the lake. It was a revealing, even prophetic moment, halting the schoolboy who was by himself, hurrying on some boyish pursuit. He later wrote about the scene at the beginning of his never-finished philosophical poem, *The Recluse*, intended to be his *magnum opus*.

> Once to the verge of yon steep barrier came
> A roving School-boy; what the Adventurer's age
> Hath now escaped his memory—but the hour,
> One of a golden summer holiday,
> He well remembers, though the year be gone.
> Alone and devious from afar he came;
> And, with a sudden influx overpowered
> At sight of this seclusion, he forgot
> His haste, for hasty had his footsteps been
> As boyish his pursuits; and, sighing said,
> 'What happy fortune were it here to live!
> And, if a thought of dying, if a thought
> Of mortal separation, could intrude
> With paradise before him, here to die!'
> No Prophet was he, had not even a hope,
> Scarcely a wish, but one bright pleasing thought,
> A fancy in the heart of what might be
> The lot of Others, never could be his.
>
> The Station whence he look'd was soft and green,
> Not giddy yet aerial, with a depth
> Of Vale below, a height of hills above.

[1] Map on p. 234.

'GRASMERE FROM RED BANK', showing two of Wordsworth's homes. The Rectory is just left of the Church, and Allan Bank is further left, higher than the other buildings.

> For rest of body, perfect was the Spot,
> All that luxurious nature could desire,
> But stirring to the Spirit; . . . here
> Must be his Home, this Valley be his World.

When he wrote this, the thought of the schoolboy had become a fact for the poet in his early thirties.

> And now 'tis mine, perchance for life, dear Vale,
> Beloved Grasmere (let the Wandering Streams
> Take up, the cloud-capt hills repeat, the Name),
> One of thy lowly Dwellings is my Home.

The poem, which was the first part of his philosophical poem, he called *Home at Grasmere*.[2]

Grasmere was more than a beautiful place for Wordsworth; it was an imaginative act, a union of the individual mind 'wedded to this outward frame of things | In love'. Not just a place but a 'Spot', to use his charged word, where the mind and world are 'blended'.

> Embrace me then, ye Hills, and close me in,
> Now in the clear and open day I feel
> Your guardianship; I take it to my heart;
> 'Tis like the solemn shelter of the night.
> But I would call thee beautiful, for mild
> And soft, and gay, and beautiful thou art,
> Dear Valley, having in thy face a smile
> Though peaceful, full of gladness. Thou art pleased,
> Pleased with thy crags, and woody steeps, thy Lake,
> Its one green Island and its winding shores;
> The multitude of little rocky hills,
> Thy Church and Cottages of mountain stone
> Clustered like stars some few, but single most,
> And lurking dimly in their shy retreats,
> Or glancing at each other chearful looks,
> Like separated stars with clouds between.
> What want we? have we not perpetual streams,
> Warm woods, and sunny hills, and fresh green fields,
> And mountains not less green, and flocks, and herds,

---

[2] I quote from the version printed in *PW*, v. 313–39. The Cornell Wordsworth, *Home at Grasmere*, edited by Beth Darlington (1977), contains two reading texts of the poem and facsimiles of the manuscripts.

And thickets full of songsters, and the voice
Of lordly birds, an unexpected sound
Heard now and then from morn till latest eve,
Admonishing the man who walks below
Of solitude, and silence in the sky?
These have we, and a thousand nooks of earth
Have also these, but no where else is found,
No where (or is it fancy?) can be found
The one sensation that is here; 'tis here,
Here as it found its way into my heart
In childhood, here as it abides by day,
By night, here only; or in chosen minds
That take it with them hence, where'er they go.
'Tis, but I cannot name it, 'tis the sense
Of majesty, and beauty, and repose,
A blended holiness of earth and sky,
Something that makes this individual Spot,
This small Abiding-place of many Men,
A termination, and a last retreat,
A Centre, come from wheresoe'er you will,
A Whole without dependence or defect,
Made for itself; and happy in itself,
Perfect Contentment, Unity entire.

Grasmere was Wordsworth's new paradise. He had spent five days
there with Coleridge on their walking tour in November of 1799,
during which he concocted a plan of building a house for himself
and Dorothy by the lakeside. But there was a cottage already
available at a modest rent—£5 per year—and before he left the
area, Wordsworth had taken it. In late December he returned with
Dorothy from Sockburn-upon-Tees in Yorkshire, and they moved
into what is now (but was never in Wordsworth's time) known as
Dove Cottage [A] at Town End. Their new home was in their minds
a 'hallowed spot', a type of what the common world might some day
become, and they were a type of the new Adam and Eve:

Both in the sadness and the joy we found
A promise and an earnest that we twain,
A pair receding from the common world,
Might in that hallow'd spot to which our steps
Were tending, in that individual nook,

> Might, even thus early, for ourselves secure,
> And in the midst of these unhappy times,
> A portion of the blessedness which love
> And knowledge, will, we trust, hereafter give
> To all the vales of Earth and all mankind.

I call this a 'new' paradise because Grasmere was no Eden exempt from pain and sorrow ('Nature to this favourite spot of ours | Yields no exemption . . . [from] | Her tribute of inevitable pain'); the two were not placed here in innocence but had to 'secede' from the common world by choice, and they were not alone.

> No, we are not alone, we do not stand,
> My Sister, here misplaced and desolate,
> Loving what no one cares for but ourselves;
> . . . this whole Vale,
> Home of untutored Shepherds as it is,
> Swarms with sensation. . . .

And before long there were more than shepherds to share their vale: to Dove Cottage came their brother John, 'A never-resting Pilgrim of the Sea, | Who finds at last an hour to his content | Beneath our roof', the Hutchinson girls, Mary (who was to become Wordsworth's wife), Sara, and Joanna—'Sisters of our hearts'— and 'One, like them, a Brother of our hearts, | Philosopher and Poet', Samuel Taylor Coleridge. They were in truth 'a happy Band', and Grasmere was to them an improvement over the old paradise:

> The boon is absolute; surpassing grace
> To me hath been vouchsafed; among the bowers
> Of blissful Eden this was neither given,
> Nor could be given, possession of the good
> Which had been sighed for, ancient thought fulfilled
> And dear Imaginations realized
> Up to their highest measure, yea and more.

Seeing Grasmere as a type of paradise is not for Wordsworth poetic hyperbole, nor is it simply a strongly felt tribute to an extraordinarily beautiful place. It is rather the celebration of a chosen beloved spot, the celebration of a life of imagination, where mind is wedded to the world in love.

By 1802 Wordsworth had come to see that he could not marry the Frenchwoman Annette Vallon, as he had intended and promised. He married instead Mary Hutchinson, whom he had known and loved from childhood. William and Dorothy left Dove Cottage to return to Yorkshire for the marriage and to bring Mary back to the cottage. The best poetic description of Dove Cottage and its garden is the poem which Dorothy referred to as the 'poem on Going for Mary'.

A FAREWELL

Farewell, thou little Nook of mountain-ground,
Thou rocky corner in the lowest stair
Of that magnificent temple which doth bound
One side of our whole vale with grandeur rare;
Sweet garden-orchard, eminently fair,
The loveliest spot that man hath ever found,
Farewell!—we leave thee to Heaven's peaceful care,
Thee, and the Cottage which thou dost surround.

Our boat is safely anchored by the shore,
And there will safely ride when we are gone;
The flowering shrubs that deck our humble door
Will prosper, though untended and alone:
Fields, goods, and far-off chattels we have none:
These narrow bounds contain our private store
Of things earth makes, and sun doth shine upon;
Here are they in our sight—we have no more.

Sunshine and shower be with you, bud and bell!
For two months now in vain we shall be sought;
We leave you here in solitude to dwell
With these our latest gifts of tender thought;
Thou, like the morning, in thy saffron coat,
Bright gowan, and marsh-marigold, farewell!
Whom from the borders of the Lake we brought,
And placed together near our rocky Well.

We go for One to whom ye will be dear;
And she will prize this Bower, this Indian shed,
Our own contrivance, Building without peer!

—A gentle Maid, whose heart is lowly bred,
Whose pleasures are in wild fields gatherèd,
With joyousness, and with a thoughtful cheer,
Will come to you; to you herself will wed;
And love the blessed life that we lead here.

Dear Spot! Which we have watched with tender heed,
Bringing thee chosen plants and blossoms blown
Among the distant mountains, flower and weed,
Which thou hast taken to thee as thy own,
Making all kindness registered and known;
Thou for our sakes, though Nature's child indeed,
Fair in thyself and beautiful alone,
Hast taken gifts which thou dost little need.

And O most constant, yet most fickle Place,
That hast thy wayward moods, as thou dost show
To them who look not daily on thy face;
Who, being loved, in love no bounds dost know,
And say'st, when we forsake thee, 'Let them go!'
Thou easy-hearted Thing, with thy wild race
Of weeds and flowers, till we return be slow,
And travel with the year at a soft pace.

Help us to tell Her tales of years gone by,
And this sweet spring, the best beloved and best;
Joy will be flown in its mortality;
Something must stay to tell us of the rest.
Here, thronged with primroses, the steep rock's breast
Glittered at evening like a starry sky;
And in this bush our sparrow built her nest,
Of which I sang one song that will not die.

O happy Garden! whose seclusion deep
Hath been so friendly to industrious hours;
And to soft slumbers, that did gently steep
Our spirits, carrying with them dreams of flowers,
And wild notes warbled among leafy bowers;
Two burning months let summer overleap,
And, coming back with Her who will be ours,
Into thy bosom we again shall creep.

Grasmere is still described as a paradise here and even more explicitly in another poem of departure, recording the beginning of his trip to Scotland in 1803, but written in 1811 (*PW*, iii. 64).

The garden and orchard behind the cottage were created by William and Dorothy with help from their friends ('This plot of orchard-ground is ours; | My trees they are, my Sister's flowers', he wrote in 'To a Butterfly'). Many of his poems were written in and some even about the garden and orchard.

> Beneath these fruit-tree boughs that shed
> Their snow-white blossoms on my head,
> With brightest sunshine round me spread
>   Of spring's unclouded weather,
> In this sequestered nook how sweet
> To sit upon my orchard-seat!
> And birds and flowers once more to greet,
>   My last year's friends together. . . .
>
> ('The Green Linnet')

Years later he said that 'The Redbreast Chasing the Butterfly' had been 'observed and described in the then beautiful Orchard at Town-End'—the phrase 'then beautiful' being an allusion to De Quincey's devastation of their garden and Moss Hut. De Quincey, who had taken Dove Cottage after the Wordsworths moved, had cut down trees and plants in order to gain more light for the apple trees and had also destroyed the Moss Hut that they were fond of (the present hut is on the same site). On Christmas Day 1804 Wordsworth wrote to Sir George Beaumont, 'We have lately built in our little rocky orchard a little circular Hut, lined with moss, like a wren's nest, and coated on the outside with heath, that stands most charmingly, with several views from the different sides of it, of the Lake, the Valley and the Church. . . . The little retreat is most delightful.' Enclosed in the letter was Wordsworth's 'dwarf inscription' for the hut:

> No whimsy of the purse is here,
> No Pleasure-House forlorn,
> Use, comfort, do this roof endear;
> A tributary Shed to chear
> The little Cottage that is near,
> To help it and adorn.

Destroying this beautiful spot was akin to sacrilege. Dorothy, Sara Hutchinson wrote, 'is so hurt and angry that she can never speak to him more: & truly it was a most unfeeling thing when he knew how much store they set by that orchard'.

De Quincey, until this time, had been an ardent friend and admirer of Wordsworth, and his account of their meeting in November 1807 provides a fine description of Dove Cottage as the Wordsworths knew it: 'A little semi-vestibule between two doors prefaced the entrance into what might be considered the principal room of the cottage. It was an oblong square, not above eight and a half feet high, sixteen feet long, and twelve broad; very prettily wainscotted from the floor to the ceiling with dark polished oak, slightly embellished with carving. One window there was—a perfect and unpretending cottage window, with little diamond panes, embowered, at almost every season of the year, with roses; and, in the summer and autumn, with a profusion of jessamine and other fragrant shrubs. . . . I was ushered up a little flight of stairs, fourteen in all, to a little dining-room. . . . It was not fully seven feet six inches high, and, in other respects, pretty nearly of the same dimensions as the rustic hall below. There was, however, in a small recess, a library of perhaps 300 volumes. . . .'[3] After they had to move out of Dove Cottage because of their growing family, the Wordsworths volunteered to lease and furnish the cottage for De Quincey, eager, most likely, to have someone there who they thought could properly appreciate it.

The years at Dove Cottage, from late 1799 to 1808, were perhaps the mature Wordsworth's happiest years and certainly his greatest years for composing poetry. Three self-portraits offer views of the poet at home in Grasmere. The beginning of a sonnet-sequence entitled 'Personal Talk' portrays him in front of the fire in the ground-floor room.

> I am not One who much or oft delight
> To season my fireside with personal talk,—
> Of friends, who live within an easy walk,
> Or neighbours, daily, weekly, in my sight:
> And, for my chance-acquaintance, ladies bright,

[3] De Quincey, pp. 128, 134.

Sons, mothers, maidens withering on the stalk,
These all wear out of me, like Forms, with chalk
Painted on rich men's floors, for one feast-night.
Better than such discourse doth silence long,
Long, barren silence, square with my desire;
To sit without emotion, hope, or aim,
In the loved presence of my cottage-fire,[4]
And listen to the flapping of the flame,
Or kettle whispering its faint undersong.

A second portrait, written in the manner of the eighteenth-century poet James Thomson, describes Wordsworth in the first four stanzas and Coleridge in the next three. 'Coleridge was living with us much of the time', Wordsworth said; 'his son Hartley has said, that his father's character and habits are here preserved in a livelier way than anything that has been written about him' (I.F.).

STANZAS

WRITTEN IN MY POCKET-COPY OF THOMSON'S 'CASTLE OF INDOLENCE'

Within our happy Castle there dwelt One
Whom without blame I may not overlook;
For never sun on living creature shone
Who more devout enjoyment with us took:
Here on his hours he hung as on a book,
On his own time here would he float away,
As doth a fly upon a summer brook;
But go to-morrow, or belike to-day,
Seek for him,—he is fled; and whither none can say.

Thus often would he leave our peaceful home,
And find elsewhere his business or delight;
Out of our Valley's limits did he roam:
Full many a time, upon a stormy night,
His voice came to us from the neighbouring height:
Oft could we see him driving full in view

---

[4] The original line, which Wordsworth preferred, was 'By my half-kitchen and half-parlour fire'. 'My Sister and I', he said, 'were in the habit of having the tea-kettle in our little sitting-room' (I.F.).

At mid-day when the sun was shining bright;
What ill was on him, what he had to do,
A mighty wonder bred among our quiet crew.

Ah! piteous sight it was to see this Man
When he came back to us, a withered flower,—
Or like a sinful creature, pale and wan.
Down would he sit; and without strength or power
Look at the common grass from hour to hour:
And oftentimes, how long I fear to say,
Where apple-trees in blossom made a bower,
Retired in that sunshiny shade he lay;
And, like a naked Indian, slept himself away.

Great wonder to our gentle tribe it was
Whenever from our Valley he withdrew;
For happier soul no living creature has
Than he had, being here the long day through.
Some thought he was a lover, and did woo:
Some thought far worse of him, and judged him wrong;
But verse was what he had been wedded to;
And his own mind did like a tempest strong
Come to him thus, and drove the weary Wight along.

With him there often walked in friendly guise,
Or lay upon the moss by brook or tree,
A noticeable man with large grey eyes,
And a pale face that seemed undoubtedly
As if a blooming face it ought to be;
Heavy his low-hung lip did oft appear,
Deprest by weight of musing Phantasy;
Profound his forehead was, though not severe;
Yet some did think that he had little business here:

Sweet heaven forefend! his was a lawful right;
Noisy he was, and gamesome as a boy;
His limbs would toss about him with delight,
Like branches when strong winds the trees annoy.
Nor lacked his calmer hours device or toy
To banish listlessness and irksome care;
He would have taught you how you might employ

Yourself; and many did to him repair,—
And certes not in vain; he had inventions rare.

Expedients, too, of simplest sort he tried:
Long blades of grass, plucked round him as he lay,
Made, to his ear attentively applied,
A pipe on which the wind would deftly play;
Glasses he had, that little things display,
The beetle panoplied in gems and gold,
A mailèd angel on a battle-day;
The mysteries that cups of flowers enfold,
And all the gorgeous sights which fairies do behold.

He would entice that other Man to hear
His music, and to view his imagery:
And, sooth, these two were each to the other dear:
No livelier love in such a place could be:
There did they dwell—from earthly labour free,
As happy spirits as were ever seen;
If but a bird, to keep them company,
Or butterfly sate down, they were, I ween,
As pleased as if the same had been a Maiden-queen.

The third 'portrait' is more obviously a description of the rocky
prominence overlooking Grasmere, called Stone Arthur [N], but to
Dorothy the rock *was* William, for the reasons given in the poem.

There is an Eminence,—of these our hills
The last that parleys with the setting sun;
We can behold it from our orchard seat;
And, when at evening we pursue our walk
Along the public way, this Peak, so high
Above us, and so distant in its height,
Is visible; and often seems to send
Its own deep quiet to restore our hearts.
The meteors make of it a favourite haunt:
The star of Jove, so beautiful and large
In the mid heavens, is never half so fair
As when he shines above it. 'Tis in truth
The loneliest place we have among the clouds.
And She who dwells with me, whom I have loved

> With such communion, that no place on earth
> Can ever be a solitude to me,
> Hath to this lonely Summit given my Name.

Later, Wordsworth pointed out that one of the assertions was wrong—'It is not accurate that the Eminence here alluded to could be seen from our orchard-seat'—but the imaginative truth of it is undisputed, and tantalizing.

As the boy had wished, Grasmere vale became 'his Home, . . . his World'. Wordsworth came to know the neighbours and the landscape, making them a part of his mind and his poetry. How this happened with a particular stretch of land along the lake a short distance from Dove Cottage is the subject of another poem, like the preceding one, in the series 'Poems on the Naming of Places'. The place is still there but hardly recognizable, for the road which now runs along the shore has changed it drastically [E]. In Wordsworth's time, there were no large buildings between Dove Cottage and the lake: the boathouse [D], the tall terrace houses, and the hotel came later, after the new road was built in about 1831.[5] Before that, the lake and Silver How were visible from Dove Cottage and the shore was an isolated, favourite walking spot.

> A narrow girdle of rough stones and crags,
> A rude and natural causeway, interposed
> Between the water and a winding slope
> Of copse and thicket, leaves the eastern shore
> Of Grasmere safe in its own privacy:
> And there myself and two beloved Friends . . .
> Sauntered on this retired and difficult way.
>
> (*PW*, ii. 115)

Of this poem Wordsworth said, 'The character of the eastern shore is quite changed, since these verses were written, by the public road being carried along its side. The friends spoken of were Coleridge and my Sister, and the fact occurred strictly as recorded.' The change by this part of the lake was particularly lamented by De Quincey, who extolled the 'exquisite outline' of this shore, with 'all

---

[5] This is the date usually given for it, though the road appears on Hodgson's 1828 map of Westmorland. On 14 July 1824 Mary Wordsworth wrote to a friend that 'the new road will pass thro' that delightful tract', Bainriggs.

its little bays and wild sylvan margin, feathered to the edge with wild flowers and ferns', but in 1854 he added, 'All which inimitable graces of nature have, by the hands of mechanic art, by solid masonry, by whitewashing, etc., been exterminated, as a growth of weeds and nuisances, for thirty years.'[6] In the same year (1800) that De Quincey first wrote about this shore-line, Wordsworth wrote an inscription for the island [F] in the lake and its barn, to which he often rowed.

WRITTEN WITH A PENCIL UPON A STONE
IN THE WALL OF THE HOUSE (AN OUT-HOUSE), ON THE ISLAND AT GRASMERE

Rude is this Edifice, and Thou hast seen
Buildings, albeit rude, that have maintained
Proportions more harmonious, and approached
To closer fellowship with ideal grace.
But take it in good part:—alas! the poor
Vitruvius of our village had no help
From the great City; never, upon leaves
Of red Morocco folio saw displayed,
In long succession, pre-existing ghosts
Of Beauties yet unborn—the rustic Lodge
Antique, and Cottage with verandah graced,
Nor lacking, for fit company, alcove,
Green-house, shell-grot, and moss-lined hermitage.
Thou see'st a homely Pile, yet to these walls
The heifer comes in the snow-storm, and here
The new-dropped lamb finds shelter from the wind.
And hither does one Poet sometimes row
His pinnace, a small vagrant barge, up-piled
With plenteous store of heath and withered fern,
(A lading which he with his sickle cuts,
Among the mountains) and beneath this roof
He makes his summer couch, and here at noon
Spreads out his limbs, while, yet unshorn, the Sheep,
Panting beneath the burthen of their wool,
Lie round him, even as if they were a part

---

[6] De Quincey, pp. 122, 403.

Of his own Household: nor, while from his bed
He looks, through the open door-place, toward the lake
And to the stirring breezes, does he want
Creations lovely as the work of sleep—
Fair sights, and visions of romantic joy!

By 1808 Dove Cottage was overflowing; there was not only the poet and his sister, but also his wife, three small children, and at various times other Wordsworth and Hutchinson relatives, Coleridge, De Quincey, and many other visitors, who often had to be put up across the road at the Ashburners. They had to find a larger place, and they reluctantly moved to Allan Bank [L]. Perhaps the move was doomed before it took place. When Allan Bank was about to be built in 1805, Wordsworth had voiced his disapproval of it in no uncertain terms.

Woe to poor Grasmere for ever and ever! A wretched Creature, wretched in name and Nature, of the name of *Crump*, goaded on by his still more wretched Wife (for by the bye the man though a Liverpool attorney is, I am told, a very good sort of Fellow but the Wife as ambitious as Semiramis) this same Wretch has at last begun to put his long impending threats in execution; and when you next enter the sweet paradise of Grasmere you will see staring you in the face upon that beautiful ridge that elbows out into the vale (behind the church and towering far above its steeple) a temple of abomination, in which are to be enshrined Mr and Mrs Crump.

(*Letters*, 7 February 1805)

How different from his love of Dove Cottage! Could paradise survive with a temple of abomination staring over it? Could a poet, who 'looks at the world in the spirit of love', enshrine himself in such a place with impunity? The happy band tried. Since they were the first tenants, Wordsworth was allowed to plant the grounds, and many of the trees at Allan Bank today were put there by Wordsworth. Mr Crump turned out to be 'a most kind-hearted and good-natured man', in Dorothy's words, and the children (two more were born at Allan Bank) enjoyed playing in the grounds. But all of the chimneys smoked so much as to be useless on a windy day, making the house bitterly cold and uncomfortable, and it was too expensive for them to maintain. Far worse, the friendship between

Wordsworth and Coleridge grew increasingly strained; in 1810 and 1811 anger and estrangement replaced one of the greatest of all literary friendships. When Coleridge returned to the Lake District in 1812, he picked up his sons, Hartley and Derwent, from their school at Ambleside, and drove in the chaise right past the Wordsworths' new residence without stopping—Hartley stunned and white-faced, and Derwent crying.

It is painful to think about this time in Wordsworth's life. Allan Bank had been intolerable and in June 1811 they had moved into the Rectory [J] opposite the church. It was no better. In early 1812, Sara Hutchinson, who was living with them, felt the urgent need for 'a healthier house—for I verily believe that this is in a deadly situation, and you would all say the same if you knew the *bog* which it stands in—add to this the comforts of the smoke within'—more smoking chimneys—'and it is without doubt a hateful house'. In June the Wordsworths' three-year-old daughter Catharine died suddenly while both parents were away from home. She was buried days before her parents knew of the death. In early December another death—this time their six-year-old boy—was almost more than the strong family could bear. Looking across the road daily at the churchyard where their children had played and where two of them now lay buried was too much: they wanted only to leave Grasmere vale. They had known that the new paradise would have its inevitable pain, but they had not counted on this much.

The church and churchyard across the road from the Rectory was the Wordsworths' place of worship, their children's playground and school, and their final resting place. The churchyard [I] still bears the stamp of Wordsworth's presence: there are the much-visited graves of the poet, his wife, their children, and the nearby grave of Hartley Coleridge, which Wordsworth picked out, saying, 'Let him lie as near to us as possible, leaving room for Mrs Wordsworth and myself. It would have been his wish.' And there still remain the eight yew trees that the poet planted and nurtured. He was proud of these, for they improved the appearance of the churchyard that had been declining: 'the whole eight are now thriving', he said over twenty years after planting the trees, 'and are already an ornament to a place which, during late years, has lost much of its rustic simplicity by the introduction of iron palisades to fence off family burying-grounds, and by numerous monuments, some of them in very bad taste; from which this place of burial was in my memory quite free' (I.F.). The churchyard that he knew in 1800 is the one described in *The Excursion*:

> Green is the Churchyard, beautiful and green,
> Ridge rising gently by the side of ridge,
> A heaving surface, almost wholly free
> From interruption of sepulchral stones,
> And mantled o'er with aboriginal turf
> And everlasting flowers.
>
> (vi. 605–10)

To the north of the church, not far from the present ginger-bread shop, is the grave of George and Sarah Green, who died on the fells while six of their eight children waited at home for them. Wordsworth's poem about them, 'Elegiac Stanzas composed in the Churchyard of Grasmere' ('*composed* I have said, I ought rather to have said effused, for it is the mere pouring out of my own feeling'), was written on a beautiful day in early April, altogether unlike the snowstorm in which they had died less than three weeks earlier.[7]

The tiny ginger-bread shop was until 1854 the village schoolhouse [K]; Wordsworth's son John had lessons there, and for a time in 1811 Wordsworth taught the children for several hours each day. The churchyard next to the schoolhouse, which had as yet no graves, was their playground. Wordsworth had seen children playing in it years before he moved to Grasmere, and he wrote of it in a draft of an early poem, *An Evening Walk*:

> guided by some hand unseen
> Through paths where grey huts thinly intervene,
> I seek that footworn spot of level ground
> Close by the school within the churchyard's bound
> Through every race of them who near are laid
> For children's sports kept sacred from the spade;
> Such the smooth plot that skirts the mouldering rows
> Of graves where Grasmere's rustic sons repose. . . .

---

[7] For the Greens' story, see p. 111. The poem is in *PW*, iv. 375.

The church and churchyard, indeed the whole of Grasmere vale, figure prominently in *The Excursion*. The Wanderer, Poet, and Solitary leave the Solitary's secluded room at Blea Tarn between the Langdales and unnaturally, 'as by the waving of a magic wand', the poet told Miss Fenwick, they are soon in 'the stately and comparatively spacious vale of Grasmere, its Lake, and its ancient Parish Church' [H], where they see, in Book v, the 'grey church-tower' with its 'battlements', and enter the church:

> Not raised in nice proportions was the pile,
> But large and massy; for duration built;
> With pillars crowded, and the roof upheld
> By naked rafters intricately crossed. . . .

Later, in Book ix, they row down the lake and climb 'a green hill's side'. Wordsworth imagined them as being on 'the side of Loughrigg Fell [R], at the foot of the lake, and looking down upon it and the whole vale and its encompassing mountains' (I.F.). Here they gaze on the setting sun and hear the eloquent words of the Pastor, mindful of human pain, strife, falsehood, mortality, and barbarity, at a time and place so beautiful that

> a willing mind
> Might almost think, at this affecting hour,
> That paradise, the lost abode of man,
> Was raised again: and to a happy few,
> In its original beauty, here restored.

Not far from this spot a schoolboy had once paused, gazed, and thought that 'here | Must be his Home, this Valley be his World'.

9

Easedale[1]

'There are delightful walks in that part of Grasmere, called Easedale', Wordsworth wrote, and he may be regarded as an authority on the subject. He and Dorothy had not been in Grasmere more than four days before they discovered a terrace walk at Lancrigg 'which long remained our favourite haunt'. Dorothy's journals are filled with reports of walks to Easedale, sometimes referred to as the Black Quarter because of the clouds and storms that gather there, and William claimed to have written 'thousands of verses by the side of' Easedale Beck (I.F.). De Quincey also had a special affection for the place. 'The little valley of Easedale', he wrote, 'is, on its own account, one of the most impressive solitudes amongst the mountains of the lake district.' He praises at length its seclusion, its lovely 'small fields and miniature meadows', its level floor, and 'the sublimity of its mountain barriers'. Above the valley are the Sour Milk Gill waterfall (which Dorothy refers to as Churn Milk force) and Easedale Tarn [C]—both part of its attractiveness to De Quincey: 'In one of its many rocky recesses is seen a "force", (such is the local name for a cataract,) white with foam, descending at all seasons with respectable strength, and, after the melting of snows, with an Alpine violence. Follow the leading of this "force" for three quarters of a mile, and you come to a little mountain lake, locally termed a "tarn", the very finest and most gloomily sublime of its class.'[2]

Further down on Easedale Beck, however, the scene is quite different—joyously beautiful, perhaps, rather than gloomily sublime. 'It was an April morning' is the first of Wordsworth's 'Poems on the Naming of Places'; it 'was suggested', Wordsworth said, 'on the banks of the brook that runs through Easedale, which

---

[1] Map on p. 240.   [2] De Quincey, pp. 250–1.

'Easedale from Butterlip How'. Easedale Beck, which is not visible from this vantage point, flows from Easedale Tarn,

is, in some parts of its course, as wild and beautiful as brook can be'
(I.F.). One spot, particularly dear to him, became 'my other
home, │ My dwelling, and my out-of-doors abode'. He named it, in
this poem, Emma's Dell—Emma being his pseudonym for
Dorothy. It pictures the poet, 'Alive to all things', roaming up the
brook, beginning at Goody Bridge, or somewhere below it, walking
up to the 'sudden turning' of the stream and to the small waterfall
[A], where he 'gazed and gazed' and then dedicated the wild nook to
Emma.

> It was an April morning: fresh and clear
> The Rivulet, delighting in its strength,
> Ran with a young man's speed; and yet the voice
> Of waters which the winter had supplied
> Was softened down into a vernal tone.
> The spirit of enjoyment and desire,
> And hopes and wishes, from all living things
> Went circling, like a multitude of sounds.
> The budding groves seemed eager to urge on
> The steps of June; as if their various hues
> Were only hindrances that stood between
> Them and their object: but, meanwhile, prevailed
> Such an entire contentment in the air
> That every naked ash, and tardy tree
> Yet leafless, showed as if the countenance
> With which it looked on this delightful day
> Were native to the summer.—Up the brook
> I roamed in the confusion of my heart,
> Alive to all things and forgetting all.
> At length I to a sudden turning came
> In this continuous glen, where down a rock
> The Stream, so ardent in its course before,
> Sent forth such sallies of glad sound, that all
> Which I till then had heard, appeared the voice
> Of common pleasure: beast and bird, the lamb,
> The shepherd's dog, the linnet and the thrush,
> Vied with this waterfall, and made a song,
> Which, while I listened, seemed like the wild growth
> Or like some natural produce of the air,
> That could not cease to be. Green leaves were here;

But 'twas the foliage of the rocks—the birch,
The yew, the holly, and the bright green thorn,
With hanging islands of resplendent furze:
And, on a summit, distant a short space,
By any who should look beyond the dell,
A single mountain-cottage might be seen.
I gazed and gazed, and to myself I said,
'Our thoughts at least are ours; and this wild nook,
My Emma, I will dedicate to thee.'
—Soon did the spot become my other home,
My dwelling, and my out-of-doors abode.
And, of the Shepherds who have seen me there,
To whom I sometimes in our idle talk
Have told this fancy, two or three, perhaps,
Years after we are gone and in our graves,
When they have cause to speak of this wild place,
May call it by the name of EMMA'S DELL.

When Wordsworth wrote this poem, he was thirty years old; he and Dorothy had been in Grasmere less than a year. Thirty-six years later, he took Coleridge's nephew and four others to this very spot, though by a different route. Its beauty was still undeniable, but in the intervening years a calamity had happened. Justice Coleridge, the poet's nephew, reported the episode:

He turned aside at a little farm-house [Goody Bridge Farm] and took us into a swelling field, to look down on the tumbling stream which bounded it, and which we saw precipitated at a distance, in a broad white sheet, from the mountain [the Sour Milk Gill waterfall]. A beautiful water-break of the same stream was before us at our feet, and he noticed the connection which it formed in the landscape with the distant waterfall. Then, as he mused for an instant, he said, 'I have often thought what a solemn thing it would be, if we could have brought to our mind, at once, all the scenes of distress and misery, which any spot, however beautiful and calm before us, has been witness to since the beginning. That water-break, with the glassy, quiet pool beneath it, that looks so lovely, and presents no images to the mind but of peace,—there, I remember, the only son of his father, a poor man, who lived yonder, was drowned. He missed him, came to search, and saw his body dead in the pool.'

(Grosart, iii. 431)

Another calamity, with which the Wordsworths were much concerned, happened further up Easedale in 1808. George and Sarah Green, whose graves are in the Grasmere Churchyard, lived in a cottage with six children, the oldest eleven years old and the youngest an infant. The cottage [B] still stands on Blindtarn Gill. They were 'the poorest people in the vale', with a small estate heavily mortgaged, one nearly dry cow, and few possessions, but they were cheerful and well liked, and the children were, in Wordsworth's words, 'the admiration of every Body for their innocence, affectionate dispositions, and good behaviour'. In March George and Sarah Green went over the fell into Langdale to a farm sale—it was for them a social occasion rather than a commercial one—and on their way home they became lost in a snowstorm, fell on the crags and perished. Dorothy explained in a letter that they

went to a sale in Langdale in the afternoon; and set off homewards in the evening, intending to cross the fells and descend just above their own cottage, a lonely dwelling in Easedale. They had left a daughter at home eleven years old, with the care of five brothers and sisters younger than herself, the youngest an infant at the breast. These dear helpless creatures sate up till 11 o'clock expecting their parents, and then went to bed thinking that they had stayed all night in Langdale because of the weather. All next day they continued to expect them, and on Monday morning one of the boys went to a house on the opposite side of the dale to borrow a cloak. On being asked for what purpose he replied that his sister was going to Langdale to *lait* [seek] *their Folk* who had never come home. The man of the house started up, and said that they were lost; and immediately spread the alarm. As long as daylight lasted on that day, and on Monday and till Tuesday afternoon, all the men of Grasmere and many from Langdale were out upon the Fells. On Tuesday afternoon the bodies were found miserably mangled, having been cut by the crags. They were lying not above a quarter of a mile above a house in Langdale where their shrieks had been distinctly heard by two different persons who supposed that the shrieks came from some drunken people who had been at the sale. The bodies were brought home in a cart, and buried in one grave last Thursday. The poor children all the time they had been left by themselves suspected no evil; and as soon as it was known by others that their father and mother were missing the truth came upon them like a thunder-stroke.

(28 March 1808)

William was in London at the time, but all the men in Grasmere stopped their work to look for the bodies until they were found, and the women took care of the children. Mary Wordsworth and others formed a committee to place the children with local families (the Wordsworths themselves took in one daughter, Sally), Dorothy wrote a full account of the accident and the family, and, when he arrived home three weeks after the accident, William visited the grave (which inspired his elegiac stanzas on the Greens) and wrote letters to his 'more rich and powerful Friends' to raise money to clothe the orphans and send them to school.

Wordsworth, always quick to help an unknown beggar, no doubt felt more strongly when the needy were local people known to him. But he must have been deeply moved on this occasion. It was a sad enough story to elicit help from all over England, but for Wordsworth it aroused painful memories of his life in the Lake Country. He and Dorothy were orphaned themselves when he was a schoolboy, and Dorothy suffered from being sent to live with unloving relations at Penrith. Furthermore, they were orphaned by a similar accident: their father, returning from business in Millom, became lost in the mountains and had to spend a winter's night on the fellside. He made his way out the next day, but died in his home at Cockermouth not long after. Wordsworth may also have recalled another event, though it is possible that this happened later. When he took Justice Coleridge to Easedale he pointed to Blea Rigg, where the Greens had perished, and told of an occasion when he and Dorothy were returning from Langdale. 'He having for some reason parted, she encountered a fog, and was bewildered. At last, she sat down and waited; in a short time it began to clear; she could see that a valley was before her. In time, she saw the backs of cattle feeding, which emerged from the darkness, and at last the Tarn [Easedale Tarn]; and then found she had stopped providentially, and was sitting nearly on the edge of the precipice.'[3]

Soon after his arrival in Grasmere, the poet found a favourite haunt at Lancrigg terrace [D] on the hillside above the floor of Easedale. He wrote much of *The Prelude* while walking at Lancrigg, and he wrote a sonnet ('Mark the concentred hazels', *PW*, iii. 24)

[3] Grosart, iii. 432.

which, he said, was 'suggested in the wild hazel-wood at the foot of Helm-crag, where the stone still lies, with others of like form and character, though much of the wood that veiled it from the glare of day has been felled' (I.F.). In 1840 the land was purchased by his friend Mrs Fletcher, who built a larger house where the old cottage stood, taking advice about the building from the poet. Wordsworth had particularly strong opinions about chimneys; those on the present building at Lancrigg, it is said, were built to his specifications. Canon H. D. Rawnsley recorded a conversation with an old man who had built Fox How for Dr Thomas Arnold and had seen Wordsworth often. 'He and the Doctor', said George the waller,

'you've mappen hard tell o' t' Doctor,—well, he and the Doctor was much i' yan anudder's company; and Wudsworth was a girt un for chimleys, had summut to saay in the makkin' of a deal of 'em hereaboot. There was 'maist all the chimleys Rydal way built efter his mind. I can mind he and the Doctor had girt argiments aboot the chimleys time we was building Foxhow, and Wudsworth sed he liked a bit o' colour in 'em. And that the chimley coigns sud be natural headed and natural bedded, a lile bit red and a lile bit yallar. For there is a bit of colour i' t' quarry stean up Easedale way. And heèd a girt fancy an' aw for chimleys square up hauf way, and round t'other. And so we built 'em that road.[4]'

This description has the ring of truth to it: in his *Guide* Wordsworth writes, 'Nor will the singular beauty of the chimneys escape the eye of the attentive traveller', and he describes various types, noting 'a pleasing harmony between a tall chimney of this circular form, and the living column of smoke, ascending from it through the still air'. Wordsworth is a poet even when writing prose: the 'living column of smoke' has the principle of life that the living rocks have in his poems. Cottages, too, are animated in the *Guide;* he writes of the lichens, mosses, ferns, and flowers that make their way into the rough unhewn stones of the cottage walls and into the irregular slates of the roofs. 'Hence buildings', he adds, 'which in their very form call to mind the processes of Nature, do thus, clothed in part in a vegetable garb, appear to be received into the bosom of the living principle of things, as it acts and exists among

4 H. D. Rawnsley, *Lake Country Sketches* (1903), pp. 19–20.

the woods and fields'. George and Sarah Green's cottage in
Easedale was just such a place, as he described it in a letter to a
friend: 'The house itself is of grey mountain stone, as if it had
grown out of the mountain, an indigenous Dwelling, for indigenous
Inhabitants.'

10

Rydal[1]

Having been home at Grasmere, with an 'out-of-doors abode' in
Easedale, for thirteen years, the Wordsworths wanted to leave—a
desire almost unthinkable when *Home at Grasmere* was written. But
they had outgrown Dove Cottage; they had never liked Allan Bank;
and, most especially, the gloomy Rectory, right across from the
churchyard, had painful associations after the deaths of the two
children, Catharine and Thomas, in 1812. When they heard that
Rydal Mount [G], in the neighbouring vale two miles away, had
been sold to Lady Fleming of Rydal Hall and that she intended to
let it, they immediately made arrangements to obtain it. 'There is
no objection to it', Dorothy wrote, 'but that from the garden we
shall view the Grasmere hills; yet on the other hand we should wish
to be within a walk of Grasmere—and should wish to keep up that
bond betwixt the living and the dead by going weekly to the parish
Church beside which their bodies are laid. . . .' It was a sad and
difficult time for the family. William looked to Dorothy as if he had
aged ten years within a short time of the deaths of his two children,
and Mary fell into a profound depression that worried them all.

There were still three children, however, a large family both in
and beyond Grasmere, and caring friends. Coleridge, in spite of
their estrangement, wrote a compassionate letter full of his former
affection and even promised to visit them, though he never did.
Wordsworth's finances received a welcomed improvement through

[1] Map on p. 243.

'RYDAL WATER AND GRASMERE, FROM RYDAL PARK'. Rydal Hall is the large house to the left of centre; beyond it the tower of Rydal Chapel is visible. Loughrigg is to the left of Rydal Water, the lower lake, and Silver How is to the left of Grasmere.

his appointment as Distributor of Stamps several months before
they left Grasmere. And the excitement of moving and furnishing
the new house proved salutary. They moved to Rydal Mount in
May, 1813. Dorothy wrote to a friend after they had been there
some months, 'Now I must tell you of our grandeur. We are going
to have a *Turkey*!!! carpet—in the dining room, and a Brussels in
William's study. You stare, and the simplicity of the dear Town
End Cottage [Dove Cottage] comes before your eyes, and you are
tempted to say, "are they changed, are they setting up for fine Folks?
for making parties—giving Dinners etc etc?" No no, you do not
make such a guess. . . .' But in the next paragraph, describing the
garden at their new house, her thoughts go back to the lost boy:
'Thomas was a darling in the garden—our best helper—steady to
his work—always pleased. God bless his memory! I see him
wherever I turn' (*Letters*, *c*. 14 September 1813).

Rydal Mount was, and is, a beautiful place, and the
Wordsworths were the right people to appreciate its particular,
quiet beauty. It was right for them too because, like Dove Cottage,
it had a garden which could be shaped by the poet's hand.
Wordsworth thought that if he had not become a poet, he could
have been an art critic or a landscape designer. The present garden
at Rydal Mount—still much the same as it was when Wordsworth
died—is living proof of his talent at the latter, and his labour here,
as well as in Grasmere and Coleorton (Sir George Beaumont's
estate in Leicestershire), shows how passionate an avocation it was.
When he moved in, the grounds had not been the object of much
attention, though there was an ancient Norse mound in front
(hence the name of the house), a large kitchen garden with
cabbages, onions, and carrots, one terrace, and many shrubs and
trees. Over the years he improved the land through a labour of love.
His avocation, moreover, was not distinct from his vocation, for the
landscape was not only his place for composing poetry but also the
subject of many poems.

The mound, or mount, in front of the house was used as a look-
out during and after the ninth century, when it was built; there
were few trees at the time and the view would have been even more
extensive than it is today. Wordsworth raised the mound, built
accesses to it, and it became a favourite spot for viewing the valley

and its surrounding mountains, such as the one to the south-east, above Ambleside:

> Wansfell! this Household has a favoured lot,
> Living with liberty on thee to gaze. . . .

One of his 'Evening Voluntaries' (entitled 'Composed upon an Evening of Extraordinary Splendour and Beauty') was, he said, 'felt and in a great measure composed upon the little mount in front of our abode at Rydal' (I.F.). It was written in the summer of 1817, when, because of a peculiar effect of the sun and haze, the mountain ridges appeared to be multiplied, a series of steps, or Jacob's Ladder, leading to heaven.

> But, rooted here, I stand and gaze
> On those bright steps that heavenward raise
> Their practicable way.

Over ten years after the 'Immortality Ode', he catches again a 'glimpse of glory', perhaps 'a vestige of those gleams' so powerful in childhood, before 'the visionary splendour fades'.

A less visionary image of stars just above the mountain ridges seen from Rydal Mount on a winter's night provided Wordsworth with an emblem of himself as poet in a poem that he placed at the beginning of his collected poems, 'as a sort of Preface':

> If thou indeed derive thy light from Heaven,
> Then, to the measure of that heaven-born light,
> Shine, Poet! in thy place, and be content:—
> The stars pre-eminent in magnitude,
> And they that from the zenith dart their beams,
> (Visible though they be to half the earth,
> Though half a sphere be conscious of their brightness)
> Are yet of no diviner origin,
> No purer essence, than the one that burns,
> Like an untended watch-fire, on the ridge
> Of some dark mountain; or than those which seem
> Humbly to hang, like twinkling winter lamps,
> Among the branches of the leafless trees;
> All are the undying offspring of one Sire:
> Then, to the measure of the light vouchsafed,
> Shine, Poet! in thy place, and be content.

Talking about this poem with Isabella Fenwick, Wordsworth mentioned the beauty of Rydal Mount, 'backed and flanked by lofty fells, which bring the heavenly bodies to touch, as it were, the earth upon the mountain-tops, while the prospect in front lies open to a length of level valley, the extended lake, and a terminating ridge of low hills; so that it gives an opportunity to the inhabitants of the place of noticing the stars in both the positions here alluded to, namely on the tops of the mountains, and as winter-lamps at a distance among the leafless trees'.

Under the poet's gaze, the beauty of Rydal Mount became emblematic of what was most important in life. 'All just and solid pleasure in natural objects', he wrote in the *Guide*, 'rests upon two pillars, God and Man.' The lawn below the house, with its 'crowd of daisies', became at evening 'An emblem . . . of what the sober Hour | Can do for minds disposed to feel its power!' ('Soft as a Cloud', in *PW*, iv. 7). Or, at other times, other things could be seen in the same lawn: 'This Lawn is the sloping one approaching the kitchen-garden, and was made out of it. Hundreds of times have I watched the dancing of shadows and a press of sunshine, and other beautiful appearances of light and shade, flowers and shrubs' (I.F.). In this poem it becomes an emblem of those engaged in 'strenuous idleness'—one of the few phrases Wordsworth liked well enough to use more than once.

> This Lawn, a carpet all alive
> With shadows flung from leaves—to strive
>   In dance, amid a press
> Of sunshine, an apt emblem yields
> Of Worldlings revelling in the fields
>   Of strenuous idleness;
>
> Less quick the stir when tide and breeze
> Encounter, and to narrow seas
>   Forbid a moment's rest;
> The medley less when boreal Lights
> Glance to and fro, like aery Sprites
>   To feats of arms addrest!
>
> Yet, spite of all this eager strife,
> This ceaseless play, the genuine life
>   That serves the stedfast hours,

Is in the grass beneath, that grows
Unheeded, and the mute repose
Of sweetly-breathing flowers.

The landscape at Rydal Mount gave rise to poems and sometimes the poems became part of the landscape. Inscriptions were a favourite literary form for Wordsworth because the word becomes a part of the living land, which came, according to St. John, from the Word. In Dora's Field [F], immediately below Rydal Mount, some stone steps make a difficult path down a slope. Still inscribed on the rock next to the steps are Wordsworth's lines:

Wouldst thou be gathered to Christ's chosen flock,
Shun the broad way too easily explored,
And let thy path be hewn out of the Rock,
The living Rock of God's eternal Word.

Above the steps and near the gate to Rydal Mount is another inscription. When he was in Italy, his family had his lines engraved on brass and inserted in the stone.

In these fair vales hath many a Tree
    At Wordsworth's suit been spared;
And from the builder's hand this Stone,
For some rude beauty of its own,
    Was rescued by the Bard:
So let it rest; and time will come
    When here the tender-hearted
May heave a gentle sigh for him,
    As one of the departed.

Near the end of 1825, after the Wordsworths had lived in Rydal Mount for twelve years, the owner decided to let the house to a relative; the Wordsworths would have to move. They emphatically did not want to move, and Wordsworth did what he could to prevent it. Upon first hearing of the possibility, he immediately purchased the land just below Rydal Mount—now called Dora's Field—'at an extravagant fancy price', he admitted. The price did not seem to matter: Wordsworth wanted a place in Rydal to build on if they should be evicted from Rydal Mount, and, more importantly, he thought that the threat of a building adjacent to Lady Fleming's property and chapel might lead her to change her mind. Lady Fleming, however, was not easily intimidated.

Wordsworth wrote to her asking about the possibility of their losing the lease, at the same time informing her of his purchase of the adjacent property, but she affirmed that her relative would have Rydal Mount in 1827. Wordsworth hired an architect who drew up plans for a house. Lady Fleming remained adamant, even refusing to affirm that the Wordsworths could stay if her relative changed her mind. The Wordsworths did not wish to move, but for a while it seemed that they would have to. All of Wordsworth's landscaping on the property around the house would pass into other hands—the sloping terrace above the house leading to the summer-house (an arbour lined with fir cones), the far terrace, the many trees, shrubs, and flowers he had planted, the lawn, and the mound. Not long before hearing that they might lose Rydal Mount, Wordsworth had celebrated the summer-house in a poem contrasting a parrot, living in a gilded cage within doors, with a wren 'that haunted for many years the Summerhouse between the two terraces at Rydal Mount' (I.F.). Addressed to his daughter Dora, the poem ends with four stanzas describing the wren and its home in their mossy shed:

> This moss-lined shed, green, soft, and dry,
> Harbours a self-contented Wren,
> Not shunning man's abode, though shy,
> Almost as thought itself, of human ken.
>
> Strange places, coverts unendeared,
> She never tried; the very nest
> In which this Child of Spring was reared
> Is warmed, thro' winter, by her feathery breast.
>
> To the bleak winds she sometimes gives
> A slender unexpected strain;
> Proof that the hermitess still lives,
> Though she appear not, and be sought in vain.
>
> Say, Dora! tell me, by yon placid moon,
> If called to choose between the favoured pair,
> Which would you be,—the bird of the saloon,
> By lady-fingers tended with nice care,
> Caressed, applauded, upon dainties fed,
> Or Nature's DARKLING of this mossy shed?
>   ('The Contrast: The Parrot and the Wren')

The next year, convinced that they would have to move, Wordsworth wrote an inscription for the far terrace, which he had built from the summer-house, leading to Nab Well.

> The massy Ways, carried across these heights
> By Roman perseverance, are destroyed,
> Or hidden under ground, like sleeping worms.
> How venture then to hope that Time will spare
> This humble Walk? Yet on the mountain's side
> A Poet's hand first shaped it; and the steps
> Of that same Bard—repeated to and fro
> At morn, at noon, and under moonlight skies
> Through the vicissitudes of many a year—
> Forbade the weeds to creep o'er its grey line.
> No longer, scattering to the heedless winds
> The vocal raptures of fresh poesy,
> Shall he frequent these precincts; locked no more
> In earnest converse with belovèd Friends,
> Here will he gather stores of ready bliss,
> As from the beds and borders of a garden
> Choice flowers are gathered! But, if Power may spring
> Out of a farewell yearning—favoured more
> Than kindred wishes mated suitably
> With vain regrets—the Exile would consign
> This Walk, his loved possession, to the care
> Of those pure Minds that reverence the Muse.

> (PW, iv. 201)

At about the same time he wrote a poem entitled 'Composed when a probability existed of our being obliged to quit Rydal Mount as a residence', addressed to Nab Well [1], the small spring just beyond the corner of the Rydal Mount property on the upper path to Grasmere. The long poem, never published during his lifetime, begins with reflections on what will be lost:

> The doubt to which a wavering hope had clung
> Is fled; we must depart, willing or not;
> Sky-piercing Hills! must bid farewell to you
> And all that ye look down upon with pride,
> With tenderness imbosom; to your paths,
> And pleasant Dwellings, to familiar trees
> And wild-flowers known as well as if our hands

> Had tended them: and O pellucid Spring!
> Insensibly the foretaste of this parting
> Hath ruled my steps, and seals me to thy side,
> Mindful that thou (ah! wherefore by my Muse
> So long unthank'd) hast cheared a simple board
> With beverage pure as ever fix'd the choice
> Of Hermit, dubious where to scoop his cell;
> Which Persian kings might envy; and thy meek
> And gentle aspect oft has minister'd
> To finer uses. They for me must cease. . . .

> (*PW*, iv. 381)

Nab Well continues to flow, and it continued to minister to the poet, for eventually the owner's relative decided not to take the house, Lady Fleming relented, and the Wordsworths spent the rest of their lives at Rydal Mount.

The reprieve allowed Wordsworth to continue composing along the paths familiar to him. The walk past Nab Well to Grasmere had been well loved since the Grasmere days.

> A humble walk
> Here is my body doomed to tread, this path,
> A little hoary line and faintly traced,
> Work, shall we call it, of the shepherd's foot
> Or of his flock?—joint vestige of them both.
> I pace it unrepining, for my thoughts
> Admit no bondage and my words have wings.

> ('To the Clouds')

A poem from 1800, 'The Oak and the Broom', was 'suggested upon the mountain pathway that leads from Upper Rydal to Grasmere', Wordsworth said. 'The ponderous block of stone, which is mentioned in the poem, remains, I believe, a good way up Nab Scar. Broom grows under it and in many places on the side of the precipice' (I.F.). Or so it was in 1843. Today, many of the oaks [J] have, as in the poem, stopped large blocks of stone from rolling downhill (this is best seen from 'a good way up'), but the broom has not survived. Although the weak broom outlasts the pompously 'sage' oak in the poem, Wordsworth observed the contrary as well: in a companion-poem, 'The Waterfall and the Eglantine', also

suggested on the same path, 'nearer to Grasmere', the weak
eglantine succumbs to the powerful waterfall.

Even closer to home, the walks at Rydal Mount were especially
dear to the poet; the sloping terrace, the far terrace, and the level
terrace below, built for Isabella Fenwick and used by the poet in his
old age, were all built, or improved, by Wordsworth, and many of
his poems were written there. 'Nine-tenths of my verses have been
murmured out in the open air', he said. He himself told these
anecdotes of his famous, or notorious, habit of composing out of
doors.

One day a stranger having walked round the garden and grounds of Rydal
Mount asked one of the female servants who happened to be at the door,
permission to see her master's study. 'This', said she, leading him
forward, 'is my master's library, where he keeps his books, but his study is
out of doors.' After a long absence from home it has more than once
happened that some one of my cottage neighbours has said—'Well, there
he is; we are glad to hear him *booing* about again.'

(I.F.)

As in the Hawkshead days, the local folks thought his muttering
poetry to himself while walking very strange, to say the least. One
morning Hartley Coleridge passed a poor man breaking stones near
Rydal. 'Good morning, John, what news have you this morning?'
he asked, and John answered, 'Why, nowte varry particler only ald
Wadswurth's brocken lowce ageean.' Indeed, some thought the real
credit for the poetry belonged to Dorothy. Wordsworth himself
was 'turble fond o' study ont' rwoads, specially at night time, and
wi' a girt voice bumming awaay fit to flayte aw the childer to death
ameaast, not but what Miss Dorothy did best part o' putting his
potry togidder. He let it fa' and she cam efter and gethered it opp
fur him ye kna.' A local man, hearing that the Poet Laureate was to
address a meeting at Appleby, went all the way there only to find
that the speaker was his neighbour, the Stamp Distributor. 'Schaff
on it, its nobbut old Wadsworth o' Rydal efter aw!'[2]

According to Wordsworth's gardener, who knew nothing about
the connection between poetry and laurels, laurels were what grew

[2] H. D. Rawnsley, *Literary Associations of the English Lakes* (1901), ii,
136–8.

best at Rydal. Wordsworth took leave of them temporarily—Lady Fleming made no more threats to evict them—when he left for his Scottish tour in 1833.

> Adieu, Rydalian Laurels! that have grown
> And spread as if ye knew that days might come
> When ye would shelter in a happy home,
> On this fair Mount, a Poet of your own. . . .

Ten years later he became the Poet Laureate.

When the land Wordsworth had purchased was no longer needed for a house, he gave it to his daughter, and what was the Rash has since been called Dora's Field. The year before Wordsworth bought it, Lady Fleming had built a chapel [E] adjacent to it, on a site that Wordsworth helped to choose. When the foundations were being laid, Wordsworth wrote a poem, 'To the Lady Fleming', praising her and her building:

> How fondly will the woods embrace
> This daughter of thy pious care,
> Lifting her front with modest grace
> To make a fair recess more fair. . . .

When it was opened on a stormy Christmas Day 1824, his praise was more reserved: 'When time has softened down the exterior a little it will prove a great ornament to the Village.' Twenty years later, Wordsworth liked the *idea* of the chapel better than its execution. The exterior, he thought, was ill-suited 'to the site in a narrow mountain-pass', and the interior left much to be desired: 'It has no chancel; the altar is unbecomingly confined; the pews are so narrow as to preclude the possibility of kneeling; there is no vestry; and . . . the font, instead of standing at its proper place at the Entrance, is thrust into the farther end of a little Pew' (I.F.). The building was remodelled in 1884, and most of these defects were corrected. Wordsworth would probably have liked it better as it is now. Architecture aside, the chapel was welcomed by Wordsworth; at the outset it allowed '60 or 70 persons at least . . . an opportunity of attending public worship' and the clergyman, a relative of 'the munificent Foundress', proved to be exceptionally good in what Wordsworth described as a generally ill-parson'd land.

An ancestor of Lady Fleming—Sir William Fleming, who died in 1736—almost perpetrated an architectural outrage by starting to build a pleasure-house on the largest island in Rydal Water [C]. On discovering, however, that a man could wade to the island, Sir William desisted. The unfinished ruin occasioned a Wordsworth inscription—'Written with a slate pencil upon a stone, the largest of a heap lying near a deserted quarry, upon one of the islands of Rydal' (*PW*, iv. 200). Although the poem invokes us to 'blame him not, | For old Sir William was a gentle Knight, | Bred in this vale', it does register the poet's disdain for white buildings which 'blaze in snow-white splendour'. The antithesis is a home observed on the same island years later, 'The Wild Duck's Nest'.

> Words cannot paint the o'ershadowing yew-tree bough,
> And dimly-gleaming Nest,—a hollow crown
> Of golden leaves inlaid with silver down,
> Fine as the mother's softest plumes allow;
> I gazed—and, self-accused while gazing, sighed
> For human-kind, weak slaves of cumbrous pride!

No doubt the self-accused poet felt some cumbrous pride in Rydal Mount, with its Turkey carpet in the dining-room and Brussels in the study, but it was a comfortable home which served him well, worth putting up a fight to keep. What inspired his genuine love in Rydal vale, and what he wrote his poems about, was not the house but the life, natural and supernatural, that he found in the lake, clouds, stars, moon, and echoes. The last led to a memorable poem written in 1806, before he had moved to Rydal. 'The echo', he said, 'came from Nab-Scar, when I was walking on the opposite side of Rydal Mere' (I.F.).

> Yes, it was the mountain Echo,
> Solitary, clear, profound,
> Answering to the shouting Cuckoo,
> Giving to her sound for sound!
>
> Unsolicited reply
> To a babbling wanderer sent;
> Like her ordinary cry,
> Like—but oh, how different!

Hears not also mortal Life?
Hear not we, unthinking Creatures!
Slaves of folly, love or strife—
Voices of two different natures?

Have not *we* too?—yes, we have
Answers, and we know not whence;
Echoes from beyond the grave,
Recognised intelligence!

Such rebounds our inward ear
Catches sometimes from afar—
Listen, ponder, hold them dear;
For of God,—of God they are.

iii. Over Kirkstone Pass

11

Patterdale and Place Fell[1]

Since the Wordsworths had friends and relatives living near Ullswater, they travelled from Grasmere or Rydal through Patterdale on many occasions. There were two direct routes which they could take: one went north out of Grasmere, following the pack-horse road up Little Tongue Gill to Grisedale Tarn (the route leading to Helvellyn), then down Grisedale into Patterdale; the other went from Ambleside, up Stock Ghyll to Kirkstone Pass and down past Brothers Water into Patterdale. The first was 'a path for foot-travellers, and along which a horse may be led', Wordsworth wrote in the *Guide*, but the second was a proper, though rugged, road locally known as 'The Struggle'. De Quincey recalled being taken by this route on his first visit with the Wordsworths:

I had heard of no horses, and took it for granted that we were to walk; however, at the moment of starting, a cart—the common farmers' cart of the country—made its appearance; and the driver was a bonny young woman of the vale. Such a vehicle I had never in my life seen used for such a purpose; but what was good enough for the Wordsworths was good enough for me; and, accordingly, we were all carted along to the little town, or large village, of Ambleside. . . . From Ambleside—and without one foot of intervening flat ground—begins to rise the famous ascent of Kirkstone; after which, for three long miles, all riding in a cart drawn by one horse becomes impossible. The ascent is . . . [in some parts] almost frightfully steep; for the road, being only the original mountain track of shepherds, gradually widened and improved from age to age (especially since the era of tourists began), is carried over ground which no engineer, even in alpine countries, would have viewed as practicable. . . . The

[1] Map on p. 248.

'ULLSWATER', viewed from the old Matterdale road, looking towards Glenridding on the far shore in the centre. Stybarrow Crag is the steep cliff which goes into the lake to the right of Glenridding. Glencoyne Wood is on the hillside between Stybarrow Crag and

innkeeper of Ambleside, or Low-wood, will not mount this formidable hill without four horses.

(De Quincey, pp. 211–12)

A couple of hundred yards beyond the crest, on the left, is the Kirkstone, or church-stone, 'whose church-like frame | Gives to this savage Pass its name', according to Wordsworth's poem, 'The Pass of Kirkstone'. At that time, there was nothing on the Pass but a sign post, the Kirkstone, and more rocks—no pub or tearoom or car parks. De Quincey's description sets the scene for the part of Wordsworth's poem about its desolation:

The church [i.e., the Kirkstone]—which is but a phantom of man's handiwork—might, however, really be mistaken for such, were it not that the rude and almost inaccessible state of the adjacent ground proclaims the truth. As to size, *that* is remarkably difficult to estimate upon wild heaths or mountain solitudes, where there are no leadings through gradations of distance, nor any artificial standards, from which height or breadth can be properly deduced. This mimic church, however, has a peculiarly fine effect in this wild situation, which leaves so far below the tumults of this world: the phantom church, by suggesting the phantom and evanescent image of a congregation, where never congregation met; of the pealing organ, where never sound was heard except of wild natural notes, or else of the wind rushing through these mighty gates of everlasting rock—in this way, the fanciful image that accompanies the traveller on his road, for half a mile or more, serves to bring out the antagonist feeling of intense and awful solitude, which is the natural and presiding sentiment—the *religio loci*—that broods for ever over the romantic pass.

(De Quincey, pp. 213–14)

The Wordsworths crossed the Pass by cart or on foot in various kinds of weather and even welcomed bad weather because of what it revealed about the place. On their excursion in 1805, recorded in Dorothy's journal and later in the *Guide*, heavy mists gathered as William and Dorothy approached the Pass. They could not see far ahead, but they were delighted by the rocks nearby, 'magnified, though obscured, by the vapour'. The rocks seemed to be living companions, and they observed a pile of stones that they had never noticed before, though they had passed it many times. In 'The Pass of Kirkstone', Wordsworth incorporates 'thoughts and feelings of many walks in all weathers by day and night over this pass, alone and with beloved friends' (I.F.), but he moulds them into one poetic experience, beginning with the fancies and mockeries (De Quincey's phantoms and mimics) that the rocks suggest to the mind in this desolation—notions of the Flood, of Druids, of ancient warriors. This leads the poet to thoughts of the Genius of the Place—'Most potent when mists veil the sky, | Mists that distort and magnify'—who can subdue the memory of common life, and he recalls the Roman legions that once marched along this road. When the mist vanishes, however, thoughts of common life return, and he views the cultivation and other signs of humanity below with new pleasure:

> —Who comes not hither ne'er shall know
> How beautiful the world below.

The desolation of the Pass yields to hope; the inhuman and savage shapes heighten his attachment to human toil and pity and love. The poem was written, according to a note on a manuscript, 'chiefly in a walk from the top of Kirkstone to Patterdale' during June 1817.

Wordsworth often passed through Patterdale on his way to visit various friends: John Marshall, who had married one of Dorothy's close friends and who lived half-way down Ullswater at Hallsteads (now an Outward Bound Mountain School); his anti-slavery friend Thomas Clarkson at Eusemere in Pooley Bridge; his in-laws the Hutchinsons at Park House, two miles north of Pooley Bridge; Lord Lonsdale, whom he met in 1807, at Lowther Castle; his brother Richard at Sockbridge; the Quaker Thomas Wilkinson at Yanwath near Penrith—and, after 1813, he travelled through Westmorland and Cumberland in his capacity as Distributor of Stamps. In 1805 he went to Patterdale with Walter Scott, intending to climb Helvellyn the next day. There were no beds available in the Patterdale inn [C], but the innkeeper gave them permission to sleep on the floor of the sitting-room after all the guests had retired. Some of the ladies, however, were determined to talk into the very late hours. Wordsworth and Scott did their best to move them: pretending to be watchmen, they walked back and forth under the windows outside the room, calling out the half-hours. The ardent conversationalists ignored the calls and did not so much as look at the supposed watchmen. One of these ladies was on her way to Scotland in great hopes of being introduced to the famous poet, Walter Scott. Wordsworth and Scott did eventually get to sleep on the floor, although later than they had intended, and took their memorable walk up Helvellyn the next day.

Patterdale was, however, more than a place for Wordsworth to pass through. He admired its beauty and liked to stop there, often staying with his friends, Mr and Mrs Luff, at Side, or what is now Side Farm [1]. 'This is a wonderful country', Dorothy wrote from the Luffs' house, 'the more wonderful, the more we know of it.' Wordsworth was so impressed with the beauty of Patterdale that in 1804 he decided to buy nineteen acres of land at Broad How [D]. Dove Cottage was by then full to overflowing with his growing family and their guests. The house now called Broad How was not there at the time; William intended to build on a spot where there was nothing but a 'rock and grove', or to add to the farmhouse which still stands. During an evening walk he (in Dorothy's words) 'pitched upon the spot where he should like to build a house better than in any other he had yet seen'. Two days later they 'returned by William's rock and grove, and were so much pleased with the spot that William determined to buy it if possible'.

That same day, they took the path under Place Fell, past Blowick to Sandwick, Pooley Bridge, and Park House, and later to Yanwath to ask Thomas Wilkinson to negotiate the purchase for them.[2] The transaction, as it turned out, proved an embarrassing one for Wordsworth. He was willing to pay £800 and no more for the property, but when another potential buyer appeared, the owner raised the price to £1000. Both Wordsworth and the owner were adamant. Wilkinson, determined that Wordsworth should have the property, appealed to Lord Lonsdale, whom Wordsworth had never met, to make up the difference, which he did generously and tactfully. Wordsworth was justifiably chagrined. 'Strange it is', he wrote to a friend, 'that W[ilkinson] could not perceive, that if I was unwilling to pay an exorbitant price out of my own money, I should

[2] This extraordinary Quaker is the friend, or Friend, of Wordsworth's poem, 'To the Spade of a Friend (An Agriculturalist)'. Wilkinson's *Tour of Scotland* suggested the incident (and the last line) of 'The Solitary Reaper', which Wordsworth had written a few days before this visit.

be still more unwilling to pay it out of another's. . . .' The transaction was completed, however, before he was told of the arrangement. Partly no doubt because of his uneasiness over the terms, he never built his house at Broad How, and in 1834 he sold the property to the Patterdale innkeeper.

During the same visit with the Luffs, Wordsworth heard a story from Charles Luff and saw the ruins of an old stone chapel in Boardale Hause [E], where it occurred. It clearly made a deep impression on him, for the next summer he used the site and the tale in an important and moving segment of *The Excursion* (ii. 730–897). Near the end of their walk (the route is described in the next chapter), Luff showed William and Dorothy the ruins of the old chapel, which had once served both Patterdale and Martindale, and he told the story about an event which had occurred there only several months earlier. A Patterdale woman who was in the habit of taking advantage of an old man sent him up the fell to collect peat. When he could not find his way down because of a long and violent storm, he took refuge for the rest of the day and all night in the ruins of the Chapel in the Hause. Dorothy recorded the story and her description of the chapel in her journal:

Luff then took us aside, before we had begun to descend, to a small ruin, which was formerly a Chapel, or place of worship where the inhabitants of Martindale and Patterdale were accustomed to meet on Sabbath days. There are now no traces by which you could distinguish that the building had been different from a common sheepfold; the loose stones and the few which yet remain piled up are the same as those which lie elsewhere on the mountain; but the shape of the building being oblong is not that of a common sheepfold, and it stands east and west. Whether it was ever consecrated ground or not I do not know; but the place may be kept holy in the memory of some now living in Patterdale; for it was the means of preserving the life of a poor old man last summer, who, having gone up the mountain to gather peats together, had been overtaken by a storm, and could not find his way down again. He happened to be near the remains of the old Chapel, and, in a corner of it, he contrived, by laying turf and ling and stones in a corner of it from one wall to the other, to make a shelter from the wind, and there he sate all night. The woman who had sent him on his errand began to grow uneasy towards night, and the neighbours went out to seek him. At that time the old man had housed himself in his nest, and he heard the voices of the men, but could not make himself heard, the wind being so loud, and he was afraid to leave the spot lest he should not be able to find it again, so he remained there all night; and they returned to their homes, giving him up for lost: but the next morning the same persons discovered him huddled up in the sheltered nook. He was at first stupefied and unable to move; yet after he had eaten and drunk, and recollected himself a little, he walked down the mountain, and did not afterwards seem to have suffered.

(P.W. v. 418)

In creating the tale in *The Excursion*, Wordsworth used this story very much as he heard it from Luff, though he changed the location from Patterdale to a site based on Blea Tarn, used the character of a Grasmere man, and ended his tale with the death of the old man three weeks later, which did not in fact occur. Otherwise, the events of the poem are true, Wordsworth told Isabella Fenwick: 'all that belongs to the character of the Old Man, was taken from a Grasmere Pauper, who was boarded in the last house quitting the vale on the road to Ambleside; the character of his hostess, and all that befell the poor man on the mountain, belong to Patterdale; the woman I knew well; her name was Ruth Jackson, and she was exactly such a person as I describe [lacking in humanity and full of 'ostentatious zeal']. The ruins of the old Chapel, among which the old man was found lying, may yet be traced. . . .' In *The Excursion*, the Poet and Wanderer witness the funeral procession of the old man, thinking it to be the Solitary's funeral. When they see the Solitary, he tells them his 'dolorous tale' of the old pensioner, the landlady, the first, unsuccessful search that he and the landlady's husband made for the pensioner on the fellside, and the successful search of the following morning:

> soon as help
> Had been collected from the neighbouring vale,
> With morning we renewed our quest: the wind
> Was fallen, the rain abated, but the hills
> Lay shrouded in impenetrable mist;
> And long and hopelessly we sought in vain:
> Till, chancing on that lofty ridge to pass
> A heap of ruin—almost without walls
> And wholly without roof (the bleached remains
> Of a small chapel, where, in ancient time,

> The peasants of these lonely valleys used
> To meet for worship on that central height)—
> We there espied the object of our search,
> Lying full three parts buried among tufts
> Of heath-plant, under and above him strewn,
> To baffle, as he might, the watery storm:
> And there we found him breathing peaceably,
> Snug as a child that hides itself in sport
> 'Mid a green hay-cock in a sunny field.
>
> (ii. 805–23)

When the shepherds carried him back to the house, the Solitary saw from the fellside a glorious vision which he describes to the Poet and Wanderer (ii. 829–75); it is based partly on what Luff told them he had seen after the old Patterdale man was found, and partly on what Wordsworth himself saw two and a half miles from Boardale Hause, on the way up to Kirkstone Pass.

The most famous passage in Wordsworth's poetry associated with Patterdale tells of a childhood event—his stealing a boat and rowing on the lake—which critics formerly assumed took place at Esthwaite Water near Hawkshead, even though that lake has no 'rocky cave', 'mountain echoes', or 'craggy steep'. The publication of the 1805 text of *The Prelude* in this century confirms that Wordsworth's descriptions are remarkably accurate, for that text makes clear that Wordsworth was not describing the smooth and beautiful vale of Esthwaite but rather the mountainous and sublime Patterdale. Wordsworth was a Hawkshead schoolboy at the time, but he had travelled over Kirkstone Pass and spent the night at Patterdale on his way home for the summer holidays. He wandered from the inn in the evening when the moon was up, found a rowing boat tied to a tree [G], and rowed out on Ullswater until a huge cliff appeared as an awesome force.

> One evening (surely I was led by her[3])
> I went alone into a Shepherd's Boat,
> A Skiff that to a Willow tree was tied
> Within a rocky Cave, its usual home.
> 'Twas by the shores of Patterdale, a Vale

[3] Nature.

Wherein I was a Stranger, thither come
A School-boy Traveller, at the Holidays.
Forth rambled from the Village Inn alone
No sooner had I sight of this small Skiff,
Discover'd thus by unexpected chance,
Than I unloos'd her tether and embark'd.
The moon was up, the Lake was shining clear
Among the hoary mountains; from the Shore
I push'd, and struck the oars and struck again
In cadence, and my little Boat mov'd on
Even like a Man who walks with stately step
Though bent on speed. It was an act of stealth
And troubled pleasure; not without the voice
Of mountain-echoes did my Boat move on,
Leaving behind her still on either side
Small circles glittering idly in the moon,
Until they melted all into one track
Of sparkling light. A rocky Steep uprose
Above the Cavern of the Willow tree
And now, as suited one who proudly row'd
With his best skill, I fix'd a steady view
Upon the top of that same craggy ridge,
The bound of the horizon, for behind
Was nothing but the stars and the grey sky.
She was an elfin Pinnace; lustily
I dipp'd my oars into the silent Lake,
And, as I rose upon the stroke, my Boat
Went heaving through the water, like a Swan;
When from behind that craggy Steep, till then
The bound of the horizon, a huge Cliff,
As if with voluntary power instinct,
Uprear'd its head. I struck, and struck again,
And, growing still in stature, the huge Cliff
Rose up between me and the stars, and still,
With measur'd motion, like a living thing,
Strode after me. With trembling hands I turn'd,
And through the silent water stole my way
Back to the Cavern of the Willow tree.
There, in her mooring-place, I left my Bark,
And, through the meadows homeward went, with grave
And serious thoughts; and after I had seen

That spectacle, for many days, my brain
Work'd with a dim and undetermin'd sense
Of unknown modes of being; in my thoughts
There was a darkness, call it solitude,
Or blank desertion, no familiar shapes
Of hourly objects, images of trees,
Of sea or sky, no colours of green fields;
But huge and mighty Forms that do not live
Like living men mov'd slowly through my mind
By day and were the trouble of my dreams.

(1805 *Prelude*, i. 372–427)

This is perhaps the most compelling of Wordsworth's many living rocks. Here he celebrates the spirit that gives 'to forms and images a breath | And everlasting motion', for it is through this spirit, working sometimes by pain and fear, that the human soul is built up.

12

Martindale[1]

The tour through Martindale is one of two single-day walking tours described in some detail in Wordsworth's *Guide to the Lakes*. The other describes a walk to the top of Scafell Pike, the highest peak in England, but the poet was not present: it was done by Dorothy and her friend Miss Mary Barker and was an extraordinary trip for two women in those days. Dorothy was present on this excursion to Martindale as well, along with William and their friend Charles Luff of Patterdale. Dorothy first wrote the accounts of both excursions in her journal, and William revised and added to them for publication in his *Guide*. Their stop at the Chapel in the Hause near the end of their walk provided the important scene in *The*

[1] Map on p. 248.

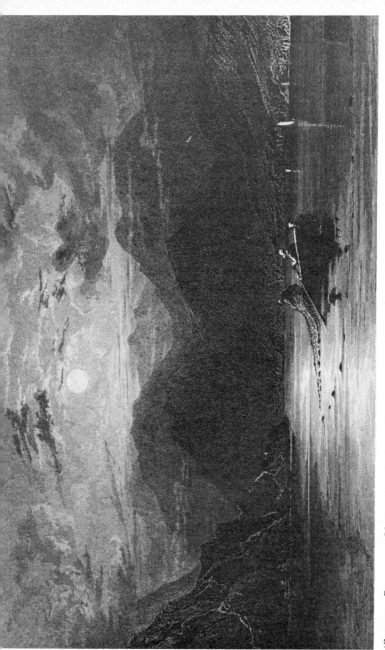

'SECOND REACH OF ULLSWATER', where Wordsworth and Dorothy, on their excursions to Martindale, passed men fishing for skellies.

Excursion mentioned in the previous chapter. In Martindale we can follow Wordsworth's footsteps more closely than anywhere else and have, in addition, his prose accounts of what interested him along the way.

The Wordsworths' excursion began on a rainy Friday morning in November 1805. By ten o'clock the rain had stopped and they set out from Patterdale in a rowing boat with Luff's servant. They watched three fishermen bringing in nets of 'skellies' (fresh-water herring) under Place Fell—'a picturesque group beneath the high and bare crags!'—and attended to a single raven: 'A raven was seen aloft; not hovering like the kite, for that is not the habit of the bird, but passing on with a straight-forward perseverance, and timing the motion of its wings to its own croaking. The waters were agitated; and the iron tone of the raven's voice, which strikes upon the ear at all times as the more dolorous from its regularity, was in fine keeping with the wild scene before our eyes.' (In *The Excursion*, iv. 1181, Wordsworth refers to the raven's sound as 'An iron knell'.) Their boat passed opposite Stybarrow Crag, the shore of Ullswater [J] where Wordsworth had seen some daffodils in April three years earlier, Aira Point, and Lyulph's Tower [L]. At Sandwick Bay [N], they left the boat for the servant to row back to Patterdale, and '[we] pursued our way towards Martindale along a pleasant path—at first through a coppice, bordering the lake, then through green fields— and came to the village (if village it may be called, for the houses are few, and separated from each other), a sequestered spot, shut out from the view of the lake'.

After passing through Sandwick, Wordsworth crossed the stream, probably at Bridge End, and went up the left side, while Luff and Dorothy followed the road and footpath on the right. They met again at Wintercrag, across the stream from the Old Church of St. Martin [O]: 'Crossed the one-arched bridge, below the chapel, with its "bare ring of mossy wall", and single yew-tree.' Martindale today is much like it was in Wordsworth's day. Not only does the Church still stand, its baptismal font (of Roman origin, probably brought down from the Roman High Street, which runs along the ridge above Martindale) was there long before Wordsworth, and the yew in the churchyard (the same 'single yew-tree') had already been there for 500 years, supplying generations of

Martindale archers with their bows. The church is still ringed by a rock wall and travellers must cross the 'one-arched bridge', just as Wordsworth did.[2]

So little has the scene changed that Wordsworth's *Guide* offers a fine description of the place today. Dale End, the house at the end of the road, still exists as a sheep farm. The trappings of the hunting-room which Wordsworth describes are no longer there, but the indigenous herd of red deer still inhabits Martindale. This is Wordsworth's *Guide* on the rest of their excursion:

At the last house in the dale we were greeted by the master, who was sitting at his door, with a flock of sheep collected round him, for the purpose of smearing them with tar (according to the custom of the season) for protection against the winter's cold. He invited us to enter, and view a room built by Mr. Hasell for the accommodation of his friends at the annual chase of red deer in his forests at the head of these dales. The room is fitted up in the sportsman's style, with a cupboard for bottles and glasses, with strong chairs, and a dining-table; and ornamented with the horns of the stags caught at these hunts for a succession of years—the length of the last race each had run being recorded under his spreading antlers. The good woman treated us with oaten cake, new and crisp; and after this welcome refreshment and rest, we proceeded on our return to Patterdale by a short cut over the mountains. On leaving the fields of Sandwyke, while ascending by a gentle slope along the valley of Martindale, we had occasion to observe that in thinly-peopled glens of this character the general want of wood gives a peculiar interest to the scattered cottages embowered in sycamore. Towards its head, this valley splits into two parts; and in one of these (that to the left) there is no house [there is now], nor any building to be seen but a cattle-shed on the side of a hill, which is sprinkled over with trees, evidently the remains of an extensive forest. Near the entrance of the other division stands the house where we were entertained [P], and beyond the enclosures of that farm there are no other. A few old trees remain, relics of the forest, a little stream hastens, though with serpentine windings, through the uncultivated hollow, where many cattle were pasturing. . . . While we paused to rest upon the hillside, though well contented with the quiet every-day sounds—the lowing of cattle, bleating of sheep, and the very gentle murmuring of the valley

---

[2] When he refers to the church's 'bare ring of mossy wall', Wordsworth is quoting himself: it is a phrase from 'The Brothers', describing the parish chapel in Ennerdale.

stream, we could not but think what a grand effect the music of the bugle-horn would have among these mountains. It is still heard once every year, at the chase I have spoken of; a day of festivity for the inhabitants of this district except the poor deer, the most ancient of them all. Our ascent even to the top was very easy; when it was accomplished we had exceedingly fine views, some of the lofty Fells being resplendent with sunshine, and others partly shrouded by clouds. Ullswater, bordered by black steeps, was of dazzling brightness; the plain beyond Penrith smooth and bright, or rather gleamy, as the sea or sea sands. Looked down into Boardale, which, like Stybarrow, has been named from the wild swine that formerly abounded here; but it has now no sylvan covert, being smooth and bare, a long, narrow, deep, cradle-shaped glen, lying so sheltered that one would be pleased to see it planted by human hands, there being a sufficiency of soil; and the trees would be sheltered almost like shrubs in a greenhouse.—After having walked some way along the top of the hill, came in view of Glenriddin and the mountains at the head of Grisdale.—Before we began to descend, turned aside to a small ruin, called at this day the chapel [E], where it is said the inhabitants of Martindale and Patterdale were accustomed to assemble for worship. There are now no traces from which you could infer for what use the building had been erected; the loose stones and the few which yet continue piled up resemble those which lie elsewhere on the mountain; but the shape of the building having been oblong, its remains differ from those of a common sheep-fold; and it has stood east and west. Scarcely did the Druids, when they fled to these fastnesses, perform their rites in any situation more exposed to disturbance from the elements. One cannot pass by without being reminded that the rustic psalmody must have had the accompaniment of many a wildly-whistling blast; and what dismal storms must have often drowned the voice of the preacher! As we descend, Patterdale opens upon the eye in grand simplicity, screened by mountains, and proceeding from two heads, Deepdale and Hartshope. . . .

In Martindale, perhaps better than any other inhabited part of the Lakes, we can fancy that time has stood still since Wordsworth and Dorothy passed through it over a hundred and seventy-five years ago.

13

Aira Force and Gowbarrow Park[1]

Where were Wordsworth's daffodils? The famous passage iden-
tifying the location is in Dorothy's journal: 'When we were in the
woods beyond Gowbarrow park we saw a few daffodils close to the
water side. . . . But as we went along there were more and yet more
and at last under the boughs of the trees, we saw that there was a
long belt of them along the shore, about the breadth of a country
turnpike road.' Given this mention of Gowbarrow Park and the bay
in the poem ('along the margin of a bay'), many have assumed that
the place was Gowbarrow Bay, almost two miles east of Lyulph's
Tower. Others, like William Knight, say it is 'below' Gowbarrow
Park not far from Lyulph's Tower. But Dorothy says '*beyond*
Gowbarrow park', and since on that occasion they were travelling
from Pooley Bridge to Patterdale, 'beyond' means on the
Patterdale, or western, side of Gowbarrow Park. Gowbarrow Bay
would be a possibility if by 'Gowbarrow park' Dorothy meant the
small area immediately surrounding Gowbarrow Hall, just east of
the Bay, but William and Dorothy always use the name to refer to
an extensive area including Lyulph's Tower and Aira Force. To
know what is 'beyond Gowbarrow park' we need to know where it
ends. On the modern Ordnance Survey maps, Gowbarrow Park
ends near Lyulph's Tower, and Glencoyne Park is west of it.
However, in Wordsworth's day they were not separate; what was
called Gowbarrow Park ends, on some early nineteenth-century
maps, nearly one and a half miles west of Lyulph's Tower, toward
Patterdale, just before Glencoyne Beck. This is stated as a matter of
fact in Wordsworth's *Guide*: '*At the outlet of Gowbarrow Park*, we
reach a third stream, which flows through a little recess called
Glencoin'. Just beyond Glencoyne Beck is Glencoyne Wood.
Dorothy's phrase 'in the woods beyond Gowbarrow park', clearly

[1] Map on p. 248.

'AIRA FORCE', in Gowbarrow Park, near Ullswater.

refers to this shoreline [J] south of Glencoyne Beck, before it reaches Stybarrow Crag—the usual locations, in the present Gowbarrow Park, notwithstanding.

The important thing, however, is not so much where the daffodils were, but rather what they did to Wordsworth and what he did with them, and these are embodied in the poem:

> I wandered lonely as a cloud
> That floats on high o'er vales and hills,
> When all at once I saw a crowd,
> A host, of golden daffodils;
> Beside the lake, beneath the trees,
> Fluttering and dancing in the breeze.
>
> Continuous as the stars that shine
> And twinkle on the milky way,
> They stretched in never-ending line
> Along the margin of a bay:
> Ten thousand saw I at a glance,
> Tossing their heads in sprightly dance.
>
> The waves beside them danced; but they
> Out-did the sparkling waves in glee:
> A poet could not but be gay,
> In such a jocund company;
> I gazed—and gazed—but little thought
> What wealth the show to me had brought:
>
> For oft, when on my couch I lie
> In vacant or in pensive mood,
> They flash upon that inward eye
> Which is the bliss of solitude;
> And then my heart with pleasure fills,
> And dances with the daffodils.

The admiration and love which this poem has inspired, and continues to inspire, witness to its success in expressing 'truths of the imagination', in Wordsworth's phrase. For the poem contains that kind of truth rather than a representation of 'matters of fact'. The facts of 15 April 1802, when William and Dorothy came upon the daffodils beyond Gowbarrow Park, had to be changed to make this particular poem. The poet was not wandering alone, as the poem says—William was walking with Dorothy—and there was a high wind ('The wind was furious', Dorothy said about the beginning of their walk, and 'The Bays were stormy' about this part) rather than a 'breeze'. But they did see daffodils at a particular time and in a particular place—a sight that surprised and delighted them both and that later inspired William to transform what he saw into a poem. Here is Dorothy's account of the scene:

When we were in the woods beyond Gowbarrow park we saw a few daffodils close to the water side. We fancied that the lake had floated the seeds ashore and that the little colony had so sprung up. But as we went along there were more and yet more and at last under the boughs of the trees, we saw that there was a long belt of them along the shore, about the breadth of a country turnpike road. I never saw daffodils so beautiful they grew among the mossy stones about and about them, some rested their heads upon these stones as on a pillow for weariness and the rest tossed and reeled and danced and seemed as if they verily laughed with the wind that blew upon them over the lake, they looked so gay ever glancing ever changing. This wind blew directly over the lake to them. There was here and there a little knot and a few stragglers a few yards higher up but they were so few as not to disturb the simplicity and unity and life of that one busy highway. We rested again and again. The Bays were stormy, and we heard the waves at different distances and in the middle of the water like the sea.

As Professor Frederick A. Pottle reminds us in a classic essay on this poem,[2] Wordsworth was not 'Nature's Boswell', following Nature around with a notebook and writing down her utterances on the spot. A close observer of nature he certainly was, but a poem— even an apparently factual one, or one based on actual facts—is something other than a record of events. This poem not only grew out of what he saw on 15 April, but out of what he later read in Dorothy's journal—the daffodils personified as a crowd, 'gay', 'dancing', and 'laughing'. And, in addition, the daffodils worked on him in a way that the poet 'little thought' of at the time, bringing the 'wealth' that comes later, away from the particular spot on Ullswater, when the daffodils 'flash upon that inward eye' and make the heart dance, as the daffodils once did (to the poet's eye)

[2] *The Yale Review*, xl (1950), 27–42.

and in some sense still do. It would be odd if such a poem were written on the spot, and 'I wandered lonely as a cloud' was not written until at least two years after Wordsworth saw the daffodils. The experience of that time and that place provided crucial raw material, but before it could become a poem it had to be transformed by memory and imagination. And this, for Wordsworth, was the usual way of composing, not the exception. 'Poetry', he wrote in the famous Preface to the *Lyrical Ballads*, 'takes its origin from *emotion* [i.e., not the daffodils themselves but the gazing on them] *recollected* in tranquillity.'

The sight of the daffodils arrested the travellers, though only the journal, and not the poem, calls attention to their stopping ('We rested again and again'). The recurrent motif in Wordsworth's poems of the halted traveller is the subject of 'Airey-Force Valley' [κ], which *is* located in Gowbarrow Park. Again, the poet is stopped by something he sees—an ash tree in this case, moving when all else in the enclosed space, except the brook, is motionless, even though the wind rages outside the vale. But the poet also hears something, not with the sensual ear (which hears nothing from Keats's urn), but with the imaginative faculty: 'A soft eye-music of slow-waving boughs'. The traveller must be attuned to more than waterfalls to stop for this:

AIREY-FORCE VALLEY

               —Not a breath of air
Ruffles the bosom of this leafy glen.
From the brook's margin, wide around, the trees
Are steadfast as the rocks; the brook itself,
Old as the hills that feed it from afar,
Doth rather deepen than disturb the calm
Where all things else are still and motionless.
And yet, even now, a little breeze, perchance
Escaped from boisterous winds that rage without,
Has entered, by the sturdy oaks unfelt,
But to its gentle touch how sensitive
Is the light ash! that, pendent from the brow
Of yon dim cave, in seeming silence makes

A soft eye-music of slow-waving boughs,
Powerful almost as vocal harmony
To stay the wanderer's steps and soothe his thoughts.

Although this poem ignores the waterfall in Aira Vale, Wordsworth himself did not. He suggested in his *Guide* that the traveller approach Ullswater at this spot (rather than from either end of the lake) because of the beauty here: 'It is better to go from Keswick through Matterdale, and descend upon Gowbarrow Park; you are thus brought at once upon a magnificent view of the two higher reaches of the Lake. Aira-force thunders down the Ghyll on the left, at a small distance from the road.' Still further to the left is Lyulph's Tower [L], which provided the inspiration for and the setting of 'The Somnambulist'. The poem begins:

> List, ye who pass by Lyulph's Tower
>   At eve; how softly then
> Doth Aira-force, that torrent hoarse,
>   Speak from the woody glen!
> Fit music for a solemn vale!
>   And holier seems the ground
> To him who catches on the gale
> The spirit of a mournful tale,
>   Embodied in the sound.

The 'mournful tale' Wordsworth made up, fancying that it took place long ago, before the relatively recent Lyulph's Tower was built, in a 'stern brow'd' house 'Not far from that fair site whereon | The Pleasure-house is reared'. The idea, however, came from something Wordsworth and his two travelling companions heard about the present building:

While we were making an excursion together in this part of the Lake District we heard that Mr. Glover, the Artist, while lodging at Lyulph's Tower, had been disturbed by a loud shriek, and upon rising he had learnt that it had come from a young woman in the house who was in the habit of walking in her sleep: in that state she had gone downstairs, and, while attempting to open the outer door, either from some difficulty or the effect of the cold stone upon her feet, had uttered the cry which alarmed him. It seemed to us all that this might serve as a hint for a poem, and the story here told was constructed, and soon after put into verse by me as it now stands.

                                                                    (I.F.)

The story, in eighteen stanzas, tells of the fair Emma's love for Sir Eglamore, who courted her among Aira's 'bowers of holly, ... | Where Fact with Fancy stooped to play'. When he leaves she takes up sleep-walking, to fatal effect ('the Stream whirled her down the dell | Along its foaming bed') and Sir Eglamore becomes a hermit 'Beside the torrent dwelling'. There is much Fancy and little Fact in all this, but Wordsworth built his fancy around the spirit of the place.

14

Penrith[1]

According to Samuel Johnson, 'No mind is much employed upon the present; recollection and anticipation fill up almost all our moments.' Wordsworth often took issue with the great critic and poet of an earlier generation—Johnson died when Wordsworth was fourteen years old—and one might think that a poet of place, as Wordsworth emphatically was and Johnson was not, would be living disproof of this sentiment. Poetry of place, one would think, ought to be the poetry of the here and now, describing or contemplating a particular landscape at a particular moment. Wordsworth as an observer of nature certainly employed himself with the present moment. He knew a yellow primrose, or even a rare moss campion, when he saw it; he studied the manners of wanderers and shepherds; and he made it the business of his soul to attend to the spirit of a place. The popular poems 'Expostulation and Reply' and 'The Tables Turned' seem to advocate something like these things to the listener: quit your books and seek a better kind of lore in the natural world around you.

[1] Map on p. 249.

'BROUGHAM
CASTLE', on the
River Eamont,
near Penrith.

Come forth into the light of things,
Let Nature be your teacher.
. . .

Come forth, and bring with you a heart
That watches and receives.

But even here it is clear that 'William' in the poem is not much
concerned with the present:

—Then ask not wherefore, here, alone,
Conversing as I may,
I sit upon this old grey stone,
And dream my time away.

The truth is that Johnson's observation can be aptly applied to
Wordsworth's poetry: recollection and anticipation fill up many, if
not almost all, of its best moments. 'I wandered lonely as a cloud'
refers to an event that happened several years in the past; 'Tintern
Abbey' begins with the past—'Five years have passed; five
summers, with the length | Of five long winters!'—and ends with
the future; and *The Prelude* is the poet's attempt to prepare for the
future (it was to be a prelude to *The Recluse*) by looking at the past.

As a child and later as a student on vacation, Wordsworth spent
much of his time in Penrith [z], but the present there was often
marred by unhappiness. Before her marriage, his mother lived
with her parents, the Cooksons, above the linen-draper's shop
which her father owned in the Market Square. The Wordsworth
family was established and grew in Cockermouth, but Ann
Wordsworth often took her children for long visits to Penrith at the
house of their grandparents and of Uncle Kit, who, when Ann and
John Wordsworth died, became the children's guardian. After
1783, Penrith was the place that technically qualified as home
whenever it came time for William to go home from Hawkshead or
Cambridge for the vacation.

Home, however, as in *Home at Grasmere*, is a word charged with
more than a technical meaning, and Penrith could not qualify for
any of the richer connotations. His brief autobiography recounts
some grim times above the draper's shop:

I was of a stiff, moody, and violent temper; so much so that I remember
going once into the attics of my grandfather's house at Penrith, upon some

indignity having been put upon me, with an intention of destroying myself with one of the foils which I knew was kept there. I took the foil in hand, but my heart failed. Upon another occasion, while I was at my grandfather's house at Penrith, along with my eldest brother, Richard, we were whipping tops together in the large drawing-room, on which the carpet was only laid down upon particular occasions. The walls were hung round with family pictures, and I said to my brother, "Dare you strike your whip through that old lady's petticoat?" He replied, "No, I won't." "Then," said I, "here goes;" and I struck my lash through her hooped petticoat, for which no doubt, though I have forgotten it, I was properly punished.

(Prose Works, iii. 372)

Dorothy wrote to a friend, 'Many a time have W[illia]m, J[ohn], C[hristopher] and myself shed tears together, tears of bitterest sorrow': their grandmother was bad-tempered, their grandfather seldom spoke to them except to scold, Uncle Kit was ill-natured and had a particular dislike for William, and the servant James insulted them with impunity (*Letters*, late July 1787). There were times of intense joy as William wandered around the environs of Penrith, but Penrith as home was a state in which much was to be endured and little to be enjoyed, as Johnson said of human life in general. That state partly explains why, according to Johnson, we spend so much of our time thinking about the past and the future rather than the present.

For Wordsworth, however, recollection was less an escape from the present than an indispensable prerequisite for poetic emotion, a source of power and strength.

> The days gone by
> Return upon me almost from the dawn
> Of life: the hiding-places of man's power
> Open; I would approach them, but they close.
> I see by glimpses now; when age comes on,
> May scarcely see at all; and I would give,
> While yet we may, as far as words can give,
> A substance and a life to what I feel:
> I would enshrine the spirit of the past
> For future restoration.

(The Prelude, xii. 277–86)

Such memories provided his famous 'spots of time', one of them a recollection of when his father's servant James (not his grandfather's insolent servant) took him riding on the large hill called Penrith Beacon [BB]. Wordsworth, five years old, was separated from James, became lost, and wandered with his horse until he came to Cowraik Quarry, where a murderer had been hanged years before. Afraid, he led his horse up the hill to a small tarn near the top where he saw 'an ordinary sight' but one which stayed in his mind with visionary power to become the material for poetry.

>   I remember well,
> That once, while yet my inexperienced hand
> Could scarcely hold a bridle, with proud hopes
> I mounted, and we journeyed towards the hills:
> An ancient servant of my father's house
> Was with me, my encourager and guide:
> We had not travelled long, ere some mischance
> Disjoined me from my comrade; and, through fear
> Dismounting, down the rough and stony moor
> I led my horse, and, stumbling on, at length
> Came to a bottom, where in former times
> A murderer had been hung in iron chains.
> The gibbet-mast had mouldered down, the bones
> And iron case were gone; but on the turf,
> Hard by, soon after that fell deed was wrought,
> Some unknown hand had carved the murderer's name.
> The monumental letters were inscribed
> In times long past; but still, from year to year,
> By superstition of the neighbourhood,
> The grass is cleared away, and to this hour
> The characters are fresh and visible:
> A casual glance had shown them, and I fled,
> Faltering and faint, and ignorant of the road:
> Then, reascending the bare common, saw
> A naked pool that lay beneath the hills,
> The beacon on the summit, and, more near,
> A girl, who bore a pitcher on her head,
> And seemed with difficult steps to force her way
> Against the blowing wind. It was, in truth,

An ordinary sight; but I should need
Colours and words that are unknown to man,
To paint the visionary dreariness
Which, while I looked all round for my lost guide,
Invested moorland waste, and naked pool,
The beacon crowning the lone eminence,
The female and her garments vexed and tossed
By the strong wind.

                    (*The Prelude*, xii. 225–61)

When he was a student at Cambridge, he returned to Penrith and walked on the Beacon with Mary Hutchinson, the girl who had attended the dame school in Penrith with Wordsworth in earlier years and was later to become his wife.

            When, in the blessed hours
Of early love, the loved one at my side,
I roamed, in daily presence of this scene,
Upon the naked pool and dreary crags,
And on the melancholy beacon fell
A spirit of pleasure and youth's golden gleam;
And think ye not with radiance more sublime
For these remembrances, and for the power
They had left behind? So feeling comes in aid
Of feeling, and diversity of strength
Attends us, if but once we have been strong.

                    (*The Prelude*, xii. 261–71)

The poet remembers a spot of time invested with imaginative power, remembers remembering it, and in the double memory finds more imaginative power—namely, these poetic lines, which become a memorial for future restoration.

When Wordsworth was seventeen, after his first year at Cambridge, he went to Penrith for the summer vacation to be with his sister Dorothy, ending a separation of nine years. Not even Uncle Kit could ruin the joy that William, Dorothy, and Mary shared in their walks on the Beacon.

                O'er paths and fields
In all that neighbourhood, through narrow lanes
Of eglantine, and through the shady woods

> And o'er the Border Beacon, and the waste
> Of naked pools, and common crags that lay
> Exposed on the bare fell, were scattered love,
> The spirit of pleasure, and youth's golden gleam.
>
> (*The Prelude*, vi. 230–6)

During that summer or the next, he climbed with Dorothy among the ruins of Brougham Castle [W], at the junction of the rivers Eamont and Lowther, as they had climbed as children among the ruins of Cockermouth Castle:

> The varied banks
> Of Emont, hitherto unnamed in song,
> And that monastic castle, 'mid tall trees,
> Low-standing by the margin of the stream, . . .
>   —that river and those mouldering towers
> Have seen us side by side, when, having clomb
> The darksome windings of a broken stair,
> And crept along a ridge of fractured wall,
> Not without trembling, we in safety looked
> Forth, through some Gothic window's open space,
> And gathered with one mind a rich reward
> From the far-stretching landscape, by the light
> Of morning beautified, or purple eve;
> Or, not less pleased, lay on some turret's head,
> Catching from tufts of grass and hare-bell flowers
> Their faintest whisper to the passing breeze,
> Given out while mid-day heat oppressed the plains.
>
> (*The Prelude*, vi. 203–6, 211–23)

Although Penrith did not have the attractions of home, it was rich in personal recollections which became the stuff of autobiographical poetry, and it was rich too in its suggestions of times past. 'This whole neighbourhood abounds in interesting traditions and vestiges of antiquity', Wordsworth wrote in a note to 'Hart's-horn Tree', 'viz. Julian's Bower; Brougham and Penrith Castles; Penrith Beacon, and the curious remains in Penrith Churchyard; Arthur's Round Table, and, close by, Maybrough; the excavation, called the Giant's Cave, on the banks of the Emont; Long Meg and her daughters, near Eden, etc., etc.' Antiquities and traditions become a significant part of a place, and Wordsworth as a poet was impelled to memorialize them as well as his own personal past. Even when the vestiges of the past are gone, the spirit of the past may remain to be given new life and form through poetry. The Hart's-horn Tree [Y], when it existed at Whinfell Park with stag horns nailed to its trunk, was the physical manifestation of an ancient story about Balliol, King of Scotland, who visited Robert Clifford at Brougham Castle in 1333. During a hunt with a single greyhound, they ran a stag from Whinfell Park to Redkirk in Scotland and back. The exhausted stag jumped a fence into the park and fell dead at the foot of the tree, and the dog, Hercules, attempted to jump but fell dead by the fence. The hunters commemorated the chase by nailing the stag's horns to the tree. The tree does not exist now, but neither did it exist when Wordsworth wrote the poem. 'The tree has now disappeared,' he wrote, 'but I well remember its imposing appearance as it stood, in a decayed state, by the side of the high road leading from Penrith to Appleby.' Its disappearance, as much as its appearance, called for a poem to perpetuate the spirit of the place.

HART'S-HORN TREE, NEAR PENRITH

Here stood an Oak, that long had borne affixed
To his huge trunk, or, with more subtle art,
Among its withering topmost branches mixed,
The palmy antlers of a hunted Hart,
Whom the Dog Hercules pursued—his part
Each desperately sustaining, till at last
Both sank and died, the life-veins of the chased
And chaser bursting here with one dire smart.
Mutual the victory, mutual the defeat!
High was the trophy hung with pitiless pride;
Say, rather, with that generous sympathy
That wants not, even in rudest breasts, a seat;
And, for this feeling's sake, let no one chide
Verse that would guard thy memory, HART'S-HORN TREE!

Likewise, Inglewood Forest, which used to surround Penrith, was the subject of another sonnet ('Suggested by a View from an Eminence in Inglewood Forest') about a place whose interest lay in the past. 'The extensive forest of Inglewood has been enclosed within my memory. I was well acquainted with it in its ancient state.' But now,

> The forest huge of ancient Caledon
> Is but a name, no more is Inglewood,
> That swept from hill to hill, from flood to flood:
> On her last thorn the nightly moon has shone. . . .

The 'last thorn' was a tree mentioned by Wordsworth in the Fenwick note on the poem and is still commemorated by the place name [AA]: 'It was single and conspicuous; and being of round shape, though it was universally known to be a Sycamore, it was always called the "Round Thorn", so difficult is it to chain fancy down to fact.' Difficult, and undesirable as well:

> Thus everywhere to truth Tradition clings,
> Or Fancy localises Powers we love.
>
>   ('Fancy and Tradition')

'Localizing Power' is an apt description of what Wordsworth does in his poetry of place, and the power that characterizes the environs of Penrith was for Wordsworth the power of the past asserting itself in the present and future. Not far from Whinfell Park is a monument which was old in Wordsworth's time and still stands [X].

COUNTESS' PILLAR

On the roadside between Penrith and Appleby, there stands a pillar with the following inscription:

'This pillar was erected, in the year 1656, by Anne Countess Dowager of Pembroke, &c. for a memorial of her last parting with her pious mother, Margaret Countess Dowager of Cumberland, on the 2d of April, 1616; in memory whereof she hath left an annuity of £4 to be distributed to the poor of the parish of Brougham, every 2d day of April for ever, upon the stone table placed hard by. Laus Deo!'

> While the Poor gather round, till the end of time
> May this bright flower of Charity display
> Its bloom, unfolding at the appointed day;
> Flower than the loveliest of the vernal prime
> Lovelier—transplanted from heaven's purest clime!
> 'Charity never faileth:' on that creed,
> More than on written testament or deed,
> The pious Lady built with hope sublime.

Alms on this stone to be dealt out, *for ever!*
'LAUS DEO.' Many a Stranger passing by
Has with that Parting mixed a filial sigh,
Blest its humane Memorial's fond endeavour;
And, fastening on those lines an eye tear-glazed,
Has ended, though no Clerk, with 'God be praised!'

An annuity of £4 to last *'for ever!'*: this is indeed 'hope sublime', but hopes for the future have their power no less than recollections of the past. Alms are in fact still distributed annually from this Pillar, as the Countess intended.

A more mysterious, more powerful, more enduring monument stands only a few miles away from Countess' Pillar, but Wordsworth did not see it until he was fifty years old. He was travelling on business, as Distributor of Stamps, when he came upon the ancient stones standing on top of a hill north-east of the Beacon. 'My Road brought me suddenly upon that ancient monument called by the Country People Long Meg and her Daughters' [CC], he wrote to Sir George Beaumont. 'Every body has heard of it, and so had I from very early childhood, but had never seen it before. Next to Stone Henge, it is beyond dispute the most noble relick of the kind that this or probably any other country contains' (*Letters*, 10 January 1821). Later he wrote (in a note to the poem about it) that since he had been taken by surprise, he might have overrated its importance as an object, but, he said, 'I must say that I have not seen any other relique of those dark ages which can pretend to rival it in singularity and dignity of appearance'. Soon after his encounter with these standing stones, he wrote this sonnet.

THE MONUMENT COMMONLY CALLED LONG MEG AND HER DAUGHTERS, NEAR THE RIVER EDEN

A weight of awe, not easy to be borne,
Fell suddenly upon my Spirit—cast
From the dread bosom of the unknown past,
When first I saw that family forlorn.
Speak Thou, whose massy strength and stature scorn
The power of years—pre-eminent, and placed
Apart, to overlook the circle vast—

Speak, Giant-mother! tell it to the Morn
While she dispels the cumbrous shades of Night;
Let the Moon hear, emerging from a cloud;
At whose behest uprose on British ground
That Sisterhood, in hieroglyphic round
Forth-shadowing, some have deemed, the infinite
The inviolable God, that tames the proud!

The encounter occurred in a particular time and at a particular place, but Wordsworth's imaginative response leads away from the here and now and toward antiquity and infinity.

While Wordsworth was still a schoolboy journeying to Penrith for his holidays, a huge cliff had loomed over him in the stolen boat on Ullswater, and it seemed to stride after him; in the night, huge and mighty forms troubled his dreams, as nature spoke to him obscurely. The ancient standing stones near Penrith, Long Meg and her Daughters, also affected Wordsworth suddenly and ominously and obscurely. But they were natural forms which had been mysteriously set in place by humans in the unknown past, offering to proud humans in the present indecipherable hieroglyphs and, perhaps, glimpses of infinity.

iv. Langdale and Beyond

15

Borrowdale[1]

As boy and man, Wordsworth associated the world of things and of human activity with trees. R. P. Graves remembered 'Mr Wordsworth saying that, at a particular stage of his mental progress, he used to be frequently so rapt into an unreal transcendental world of ideas that the external world seemed no longer to exist in relation to him, and he had to reconvince himself of its existence by clasping a tree'.[2] His first poem in *Lyrical Ballads* is about the nourishing prospect from under a yew tree along Esthwaite Water. 'Nutting', written a short time later and about a place just south of the same lake, tells of hazel trees violated by the ragged schoolboy for their nuts ('Then up I rose, | And dragged to earth both branch and bough, with crash | And merciless ravage'). *The Prelude* records a spot of time when he made his look-out on a hill near Hawkshead, by a fence, sheep, and 'one blasted tree', waiting for the horses to take him home for the Christmas holidays when his father died. In the 'Immortality Ode' there is the 'Tree, of many, one', which speaks 'of something that is gone'. Perhaps it was 'a tall ash, that near our cottage stood' outside his bedroom window when he was a schoolboy at Hawkshead, or a splendid ash 'With sinuous trunk, boughs exquisitely wreathed', at which he later gazed 'Beneath a frosty moon' when he was a student at Cambridge (*The Prelude*, iv. 85–92; vi. 76–94). Grasmere Vale had its 'CLIPPING TREE, a name which yet it bears' in 'Michael', as well as John's fir grove, opposite the Wishing Gate, and the trees in the garden at Dove Cottage ('My trees they are, my Sister's flowers').

[1] Map on p. 261.
[2] Christopher Wordsworth, *Memoirs of William Wordsworth* (1851), ii. 480.

'THE DERWENT
RIVER AND
BORROWDALE'.
The Bowder Stone
is perched above
the river on the
left. Castle Crag is
in the middle
distance on the
right, and beyond
the ridge leading to
it is Glaramara.

Rydal had a 'time-dismantled Oak' ('The Haunted Tree'), Penrith a Hart's-horn Tree, and Ullswater a Joyful Tree and a willow tree, where the boat was tied which the schoolboy stole and returned, driven back by 'a huge peak, black and huge'. Wordsworth felt the power of hills—of old Helvellyn, Place Fell, and Glaramara—and he also felt the power of trees, large or small, single or in groves.

Trees grew in his imagination. In *Lyrical Ballads*, Ruth dwells alone, 'Under the greenwood tree'; a retired seaman, no Ancient Mariner, tells the strange tale of Martha, who appears to him by the small, gnarled hawthorn that is the centre of 'The Thorn' ('some will say | She hanged her baby on the tree'); and Simon Lee works pathetically at the root of an old tree. Trees grew where the poet, as landscape designer, planted them—yew trees in the Grasmere churchyard, hollies above Lancrigg, various native kinds at Allan Bank and Rydal Mount, and birches and beeches at Fox How, Matthew Arnold's summer home. But the most famous Lake District trees are the yews of Lorton and of Borrowdale. The first, the 'pride of Lorton Vale', is a single tree, apparently indestructible, used long ago by bowmen for making weapons to use in battle in Scotland or beyond the seas. The Borrowdale Yews [H] are entirely different, a grove of four, 'Joined in one solemn and capacious grove', suggesting a building—a 'pillared shade', a place with 'sable roof' for festal purpose, and 'a natural temple'. The one yew stands alone, the others are four, united; the one contains darkness and gloom profound, the grove contains shade; the one provides weapons for war in foreign lands, the grove a meeting spot for celebration and for listening to the mountain streams; the one speaks of distant time and place ('Azincour, . . . earlier Crecy, or Poictiers'), the other of the ever-recurrent present ('at noontide'); the one attracts bands of soldiers, the other ghostly shapes of the human spirit. Both are worthy of note but, the poet tells us, the fraternal four of Borrowdale are worthier.

YEW-TREES

There is a Yew-tree, pride of Lorton Vale,
Which to this day stands single, in the midst
Of its own darkness, as it stood of yore:
Not loth to furnish weapons for the bands

Of Umfraville or Percy ere they marched
To Scotland's heaths; or those that crossed the sea
And drew their sounding bows at Azincour,
Perhaps at earlier Crecy, or Poictiers.
Of vast circumference and gloom profound
This solitary Tree! a living thing
Produced too slowly ever to decay;
Of form and aspect too magnificent
To be destroyed. But worthier still of note
Are those fraternal Four of Borrowdale,
Joined in one solemn and capacious grove;
Huge trunks! and each particular trunk a growth
Of intertwisted fibres serpentine
Up-coiling, and inveterately convolved;
Nor uninformed with Phantasy, and looks
That threaten the profane;—a pillared shade,
Upon whose grassless floor of red-brown hue,
By sheddings from the pining umbrage tinged
Perennially—beneath whose sable roof
Of boughs, as if for festal purpose decked
With unrejoicing berries—ghostly Shapes
May meet at noontide; Fear and trembling Hope,
Silence and Foresight; Death the Skeleton
And Time the Shadow;—there to celebrate,
As in a natural temple scattered o'er
With altars undisturbed of mossy stone,
United worship; or in mute repose
To lie, and listen to the mountain flood
Murmuring from Glaramara's inmost caves.

The poet and his sister saw the Lorton Yew in 1804, going from
Keswick to the west, over Whinlatter Pass, and down 'into the
fertile Vale of Lorton' to visit, in Dorothy's words, 'a Yew tree
which is the Patriarch of Yew trees, green and flourishing, in very
old age—the largest tree I ever saw. We have many large ones in
this Country, but I have never yet seen one that would not be but as
a Branch of this' (*Letters*, 7 and 10 October 1804). Today the
Lorton Yew and the Borrowdale Yews are in their decline; age and
destructive storms have taken many huge branches and much of the
main trunks, but there is still magnificence in their decay. The

Lorton Yew declined even in Wordsworth's time. In his comments on the poem in 1843 he noted this, which led him to the thought of an ancient ruin in Borrowdale which none of the trees mentioned in this poem will ever equal.

These yew-trees are still standing, but the spread of that at Lorton is much diminished by mutilation. I will here mention that a little way up the hill, on the road leading from Rosthwaite to Stonethwaite, lay the trunk of a yew-tree, which appeared as you approached, so vast was its diameter, like the entrance of a cave, and not a small one. Calculating upon what I have observed of the slow growth of this tree in rocky situations, and of its durability, I have often thought that the one I am describing must have been as old as the Christian era. The tree lay in the line of a fence. Great masses of its ruins were strewn about, and some had been rolled down the hillside and lay near the road at the bottom. As you approached the tree, you were struck with the number of shrubs and young plants, ashes, etc., which had found a bed upon the decayed trunk and grew to no inconsiderable height, forming, as it were, a part of the hedgerow. In no part of England, or of Europe, have I ever seen a yew-tree at all approaching this in magnitude, as it must have stood. By the bye, Hutton, the old Guide, of Keswick, had been so impressed with the remains of this tree that he used gravely to tell strangers that there could be no doubt of its having been in existence before the flood.

(I.F.)

When Wordsworth mentions Borrowdale in his writing, he usually dwells on its yew trees, as in *Select Views:* 'The Yew-tree has been a favourite with the former Inhabitants of Borrowdale; for the many fine old Yew-trees yet remain near the Cottages. . . . But the noblest Yew-trees to be found here, are a cluster of three, with a fourth a little detached, which do not stand in connection with any houses . . . Nothing of the kind can be conceived more solemn and impressive than the small gloomy grove formed by these trees' (*Prose Works*, ii. 275). But 'the fantastic mountains of Borrowdale', as he calls them, contain an infinite variety of beautiful objects; indeed, 'this Valley surpasses all others in variety'. There are 'Rocks and Woods . . . intermingled on the hillsides with profuse wildness', cottages 'unobtrusive as the rocks themselves, and mostly coloured like them', and lead-mines, as well as yew trees. Wordsworth loved the sublime view of the mountains looking south from Keswick. Coleridge, in a letter to a friend, described an unusual, dream-like prospect of them through a drizzle and added that 'Wordsworth, who has walked thro' Switzerland, declared that he never saw any thing superior—perhaps nothing equal—in the alps'.

The beauty of the region notwithstanding, the people of Borrowdale were said to have been extraordinary for their dissipation and stupidity. Natives were once known as Borrowdale *Gowks*, and the story circulated of one of them—a typical one, by implication—who tried to keep a cuckoo in the valley by building a stone fence around the land it had lighted on. Wordsworth, however, found the natives as intelligent and as capable as their neighbours, though he did confirm that former inhabitants, at least, were excessively devoted to gaming—thirty or forty guineas changing hands in an evening was not uncommon, he said—as a result of the wealth that came from the plumbago lead mines above the famous yew grove.

One inhabitant—a Miss Mary Barker—clearly commanded the Wordsworths' admiration for her intelligence and moral sense, at least until the time of her marriage. She had come to the Lakes as an ardent admirer of Southey and lived next door to his family in Greta Hall for several years beginning in 1812. Dorothy wrote of her: 'She is a painter & labours hard in depicting the beauties of her favorite Vale [Borrowdale]: she is also fond of Music and of reading; and has a reflecting mind: besides, . . . she is become an active Climber of the hills.' In 1814 she had an explosive falling-out with the ladies of the Southey household, which Dorothy, whose sympathies were all with Miss Barker, tried to patch up. At about the same time she wrote a poem attacking Byron for having attacked the 'Lake poets'. Wordsworth contributed substantially to the poem, though he did not want the fact to be known, and it was published as the production of 'one of the Small Fry of the Lakes'. In 1817 she built a cottage in Borrowdale where she lived alone, visited by distinguished friends like the Wordsworths, Sir George and Lady Beaumont, and the anti-slave reformer William Wilberforce. Within two years, however, she let her Borrowdale cottage and moved to Boulogne. The Wordsworths corresponded with her and even visited her there until, in 1830, she married a much younger man whom Dorothy suspected to be 'a Boulogne Swindler'. She told her so: 'I wrote my mind counselled inquiries and settlements etc etc—perhaps not very palateable' (*Letters*, 5 November 1830). Thereafter she was 'poor Miss Barker' or 'poor Soul!'

Back in her Borrowdale days, however, in October 1818, she and Dorothy made a journey which was later recounted in Wordsworth's *Guide*. Both of them were active climbers of the hills, not daunted by being in their mid and late forties or by the fact that climbing was not a conventional pastime for ladies. They took a cart from Miss Barker's house in Rosthwaite to Seathwaite, left the cart there and proceeded on foot to Esk Hause [1], accompanied by a shepherd, who served as guide, and a man who carried provisions. When they arrived at their destination, the various prospects were beautiful ('The green Vale of Esk—deep & green, with its glittering serpent stream was below us') and the autumn day was bright and clear. Since they were still full of energy, they pressed on toward Scafell Pikes. At the top was silence: 'We paused & kept silence to listen, & not a sound of any kind was to be heard.'[3] They ate their dinner in the silence and perfect clearness, wrote letters to Sara Hutchinson (as had Coleridge, the first English mountain climber, back in 1802: '*here* . . . am I now at this moment writing to you . . . surely the first Letter ever written from the Top of Sca' Fell!'), and were shepherded away as a storm suddenly blew up. The storm came and went before they reached Esk Hause again, but it did not dampen their spirits. 'Do not think we here gave up our spirit of enterprise. No! I had heard much of the grandeur of the view of Wasdale from Stye Head', Dorothy wrote, and on they went for the view into Wasdale, then down to Seathwaite and, with stars now shining above them, 'we travelled home in our Cart by Moonlight', passing below the famous Borrowdale Yews. Dorothy—and no doubt poor Miss Barker as well—was uncommonly pleased by 'our uncommon performances on this Day'.

---

[3] I have quoted from the copy of Dorothy's letter of 21 October 1818 given in *Prose Works*, ii. 364–8. Wordsworth made various changes when he adapted the letter as the 'Excursion to the Top of Scawfell' in his *Guide*.

16

Dungeon Ghyll Force and the Langdales[1]

> It was a spot which you may see
> If ever you to Langdale go.

In these lines, as in 'Michael', the poet addresses *you*, reader of poems, and traveller. You may walk up Greenhead Gill in Grasmere Vale if you care for utter solitude, unobtrusive objects like a straggling heap of unhewn stones, and a tale that will delight a few natural hearts. And a mile and a half to the west and south, over Blea Rigg and below Harrison Stickle, you may see Dungeon Ghyll Force [C]. It is an impressive sight—a secluded waterfall with a huge stone wedged above it between the walls of the ravine:

> Into a chasm a mighty block
> Hath fallen, and made a bridge of rock:
> The gulf is deep below;
> And, in a basin black and small,
> Receives a lofty waterfall.

Any traveller willing to leave the public road in search of the picturesque will find it worth seeing, 'if there be time', as Wordsworth says in his *Guide*. But if you know 'The Idle Shepherd-Boys; or, Dungeon-Ghyll Force', which, like 'Michael', is a pastoral poem, written in the same year (1800), and published in the same volume, you may see more than a waterfall: you may see 'a spot'. That humble word is charged with powerful current in Wordsworth's poetry. A spot is more than a particular place or time, more than an external matter of fact, while being emphatically particular and factual. A spot is a place that is charged with human, and sometimes more than human, significance, a place blended with the mind that observes it—whether the poet's, the shepherd's, the reader's, or the traveller's.

[1] Map on p. 268.

'Dungeon Ghyll Force', in Great Langdale, the 'lofty waterfall' and 'bridge of rock' of 'The Idle Shepherd-Boys'.

Wordsworth's favoured spot in his early years as a poet in the Lakes was Grasmere vale. The Wishing Gate overlooking the lake is 'on so fair a spot'; the vale itself is 'the calmest, fairest spot on earth' in 1800 and 'this fairest spot on earth' again in 1811. There is a 'sensation' in 'this individual Spot', he says in *Home at Grasmere*, something that abides within his heart and that 'chosen minds | Take . . . with them hence, where'er they go.' But there were many other spots besides Grasmere that made claims on Wordsworth's poetic sensibilities, and Dungeon Ghyll Force in Langdale was one of them. How it became something more than a picturesque place to Wordsworth we do not know. The tale of the lamb that is swept over the lofty waterfall because the two shepherd boys are playing instead of minding their trade might possibly have been based on fact. Wordsworth did know of lambs falling into Greenhead Gill, and perhaps he knew the same of Dungeon Ghyll. (The sheep at Greenhead Gill 'come down and feed on the little green islands in the beds of the torrents and so may be swept away', Dorothy wrote in her journal.) Perhaps he, like the Poet in 'The Idle Shepherd-Boys', actually rescued a lamb from the black pool at the bottom of the force. He told someone that 'there was some foundation in fact, however slight, for every poem he had written of a narrative kind', but the foundation, it should be noted, might be 'slight' (Grosart, iii. 426).

Whatever Wordsworth's personal associations with the place might have been, it is certain that he knew it well. The events of the poem could happen only at Dungeon Ghyll Force. But Wordsworth needed to convey some sense of the place, as well as the events, since he assumes that his reader has probably not been there ('you *may* see [it] | *If ever* you to Langdale go'). He does this not by providing a guide-book description of it but by representing its sounds at a particular time in May when the lambs are out, 'All newly born!' The reader sees Dungeon Ghyll in the poem by hearing it: 'The valley rings with mirth and joy', the echoes play, the magpie chatters, the shepherd boys play their home-made flutes (a Christmas hymn, about another joyous birth), the sand-lark chants, the thrush carols, 'both earth and sky | Keep jubilee', but the lamb in the pool below cries and the ewe high above responds with 'a cry forlorn', answering 'that plaintive sound'. The boys do not see what the reader sees, however, nor do they see Dungeon Ghyll in the way shepherds ought to see it, as a torrential threat to lambs. They are busy trimming their hats 'with that plant which in our dale | We call stag-horn, or fox's tail', playing their flutes, and challenging each other first to a foot race and then to crossing the dangerous bridge of rock over the waterfall. The challenger on the rock is 'all eyes and feet' until he hears, with his ears and heart, the plaintive cry of the lamb.

A Poet enters the poem at the end, but we are not told that he is William Wordsworth. He is, in the poem, Poet and Bard, and the old poet talking about his poems to Isabella Fenwick did not claim that he saved a lamb in such a situation. He did insist, however, on a certain kind of realism for this and other poems. He told Miss Fenwick 'a little monitory anecdote' about literal truth in his poems. He, Coleridge, and Southey were walking in the fells when Southey gave Wordsworth some free advice: if he wished to be considered a faithful painter of rural manners, he should not include such things in his poems as shepherd boys trimming their hats with stag-horn, which, Southey said, they do not do. 'Just as the words had passed his lips', Wordsworth told Miss Fenwick, 'two boys appeared with the very plant entwined round their hats'!

If ever you to Langdale go, you may not see idle shepherd boys, or three poets, or one, but you may see the scene of 'The Idle Shepherd-Boys'. It is still there—the very spot.

THE IDLE SHEPHERD-BOYS;

OR, DUNGEON-GHYLL FORCE.
A PASTORAL

The valley rings with mirth and joy;
Among the hills the echoes play
A never never ending song,
To welcome in the May.
The magpie chatters with delight;
The mountain raven's youngling brood
Have left the mother and the nest;
And they go rambling east and west
In search of their own food;

Or through the glittering vapours dart
In very wantonness of heart.

Beneath a rock, upon the grass,
Two boys are sitting in the sun;
Their work, if any work they have,
Is out of mind—or done.
On pipes of sycamore they play
The fragments of a Christmas hymn;
Or with that plant which in our dale
We call stag-horn, or fox's tail,
Their rusty hats they trim:
And thus, as happy as the day,
Those Shepherds wear the time away.

Along the river's stony marge
The sand-lark chants a joyous song;
The thrush is busy in the wood,
And carols loud and strong.
A thousand lambs are on the rocks,
All newly born! both earth and sky
Keep jubilee, and, more than all,
Those boys with their green coronal;
They never hear the cry,
That plaintive cry! which up the hill
Comes from the depth of Dungeon-Ghyll.

Said Walter, leaping from the ground,
'Down to the stump of yon old yew
We'll for our whistles run a race.'
—Away the shepherds flew;
They leapt—they ran—and when they came
Right opposite to Dungeon-Ghyll,
Seeing that he should lose the prize,
'Stop!' to his comrade Walter cries—
James stopped with no good will:
Said Walter then, exulting; 'Here
You'll find a task for half a year.
Cross, if you dare, where I shall cross—
Come on, and tread where I shall tread.'
The other took him at his word,

And followed as he led.
It was a spot which you may see
If ever you to Langdale go;
Into a chasm a mighty block
Hath fallen, and made a bridge of rock:
The gulf is deep below;
And, in a basin black and small,
Receives a lofty waterfall.

With staff in hand across the cleft
The challenger pursued his march;
And now, all eyes and feet, hath gained
The middle of the arch.
When list! he hears a piteous moan—
Again!—his heart within him dies—
His pulse is stopped, his breath is lost,
He totters, pallid as a ghost,
And, looking down, espies
A lamb, that in the pool is pent
Within that black and frightful rent.

The lamb had slipped into the stream,
And safe without a bruise or wound
The cataract had borne him down
Into the gulf profound.
His dam had seen him when he fell,
She saw him down the torrent borne;
And, while with all a mother's love
She from the lofty rock above
Sent forth a cry forlorn,
The lamb still swimming round and round,
Made answer to that plaintive sound.
When he had learnt what thing it was,
That sent this rueful cry; I ween
The Boy recovered heart, and told
The sight which he had seen.
Both gladly now deferred their task;
Nor was there wanting other aid—
A Poet, one who loves the brooks
Far better than the sages' books,
By chance had thither strayed;

And there the helpless lamb he found
By those huge rocks encompassed round.

He drew it from the troubled pool,
And brought it forth into the light:
The Shepherds met him with his charge,
An unexpected sight!
Into their arms the lamb they took,
Whose life and limbs the flood had spared;
Then up the steep ascent they hied,
And placed him at his mother's side;
And gently did the Bard
Those idle Shepherd-boys upbraid,
And bade them better mind their trade.

The path and road going up the fellside opposite Dungeon Ghyll lead to Blea Tarn, the setting of a major part of Wordsworth's long poem *The Excursion*. The title of the poem refers only in part to the fictional walking excursion made by the Wanderer, his friend the Poet, and the Solitary who joins them at Blea Tarn. The Poet and Wanderer meet at a ruined cottage on the plains in the south-west of England, wander randomly for a while, then go purposefully up Great Langdale to Blea Tarn to visit the Solitary. After spending the night at the Solitary's house, the three of them go to Grasmere vale to see the Pastor. But there is more in this poem than an excursion of human bodies, for the travellers move with active minds that habitually transform places into 'spots'. The true subject of the poem is what the Wanderer calls 'the mind's *excursive* power' (iv. 1263). The nature of that power differs from character to character: the old Wanderer is full of experience and love, 'alive | To all that was enjoyed where 'er he went, | And all that was endured' (i. 364–6); the Poet is impressionable, still learning; and the Solitary is, we would say, depressed, and for good reasons. Each mind brings to the landscape its own peculiar power, creating its own life—or death, for the mind's excursive power can be treacherous as well as beneficent.

On the fourth day of their journey, the Wanderer takes charge of their route, knowing the spot which will be their destination for the day and sensing its value for his companion:

> Then, pointing with his staff
> Raised toward those craggy summits, his intent
> He thus imparted:—
> > 'In a spot that lies
> Among yon mountain fastnesses concealed,
> You will receive, before the hour of noon,
> Good recompense, I hope, for this day's toil. . . .'
>
> > > (ii. 153–8)

They walk up Great Langdale, cross the beck, and scale the 'steep ascent' of Lingmoor Fell [F] to the top of the ridge:[2]

> > a dreary plain,
> With a tumultuous waste of huge hill tops
> Before us; savage region! which I paced
> Dispirited. . . .
>
> > > (ii. 324–7)

But the Poet does not remain long dispirited, for he suddenly comes in sight of Blea Tarn [G] and Bleatarn House below him:

> > behold!
> Beneath our feet, a little lowly vale,
> A lowly vale, and yet uplifted high
> Among the mountains; even as if the spot
> Had been from eldest time by wish of theirs
> So placed, to be shut out from all the world!
> Urn-like it was in shape, deep as an urn;
> With rocks encompassed, save that to the south
> Was one small opening, where a heath-clad ridge
> Supplied a boundary less abrupt and close;
> A quiet treeless nook, with two green fields,
> A liquid pool that glittered in the sun,
> And one bare dwelling; one abode, no more!
> It seemed the home of poverty and toil,
> Though not of want: the little fields, made green
> By husbandry of many thrifty years,
> Paid cheerful tribute to the moorland house.
> —There crows the cock, single in his domain:
> The small birds find in spring no thicket there

---

[2] See the 'Route of the Poet and Wanderer', p. 275.

> To shroud them; only from the neighbouring vales
> The cuckoo, straggling up to the hill tops,
> Shouteth faint tidings of some gladder place.
>
> (ii. 327–48)

It is, he thinks, a 'sweet Recess' and, lying down on the heather on the ridge, he transforms it into a certain kind of spot:

> —full many a spot
> Of hidden beauty have I chanced to espy
> Among the mountains; never one like this;
> So lonesome, and so perfectly secure;
> Not melancholy—no, for it is green,
> And bright, and fertile, furnished in itself
> With the few needful things that life requires.
> —In rugged arms how softly does it lie,
> How tenderly protected! . . .
> peace is here
> Or nowhere; days unruffled by the gale
> Of public news or private; years that pass
> Forgetfully; uncalled upon to pay
> The common penalties of mortal life,
> Sickness, or accident, or grief, or pain.
>
> (ii. 351–9, 364–9)

The Poet's mind and words when he first beholds Blea Tarn do justice to the view—Wordsworth later inserted it as descriptive poetry in his *Guide*—but his mind's excursive power leaves the realm of object and experience when he lies on the heather and imagines Blea Tarn to be an unearthly Eden. The notion is shattered immediately by the sounds of a funeral dirge: death exists, even in this place. They make 'a steep and difficult descent', thinking that the Solitary has died, find his copy of *Candide* in a lean-to built by children [I], and soon see the Solitary himself. The dirge, they discover, has been sung not for him but for an old inhabitant of the same house. The valley 'seems', as the Solitary tells them in his careless way, 'by Nature hollowed out to be | The seat and bosom of pure innocence', but the truth is quite different. The delusive power of the mind is brought home to the Poet again when the Solitary takes them to the cottage where he lives, Bleatarn House [H]:

> Homely was the spot;
> And, to my feeling, ere we reached the door,
> Had almost a forbidding nakedness;
> Less fair, I grant, even painfully less fair,
> Than it appeared when from the beetling rock
> We had looked down upon it.
>
> (ii. 638–43)

Inside, they eat, hear the Solitary describe the music of the winds in the Langdale Pikes [E], and hear the story of the death of the old man, which Wordsworth based on an actual event in Patterdale.

Wordsworth drew extensively on the landscape of the Langdales to create this poem, but he cannot be charged with slavish adherence to fact. The trip from south-west England to Langdale in one morning, as the Fenwick note says, or in three days, as the poem says (ii. 86), would have required 'more than seven-league boots' and the sudden issue from Blea Tarn into Grasmere in Book v, a 'magic wand' (I.F.). The trip itself was fictional and the characters fictional, though drawn in part from various people he had known and from his own character. Even the landscape was altered to fit the requirements of the poem. Outside Bleatarn House is a stream, which the Wanderer proposes to trace to its source ('a few steps may lead us to the spot | Where [it] . . . comes forth'), but they soon run into a waterfall and can make no further progress. The actual waterfall is not in fact very 'lofty' and not 'naked as a tower', as it is in the poem, though in other respects the description fits the place. But in this 'hidden nook', 'shut out from prospect of the open vale', they find monumental rocks resembling a ship, pillars, and an altar—certainly not of this particular place. There are, however, such rocks [J] on the opposite side of the valley; perhaps by imagining these two places as one, Wordsworth created the setting for an important scene.[3]

When the three men emerge from Bleatarn House, the Solitary does so unwillingly: he had wanted to stay inside to drink wine and

---

[3] William Knight identified this place as the site of the lean-to and argued that all of the elements of the 'hidden nook' scene may be found on the western side of the valley [J] (*The English Lake District as Interpreted in the Poems of Wordsworth*, 2nd ed. [1891], pp. 166–71).

is uncertain where to walk 'In spot so parsimoniously endowed'. The Wanderer therefore leads the way, sees the monumental rocks, reproves the Solitary for having 'decried the wealth which is your own', and sees 'Among these rocks and stones . . . | A semblance strange of power intelligent' (iii. 50–84). The Solitary had forgotten, or disdained them; his mind can be engaged by them, but their appearance, which gives pleasure to the Wanderer, 'is for me', he says, 'Fraught rather with depression than delight' (iii. 155–6). The conversation moves to various subjects, still in this same place, until the Solitary wants to leave: 'let us hence!' But the Poet's mind is now engaged with the problem of the Solitary's despondency, and he, 'Loth to forsake the spot, and still more loth | To be diverted from our present theme', will not leave. He is no longer deluded that Blea Tarn valley is an Eden; he has found it a place where the mind becomes engaged in surprising ways. The three men continue their conversation, revealing to the reader the causes of their different ways of viewing Blea Tarn—and, indeed, the world.

When they depart on the next day for the Parson's house and Grasmere vale, the Poet takes his solitary leave of this more isolated, naked, yet richly endowed vale, breathing

> A parting tribute to a spot that seemed
> Like the fixed centre of a troubled world.
>
> (v. 15–16)

It is, he thinks, a 'beautiful abyss', destined for 'quietness profound'. Although such places would not do for everyone, or for many, or for the best, they might provide seclusion for 'a scattered few | Living to God and nature, and content | With that communion'. Knowing that Blea Tarn is no Eden, he can still, more wisely, affirm the value of such places to their 'scattered few':

> Consecrated be
> The spots where such abide!

17

River Duddon[1]

In one of his early poems, *An Evening Walk* (1793), Wordsworth attached a note to his reader: 'Perhaps this poem may fall into the hands of some curious traveller, who may thank me for informing him, that up the Duddon . . . may be found some of the most romantic scenery of these mountains'. He never called himself, as far as I know, a Romantic poet, but he considered the Duddon valley a proper subject for the adjective. Dorothy described it in 1804 as 'one of the most romantic of all our vales and one of the wildest', and in 1830, when the poet was nearly sixty years old, she wrote that he 'tracked the Duddon almost to its source and never did he speak with more animation of the charms of his romantic country'. It was, he said, 'my favourite River'.

His introduction to the river, however, was not auspicious. When he was a twelve-year-old schoolboy, his passion for fishing led him to make the long walk from Hawkshead to the Duddon, probably up Little Langdale and over Wrynose Pass, in the company of a weaver from a neighbouring hamlet, but it poured with rain and the return proved too much for him. He related the story to Miss Fenwick:

I first became acquainted with the Duddon, as I have good reason to remember, in early boyhood. Upon the banks of the Derwent I had learnt to be very fond of angling. Fish abound in that large river; not so in the small streams in the neighbourhood of Hawkshead; and I fell into the common delusion that the farther from home the better sport would be had. Accordingly, one day I attached myself to a person living in the neighbourhood of Hawkshead, who was going to try his fortune as an angler near the source of the Duddon. We fished a great part of the day with very sorry success, the rain pouring torrents, and long before we got home I was worn out with fatigue; and, if the good man had not carried me

'WALLOWBARROW CRAG', to the left, above the River Duddon.

on his back, I must have lain down under the best shelter I could find. Little did I think then it would have been my lot to celebrate, in a strain of love and admiration, the stream which for many years I never thought of without recollections of disappointment and distress.

His love for the Duddon grew as the result of many return visits, on foot, horseback, cart, and carriage, in the company of various friends. As a schoolboy, he probably went on horseback with other boys to the Swinside Stone Circle, and during his college years he visited his cousin in Broughton [R] and walked to the Duddon. In September 1804 he and Dorothy used their one-horse 'jaunting car', which they had purchased for their trip to Scotland, to convey them to the Duddon and neighbouring vales. In 1808 he, Coleridge, and Sara Hutchinson went to the Duddon over Walna Scar, and three years later he and Mary walked the same route in the reverse direction, after having parted with their children and wagon at Duddon Bridge, and before rejoining them at Coniston.

Sometimes Wordsworth mixed pleasure with business by travelling through the vale as Distributor of Stamps. On one such occasion, in late March, he wrote, 'The Vale of Duddon I had never seen at this season, and was much charmed with it.' Once he travelled up the river in January with Mary, returning from a relative's funeral at Millom, and he commented on 'how much we were pleased with the winter appearance of my favourite River'. There were many excursions, however, simply for pleasure. On one carriage tour late in his life the party separated; Mary walked on alone and the others were to overtake her. She came to 'a rocky eminence' (Moor How Crag, below Seathwaite), climbed it, and when the others drove by on the road below, they did not hear her shouting an invitation to join her for the fine view. Naturally, they were perplexed at not overtaking her on the road. 'Then ensued vexation and distress,' the poet said, 'for I lost my temper entirely' (I.F.). They were eventually reunited in Broughton, however, 'spent a happy evening' together, and the episode proved the truth of some lines in *The River Duddon*: 'Sure, when the separation has been tried, | That we, who part in love, shall meet again' (Sonnet XXX). Four years later, when Wordsworth was seventy-four, Mary stayed at home while her husband took Lady Richardson of Lancrigg and several of his relatives on a tour of the

Duddon. This time, Lady Richardson recorded, they stopped their cart, 'getting out to ascend a craggy eminence on the right, which Mrs Wordsworth admired: the view from it is very striking' (Grosart, iii. 447). The poet was determined, or perhaps Mary charged them, *not* to miss the view on this trip.

Before the Duddon sonnets were written, he walked up the river with Mary to Ulpha. 'We dined in the Porch of Ulpha Kirk [O], and passed two Hours there and in the beautiful churchyard.' This visit perhaps inspired the sonnet which begins, 'THE KIRK OF ULPHA to the pilgrim's eye | Is welcome as a star', and celebrates the churchyard and river:

> How sweet were leisure! could it yield no more
> Than 'mid that wave-washed Church-yard to recline,
> From pastoral graves extracting thoughts divine;
> Or there to pace, and mark the summits hoar
> Of distant moon-lit mountains faintly shine,
> Soothed by the unseen River's gentle roar.
>
> (Sonnet XXXI)

Probably on the same trip he gathered information about the curate of Seathwaite, 'Wonderful' Walker, who was born a native of the vale at Under Crag [H], the youngest of twelve children, and who served as teacher and pastor at Seathwaite Chapel [I] for sixty-six years,

> A Pastor such as Chaucer's verse portrays;
> Such as the heaven-taught skill of Herbert drew;
> And tender Goldsmith crowned with deathless praise!
>
> (Sonnet XVIII)

Walker's extraordinary intellect, hospitality, frugality, and industry in this isolated spot, which he could not be tempted away from—even to accept the additional curacy of Ulpha—form the subject of Wordsworth's fascinating 'Memoir of the Rev. Robert Walker', which he attached to the poem.

The series of thirty-four sonnets entitled *The River Duddon* was, Wordsworth wrote in his note to the poem, 'the growth of many years;—the one which stands the 14th was the first produced [in 1806]; and others were added upon occasional visits to the Stream, or as recollections of the scenes upon its banks awakened a wish to describe them'. But nineteen of the sonnets were written in late 1818 and most of the rest in 1819. In a letter of 1 December 1818 to Sara Hutchinson, who had been on at least one of the poet's trips to the Duddon, Mary wrote that William 'is asleep from sheer exhaustion—he has worked so long. He has written 21 Sonnets (including 2 old ones) on the river Duddon—they all together comprise one Poem.' The 'one Poem' (and Wordsworth clearly regarded it as this rather than as a loosely connected series of poems) was published in 1820, together with his *Guide to the Lakes*, or *Topographical Description of the Country of the Lakes*, as it was called in that edition. Wordsworth was pleased by its reception: 'My sonnets to the river Duddon have been wonderfully popular', he said a year before his death. 'Properly speaking, nothing that I ever wrote has been popular, but they have been more warmly received.'

There is little about the River Duddon in the *Guide*, which is surprising, given its status as his favourite river. Perhaps he felt that the sonnets would suffice, but they of course do not provide a topographical description. Even if we expect a physical description of the poet's favourite spots on the river, we will be mildly—but not entirely—disappointed. To be sure, Wordsworth's prose head-note to the poem does offer the bare, essential facts: 'The River Duddon rises upon Wrynose Fell, on the confines of Westmorland, Cumberland, and Lancashire; and, having served as a boundary to the last two Counties for the space of about twenty-five miles, enters the Irish Sea, between the Isle of Walney and the Lordship of Millum.' In Sonnet III, the poet asks the river, 'How shall I paint thee?' and allows that he will be 'Pleased could my verse, a speaking monument, | Make to the eyes of men thy features known'. The poem is in part a descriptive one: we are shown the 'lofty waste' of its beginnings; the snake-like curves and the flowers of the upper Duddon; the grove and cottage by its side at Cockley Beck; the stepping stones; the cleft at Birks Bridge; the view of the area around Seathwaite from the top of the Pen; the chasm of Wallowbarrow Gorge, where the river deserts 'the haunts of men'; that 'Torrent white' of Tarn Beck as it hurries down to join the Duddon; the flowery plain of Dunnerdale, below Seathwaite, and the 'rough course' further down; the 'hidden pool' of Long Dub;

the ruined house on the hill above Ulpha Bridge; the blank graveyard of The Sepulchre; the Kirk of Ulpha; and at the end its 'radiant progress . . . over smooth flat sands'. But the physical description of the Duddon is not elaborate or minute; we do not come to see the river from the sonnets in anything like the way we might come to see it in paintings or photographs. The poet's 'speaking monument' speaks of things other than physical qualities of the river, and 'the eyes of men' are made to see things other than rocks, water, and plants.

For Wordsworth the beauty of Nature is 'a living Presence of the earth', not to live alone but to be wedded to the mind. 'How exquisitely the individual Mind . . . to the external World | Is fitted:—and how exquisitely, too . . . | The external World is fitted to the Mind', he wrote in the Prospectus to *The Recluse*. The subject of this poem is not properly the River Duddon but the river blended with the poet's mind, which comes stocked not only with a love of beauty, but with poetry, a sense of history, a lively fancy, traditions, superstitions, and a concern for human life from birth to death, and beyond. Hence the poet begins 'Not envying Latian shades' around Horace's spring, 'Careless of flowers' around Persian fountains, and 'Heedless of Alpine torrents'. Not until the ninth line does he get to the subject that meets the eye: 'I seek the birthplace of a native Stream'. Even here we are not invited to imagine the poet clambering about the rocks on a fact-finding mission. He told Miss Fenwick, 'It is with the little River Duddon as it is with most other rivers, Ganges and Nile not excepted,— many springs might claim the honour of being its head. *In my own fancy* I have fixed its rise near the noted Shire-stones' [A]. And in Sonnet III, Nature, Antiquity, and Fortune cannot point to the source, but the poet sees what the headwaters offer: not an exact spot marking the physical beginning of the river, but a physical object in which the poet's mind finds the essence of beginnings—a large patch of bog-moss which seems to be charged with an animating force of newness, or, as the poet says much better, 'a gleam | Of brilliant moss, instinct with freshness rare'.

When the poet considers the stepping stones [D] that cross the river, he does not number the stones or describe the place with enough exactness to leave us certain about *which* stepping stones, but rather he sees the river as a growing being, imagines the stones as part of a belt, or 'zone', worn by this being, sees the water running between the stones as a series of racers, and then imagines (not describes) the human activity that happens here when children test their mettle at floodtime and when old men think their sad thoughts as they cross with increasing feebleness.

THE STEPPING-STONES

The struggling Rill insensibly is grown
Into a Brook of loud and stately march,
Crossed ever and anon by plank or arch;
And, for like use, lo! what might seem a zone
Chosen for ornament—stone matched with stone
In studied symmetry, with interspace
For the clear waters to pursue their race
Without restraint. How swiftly have they flown,
Succeeding—still succeeding! Here the Child
Puts, when the high-swoln Flood runs fierce and wild,
His budding courage to the proof; and here
Declining Manhood learns to note the sly
And sure encroachments of infirmity,
Thinking how fast time runs, life's end how near!

(Sonnet IX)

His fancy engaged by these stepping stones, the poet continues in the next stanza to imagine youthful lovers crossing—she blushing, timid, wanting help; he teasingly holding out his hand, then drawing back, and finally helping ('the thrilling touch | Both feel'); the cupids on 'yon high rock' clapping their wings when the lovers make it across. Clearly, this is no ordinary seeing: we are in the presence not of the informative tour director, or of the guide to the picturesque, but of the poet, accompanied by a Muse who finds much to engage the fancy. At times, such as at Birks Bridge, there is so much—'Objects immense portrayed in miniature, | Wild shapes for many a strange comparison!'—that the poet has to drive her on: 'On, loitering Muse—the swift Stream chides us—on!'

Besides being blended with the poet's mind through the active working of fancy on stones and wild shapes, the river is blended with mind through history, traditions, and superstitions that are attached to the places or brought there by the poet. A 'Faery Chasm' suggests the wild dancing of baby-stealing elves (XI). Viewing a 'gloomy NICHE, capacious, blank, and cold' on the crags of Wallowbarrow Gorge (XV) brings thoughts of the Deluge and the story of ancient American Indians carving mysterious murals high on inaccessible cliffs from their boat during the time of the Great Waters (XVI). At Long Dub [L] the poet thinks of a love-lorn maid who drowns herself by diving for the reflection of a lonely primrose on the sheer rock wall. On a high hill above the Duddon an old ruined hall [P] evokes the tale of an ancient hall plagued by such lamentations, terror, and ghostly power that 'the gay, the bountiful, the bold' abandoned it for ever, leaving it to gradual decay. Still more ancient ruins lead the poet to reflect on those who 'Slept amid that lone Camp on Hardknot's height, | Whose Guardians bent the knee to Jove and Mars' [C] and on the origins of the Swinside Stone Circle [Q] (XVII). The enclosed burial ground, The Sepulchre [M], where peaceful Quakers lie in unmarked graves, inspires thoughts of the absence of lances, charging horses, bloody heroes, and more doubtful combats in this peaceful, secluded valley.

The mind may travel back to prehistory, when 'mighty forests' stood on fells roamed by bison and huge deer (II), or back to the time of the first human intruders, who were perhaps 'nursed | In hideous usages, and rights accursed, | That thinned the living and disturbed the dead' (VIII). But the poet's mind always returns to the Duddon Valley and is never far from its physical presence. At one point the poet climbs a hill, the Pen [G], and describes what he sees—for three lines. But then he imagines the place in a different season and in stormy weather; then he imagines the storm in a still-forested, wilder place; then he imagines himself back in Duddon Valley in such a storm, retreating to the ale, laughter, and stories at Newfield Inn [K], which is just under the Pen, where *he* is.

OPEN PROSPECT

Hail to the fields—with Dwellings sprinkled o'er,
And one small hamlet, under a green hill
Clustering, with barn and byre, and spouting mill!
A glance suffices;—should we wish for more,

Gay June would scorn us. But when bleak winds roar
Through the stiff lance-like shoots of pollard ash,
Dread swell of sound! loud as the gusts that lash
The matted forests of Ontario's shore
By wasteful steel unsmitten—then would I
Turn into port; and, reckless of the gale,
Reckless of angry Duddon sweeping by,
While the warm hearth exalts the mantling ale,
Laugh with the generous household heartily
At all the merry pranks of Donnerdale!

(Sonnet XIII)

The poem is the blending of mind and river, but the poet and the Duddon are two separate things. The poet is glad to drink ale while the angry river sweeps by; he chooses 'to saunter o'er the grassy plain' where the river wheels through the 'rough copse' [N]; and the true poet of the river's birth is not this poet but 'the whistling Blast', and its patron saint is Desolation (II). This poet is 'The Bard who walks with Duddon for his guide' (XII), seeking, observing, listening, imagining, praising, thanking, remembering, dreaming, reflecting, and feeling. He begins in the morning at the Three Shire Stone, hurries regretfully away from a spot near Birks Bridge, hears the 'busy hum of Noon' at Seathwaite, finds a resting place in a nook near Long Dub when 'Mid-noon is past', becomes idle and discontented because of the absence of his love, regains his pleasure in the river, rises and moves on, makes a detour away from the river at The Sepulchre, rejoins it, reaches the Kirk of Ulpha in the evening, sees the Duddon flowing over the sands into the sea, and is moved to think of his own death.

The river, a 'child of the clouds', begins its journey at some unidentifiable birthplace, falls from a dizzy steep and laughingly dares a human adventurer to do likewise. It curves down the fellside, provides calm seclusion for flowers and wrens, soothes and cleanses the violence of the unknown past, and chides travellers near Birks Bridge. It views shepherds, cottages, and tillage-ground but is not content, impelled by 'some awful Spirit' to desert the haunts of men and plunge into the Wallowbarrow Gorge. An entrancement detains the river in the flowery plains of Dunnerdale, but it breaks the chains, changes its temper, pursues a rough bacchanalian course, dancing from rock to rock. It forgives wrongs, praises the loyal and brave at The Sepulchre, and inspires scorn of power usurped. Finally, as 'Majestic Duddon', it makes its 'radiant progress toward the Deep', sinks into powerless sleep, and forgets its nature, merging into the sea.

Yet the river and poet, separate beings, do move in the same direction and in some of the same ways and toward similar ends. Both progress from obscure origins, growing, changing, displaying various tempers, sometimes apparently enchanted, sometimes impelled by something outside themselves, but moving inevitably toward an end which consists of a mingling with something infinitely more vast. The river seems an emblem of human life, and the Wanderer-Poet, in his 'Conclusion' (XXXIII), prays that he may be like the Duddon (which he addresses directly, as 'Thee'):

> And may thy Poet, cloud-born Stream! be free—
> The sweets of earth contentedly resigned,
> And each tumultuous working left behind
> At seemly distance—to advance like Thee;
> Prepared, in peace of heart, in calm of mind
> And soul, to mingle with Eternity!

But there is an 'After-thought' (XXXIV):

> I thought of Thee, my partner and my guide,
> As being past away.—Vain sympathies!

The poet looks back on the Duddon, his partner and guide, and perceives that it will abide, while we must die—'be it so!' It is enough if something from us have power to live on—for the poet, perhaps this poem—and enough if 'We feel that we are greater than we know'. This ending seems to some readers too consoling, too easy. But in Wordsworth's scheme of things, this feeling is the culmination of our contact with the river and the poem. We feel that we are greater than we know by following the River Duddon as our partner and guide, by fitting the individual mind to the external world, blending mind and river, or by following, with the imagination, the poet's imaginative journey in *The River Duddon*.

Conclusion

18

Joanna's Rock—The Place in the Poem

Wordsworth spent a lifetime observing nature in the Lakes and he wrote many poems about what he saw. But when we follow his footsteps, do we see what he saw? In some cases, we do not because the landscape has changed during the past century and a half. When the landscape has not changed radically, however, we may still not see what Wordsworth saw because we do not look with Wordsworth's eyes. Aubrey de Vere quoted Wordsworth talking about his own extraordinary way of seeing:

He proceeded to remark that many who could descant with eloquence on Nature cared little for her, and that many more who truly loved her had yet no eye to discern her—which he regarded as a sort of 'spiritual discernment.' He continued, 'Indeed I have hardly ever known any one but myself who had a true eye for Nature, one that thoroughly understood her meanings and her teachings—except' (here he interrupted himself) 'one person. There was a young clergyman, called Frederick Faber, who resided at Ambleside. He had not only as good an eye for Nature as I have, but even a better one, and sometimes pointed out to me on the mountains effects which, with all my great experience, I had never detected.'

(Grosart, iii. 488)

Most of us have not looked as closely at the Lakes as Wordsworth or the young clergyman, though our way of looking at them has altered because of what Wordsworth saw and how he wrote about what he saw. His notion of seeing as 'a sort of "spiritual discernment"' clearly requires not only external objects—rocks, daffodils, or people—but some means of perceiving them, namely, the imagination.

Wordsworth's poems, as imaginative acts, lead readers to perceive the landscape as something not merely external and

'LANGDALE PIKES', from Blea Tarn. 'I could not, ever and anon, forbear | To glance an upward look on two huge Peaks, | That from some other vale peered into this' (*The Excursion*, II. 691–3).

isolated from us, though by habit most of us begin a poem thinking that landscape *is* external and separate. Coleridge spent a lifetime waging war on what he called the 'despotism of the eye', the often unconscious assumption that the only, or primary, reality is what we see with our physical eye. To that we may add a second over-narrow view of reality, the tyranny of fact. Both Wordsworth and Coleridge were conscious of these tyrannies and struggled against them in their day, and the passage of over a century and a half has done nothing to make them any less prevalent or dangerous. In the preceding chapters I have (following Wordsworth) made much of the connections between poems and places that, for the most part, we can still see, and I have cited many facts that he claimed gave rise to the poems. But we have observed that the facts of Wordsworth's walk along Ullswater were very different from what appears in his poem about daffodils, and that the poem itself speaks of an 'inward eye' which acts long after the physical eye has done its work. Likewise, the beggar that Wordsworth and his sister met on the public road was not the same as the leech-gatherer on the lonely moor in the poem. Still, it is tempting to think of poems as descriptions or as records of facts, or to think that we cannot know a poem without knowing what *out there* is being described or what the facts *really* were.

There is no doubt that the facts of Wordsworth's experience—his seeing daffodils or meeting a beggar—gave rise to particular poems and no doubt that Wordsworth was, in ways that show up in the poems, a close observer of nature in the Lake District. Furthermore, we can be grateful that Wordsworth left us records of the personal experiences which affected his poetry and that the Lake District he knew is not altogether lost to us. But a poem, written or spoken, is different, essentially different, from an image, an experience, or a fact. It may have been 'suggested' by them (to use Wordsworth's word), or allude to them or use them, faithfully or unfaithfully, but a poem creates its own images, experiences, and facts to work on us, the readers. Wordsworth's notes dictated to Miss Fenwick can have a tendency to lead us into thinking of the poems only in relation to their origins, but Wordsworth was throughout his life scornful of verse which was nothing more than matter of fact or description.

'To Joanna', which is not essentially different from the other 'Poems on the Naming of Places', offers a useful antidote to what can become an obsession with literal analogues. Consider first only the facts in the poem itself. The poet (i.e., the speaker, or narrator) is ostensibly writing an informal 'discourse' to Joanna, whom he has not seen for 'two long years'. He tells her of a conversation he had 'some ten days past' with the Vicar, who came over from his 'gloomy house' to the fir trees by the church where the poet was sitting. The Vicar, after inquiring about Joanna, reprimands him for having defaced a rock by chiselling a name into it. The poet does not regret having done this and thinks he will have a bit of fun with the Vicar by telling him in extravagant terms why and how he came to do it; in the last half of the poem—the reply in quotation marks—he reports to Joanna what he said to the Vicar.

We learn in the poem that the chiselling of Joanna's name in the rock took place six months earlier than this meeting with the Vicar, and that he chiselled it in memory of an event which took place at the rock two years ago—or 'eighteen moons' before the chiselling. At that time two years ago Joanna was visiting the poet; they were taking a walk at daybreak; and they experienced an echoing in the mountains, which the poem describes. Here is his account of it.

TO JOANNA

Amid the smoke of cities did you pass
The time of early youth; and there you learned,
From years of quiet industry, to love
The living Beings by your own fire-side,
With such a strong devotion, that your heart
Is slow to meet the sympathies of them
Who look upon the hills with tenderness,
And make dear friendships with the streams and groves.
Yet we, who are transgressors in this kind,
Dwelling retired in our simplicity
Among the woods and fields, we love you well,
Joanna! and I guess, since you have been
So distant from us now for two long years,
That you will gladly listen to discourse,
However trivial, if you thence be taught

That they, with whom you once were happy, talk
Familiarly of you and of old times.

    While I was seated, now some ten days past,
Beneath those lofty firs, that overtop
Their ancient neighbour, the old steeple-tower,
The Vicar from his gloomy house hard by
Came forth to greet me; and, when he had asked,
'How fares Joanna, that wild-hearted Maid!
And when will she return to us?' he paused;
And, after short exchange of village news,
He with grave looks demanded, for what cause,
Reviving obsolete idolatry,
I, like a Runic Priest, in characters
Of formidable size had chiselled out
Some uncouth name upon the native rock,
Above the Rotha, by the forest-side.
—Now, by those dear immunities of heart
Engendered between malice and true love,
I was not loth to be so catechised,
And this was my reply: 'As it befell,
One summer morning we had walked abroad
At break of day, Joanna and myself.
—'Twas that delightful season when the broom,
Full-flowered, and visible on every steep,
Along the copses runs in veins of gold.
Our pathway led us on to Rotha's banks;
And when we came in front of that tall rock
That eastward looks, I there stopped short—and stood
Tracing the lofty barrier with my eye
From base to summit; such delight I found
To note in shrub and tree, in stone and flower,
That intermixture of delicious hues,
Along so vast a surface, all at once,
In one impression, by connecting force
Of their own beauty, imaged in the heart.
—When I had gazed perhaps two minutes' space,
Joanna, looking in my eyes, beheld
That ravishment of mine, and laughed aloud.
The Rock, like something starting from a sleep,
Took up the Lady's voice, and laughed again;

That ancient Woman seated on Helm-crag
Was ready with her cavern; Hammar-scar,
And the tall Steep of Silver-how, sent forth
A noise of laughter; southern Loughrigg heard,
And Fairfield answered with a mountain tone;
Helvellyn far into the clear blue sky
Carried the Lady's voice,—old Skiddaw blew
His speaking-trumpet;—back out of the clouds
Of Glaramara southward came the voice;
And Kirkstone tossed it from his misty head.
—Now whether (said I to our cordial Friend,
Who in the hey-day of astonishment
Smiled in my face) this were in simple truth
A work accomplished by the brotherhood
Of ancient mountains, or my ear was touched
With dreams and visionary impulses
To me alone imparted, sure I am
That there was a loud uproar in the hills.
And, while we both were listening, to my side
The fair Joanna drew, as if she wished
To shelter from some object of her fear.
—And hence, long afterwards, when eighteen moons
Were wasted, as I chanced to walk alone
Beneath this rock, at sunrise, on a calm
And silent morning, I sat down, and there,
In memory of affections old and true,
I chiselled out in those rude characters
Joanna's name deep in the living stone:—
And I, and all who dwell by my fireside,
Have called the lovely rock, JOANNA'S ROCK.'

The poem has its own facts—its people, places, events, and rather elaborate time scheme—and it renders an experience that readers who have grown to love the poem find deeply moving. The poet, playing with the Vicar's reprimand, becomes caught up by the recollection of the beauty he has seen in the broom and on the lofty barrier of rock. But when he recounts the echo of Joanna's laugh, he is, as Wordsworth commented, 'caught in the trap of my own imagination', apparently *participating* in an extravagant series of echoes. The Vicar 'in the hey-day of astonishment' recognizes it as an extravagance and then receives a more sober, tentative account of that 'loud uproar' and Joanna's response. And then, 'in a strain of deep tenderness', as Wordsworth described it, he tells of chiselling the rock eighteen months later.

Immediately after the poem, Wordsworth appended this:

Note.—In Cumberland and Westmoreland are several Inscriptions, upon the native rock, which, from the wasting of time, and the rudeness of the workmanship, have been mistaken for Runic. They are, without doubt Roman.

The Rotha, mentioned in this poem, is the River which, flowing through the lakes of Grasmere and Rydal, falls into Wynandermere. On Helm-crag that impressive single mountain at the head of the Vale of Grasmere, is a rock which from most points of view bears a striking resemblance to an old Woman cowering. Close by this rock is one of those fissures or caverns, which in the language of the country are called dungeons. Most of the mountains here mentioned immediately surround the Vale of Grasmere; of the others, some are at a considerable distance, but they belong to the same cluster.

A remarkably dry, factual note for a lively and extravagant poem! His comment to Miss Fenwick, too, appears to want to set the facts straight: 'Grasmere, 1800. The effect of her laugh is an extravagance; though the effect of the reverberation of voices in some parts of the mountains is very striking. There is, in *The Excursion*, an allusion to the bleat of a lamb thus re-echoed, and described without any exaggeration, as I heard it, on the side of Stickle Tarn, from the precipice that stretches on to Langdale Pikes.'

As the notes so often do, these have the tendency to pull us away from the experience of the poem itself to some analogous facts and experiences in Wordsworth's life and his surroundings: as he thinks about his own poetry, such things clearly matter. And they do clearly figure in this poem. He did know a woman named Joanna, dearly loved at the Grasmere fireside and seldom there—Joanna Hutchinson, the youngest sister of Mary. Furthermore, there were next to the Grasmere church 'lofty firs, that overtop | Their ancient neighbour, the old steeple-tower'. (When the Wordsworths returned to Grasmere in 1807 Dorothy lamented that 'all the finest firtrees that overtopped the steeple tower' had been cut down.) The

Grasmere Rectory was in fact, as in the poem, 'hard by' and 'gloomy': it sat in a bog across from the church and when the Wordsworths moved there in 1811 they found it still gloomier than they had thought. That Wordsworth was given to carving names we have already seen: he did it on the school desk in the Hawkshead Grammar School and on the Rock of Names, to mention the most famous instances. We know, too, that echoes could have a striking effect not only at Stickle Tarn but in Grasmere vale. A few weeks before he wrote this poem, he and Dorothy had this experience, reported in Dorothy's journal, while rowing on the lake:

We heard a strange sound in the Bainriggs wood as we were floating on the water it *seemed* in the wood, but it must have been above it, for presently we saw a raven very high above us—it called out and the Dome of the sky seemed to echo the sound—it called again and again as it flew onwards, and the mountains gave back the sound, seeming as if from their center a musical bell-like answering to the bird's hoarse voice. We heard both the call of the bird and the echo after we could see him no longer.

And, of course, as the poet's end-note takes pains to point out, the places mentioned in the poem do exist: Helm Crag with its Ancient Woman, Hammer-scar, the tall steep of Silver How, Loughrigg, Fairfield, Helvellyn, old Skiddaw, Glaramara, and Kirkstone.

But this is a poem, not a gazetteer or a press release or even a 'discourse' to Joanna, as it purports to be. Joanna Hutchinson did not in fact grow up amid the smoke of cities (but, we can still insist, 'Joanna' in the poem *did*); she did not visit the Wordsworths at Grasmere two years before August 1800, when the poem was written; the Wordsworths did not even live in Grasmere then. Worse yet, if we have succumbed to the tyranny of fact, there is no 'tall rock that eastward looks' on 'Rotha's banks' that fits the description in the poem. Since so much in Wordsworth's Lake District poems is based on identifiable places, it is only natural to wonder what and where the rock is. A friend walking with Wordsworth asked him about the location of Joanna's Rock. They were at that moment walking by Butterlip How, and Wordsworth replied rather casually, 'Any place that will suit; that as well as any other'. But for this poem, no factual place suits very well. Joanna's Rock is in the poem, part of an imaginative act which connects people with a landscape. That connection is not limited to poems; it can, and manifestly does, take place outside them. But these particular events at this particular place happen only in this poem: the poet, accompanied by Joanna, has responded to a view with imaginative gazing and ravishment; Joanna has responded with wonder and laughter at such gazing; the mountains have responded to her laughter; they have been bound together in delight over nature's beauty and in fear of its astonishing power. Here are beauty and sublimity, the two forces of nature that, as Wordsworth understood it, act *on* and *in* us, in moments of intense liveliness. The rocks work on us and we work on them. Joanna, the poet, and their friends are not the only 'living Beings' in this poem. The rocks live:

> . . . there . . .
> I chiselled out in those rude characters
> Joanna's name deep in the living stone

—'living' not just when it is echoing the laughter, but when he returns 'long afterwards' on that calm and silent morning to chisel his memorial. The poem is not record but imaginative act: when we, responding to the poem, have imagined it, we too have had something 'imaged in our hearts'; we have seen with an inward, not a physical, eye Wordsworth's vision of the 'connecting force' in nature and between man and nature; we have felt that the rocks live.

I have said that 'To Joanna' is essentially like the other 'Poems on the Naming of Places'. It is an altogether different poetic experience, of course, and it is the only one that is clearly not based on an identifiable place.[1] But they are all imaginative acts, not records. The wild place of Emma's Dell, the lonely solitude of Stone Arthur, the sites, at least, of a 'narrow girdle of rough stones and crags' leading to Point Rash-Judgement and of the calm recess of John's Grove can still be pointed to and admired with a livelier zeal than we might otherwise bring to them, but the precise spirit of place in the poems is still there, in the poems. When we respond to

---

[1] Mary's Nook ('Our walk was far among the ancient trees') is perhaps another, but presumably one might have located it at one time. Wordsworth stated unequivocally that it 'is in Rydal Upper Park' (I.F.), but the poem says—rightly, as it turns out—'The travellers know it not, and 'twill remain | Unknown to them'.

the spirit of place in a poem—whether it is about Joanna's Rock, which is *not* out there as a fact, or about Stone Arthur, which *is* out there, almost exactly as it was in Wordsworth's time—we are caught up in the life of a poem. If Joanna's Rock were a physical fact and we could see it, we might gaze at it in ravishment like the poet in the poem, or we might laugh at someone else's ravishment and feel fear in the midst of echoing mountains, like the wild-hearted Joanna, or we might be disgusted at the uncouth carvings on it, like the Vicar, or—far more likely—we might have our own individual response unlike any of these. If the rock lives, it is between us and the rock. If the rock lives in 'To Joanna', it is between us and the poem.

This does not mean, of course, that poetry and landscape have nothing to do with each other. Neither Joanna's Rock nor Stone Arthur could possibly live in their poems if the landscape were not alive to the extraordinary eye of William Wordsworth. And the reader who can see little in a landscape, like Peter Bell ('A primrose by the river's brim | A yellow primrose was to him, | And it was nothing more'), will no doubt miss much in a Wordsworth poem about place. Seeing and reading are different activities but they are certainly related, just as seeing and writing were certainly related for Wordsworth.

No one knows with any certainty who Louisa was in the fine little poem called 'Louisa, after Accompanying her on a Mountain Excursion'. Some say Joanna Hutchinson, some say Dorothy Wordsworth, some say Mary Wordsworth, some say that she was no single person. Nor do we know which mountain waterfalls may have inspired the poem: so many places might do, it is futile to guess. No matter. What we need to know is in the poem—a poet who boldly asserts the wonders of Louisa, and the energetic Louisa herself, who 'down the rocks can leap along | Like rivulets in May'. The enthusiastic poet is charmed by 'that lovely Maid', as well he might be, and is willing to give all just to be near her at a certain time and place:

> Take all that's mine 'beneath the moon,'
> If I with her but half a noon
> May sit beneath the walls
> Of some old cave, or mossy nook,

> When up she winds along the brook
> To hunt the waterfalls.

The poet in the poem knows that his characteristic activity of sitting beneath the walls of some old cave or nook is quite different from hers—hunting waterfalls; he has his pleasures and she has hers. Yet in their **separateness** they are linked by the way the poet sees her with love and admiration. A poet, Wordsworth said in a quite different context, is one who 'looks at the world in the spirit of love'.[2]

Hunting Wordsworthian waterfalls and reading Wordsworth's poems are also different activities—the first best done in the Lake District and the second, anywhere. The reading does not require the hunting since the poems are imaginative acts rather than matters of fact to be verified by the physical eye. Still, many have found new pleasures in the poems after they have come to know the places, and many have found new pleasures in the places from having known Wordsworth's poems. The connections abide. And they abide in the imagination, which brings primroses, rocks, and poems to life. The hunting of waterfalls and the reading of poems both require what Wordsworth called 'an eye to perceive and a heart to enjoy'.

[2] Preface to *Lyrical Ballads*, in *Prose Works*, i. 140.

PART II

In the Footsteps of Wordsworth
(*Maps and Guides*)

Those walks well worthy to be prized and loved—
Regretted!—that word, too, was on my tongue,
But they were richly laden with all good,
And cannot be remembered but with thanks
And gratitude, and perfect joy of heart—

The Prelude, iv. 131–5

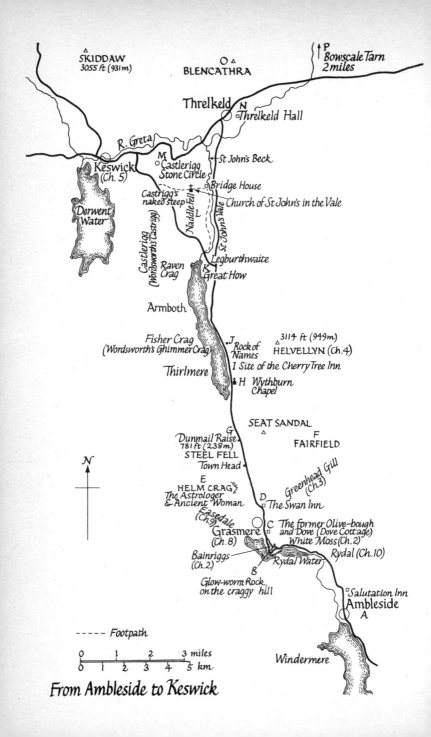

SKIDDAW
3055 ft (931m)

BLENCATHRA

P↑ Bowscale Tarn
2 miles

Threlkeld

N
Threlkeld Hall

R. Greta

M
Castlerigg
Stone Circle

St John's Beck

Keswick
(Ch. 5)

Bridge House

Castrigg's
naked steep

Church of St John's in the Vale

Derwent
Water

Castlerigg
(Wordsworth's Castrigg)

Naddle Fell

St John's Vale

Legburthwaite

Raven
Crag

K Great How

Armboth

Fisher Crag
(Wordsworth's Ghimmer Crag)

J Rock of
Names

3114 ft (949m)
HELVELLYN (Ch.4)

I Site of the Cherry Tree Inn

Thirlmere

H Wythburn
Chapel

SEAT SANDAL

Dunmail Raise
781 ft (238m)
STEEL FELL

G

F
FAIRFIELD

Town Head

Greenhead Gill
(Ch.3)

E
HELM CRAG
The Astrologer
& Ancient Woman

D
The Swan Inn

Easedale
(Ch.9)

C The former Olive-bough
and Dove (Dove Cottage)

Grasmere
(Ch. 8)

White Moss (Ch.2)

Bainriggs
(Ch.2)

Rydal (Ch.10)

Rydal Water

B

Glow-worm Rock
on the craggy hill

Salutation Inn

Ambleside
A

N

----- Footpath

0   1   2   3 miles
0   1   2   3   4   5 km

From Ambleside to Keswick

Windermere

1

From Ambleside to Keswick

Guide to places

[The capital letters correspond to the letters on the preceding map. When a letter in this key is accompanied by an asterisk (as in c*), the place to which it refers is discussed further in the first chapter of Part I: Poems and Places (p. 9). In this case, the key letter also appears in the chapter by the place name.]

A   AMBLESIDE: 'This Town or Market-village was formerly perhaps more rich in picturesque beauty, arising from a combination of rustic architecture and natural scenery than any small Town or Village in Great Britain. Many of the ancient buildings with their porches, projections, round chimnies and galleries have been displaced to make way for the docked, featureless, and memberless edifices of modern architecture; which look as if fresh brought upon wheels from the Foundry, where they had been cast. Yet this Town, if carefully noticed, will still be found to retain [a] store of picturesque materials . . .' (*Select Views*, in *Prose Works*, ii. 268). It is the 'little rural Town' of the sonnet beginning 'While beams of orient light shoot wide and high' (*PW*, iii. 60).

B   GLOW-WORM ROCK: a crag along the road where the Wordsworths often walked. For its appearances in Wordsworth's poetry, see Part I: Chapter 2 (p. 20).

c*   DOVE COTTAGE: formerly an inn, The Olive-Bough and Dove, where Benjamin the Waggoner could drink; later the home of a water-drinking poet.

> The place to Benjamin right well
> Is known, and by as strong a spell
> As used to be that sign of love
> And hope—the OLIVE-BOUGH and DOVE;
> He knows it to his cost, good Man!

It is discussed further, as Wordsworth's home, in Part I: Chapter 8 (p. 89).

D* THE SWAN INN: 'Who does not know the famous SWAN?' Benjamin knew it well, but did not pause here on this journey, 'in despite | Of open door and shining light'.

E* HELM CRAG: 'A mountain of Grasmere, the broken summit of which presents two figures, full as distinctly shaped as that of the famous Cobbler near Arroquhar in Scotland', Wordsworth wrote in a note to *The Waggoner*. In the poem Benjamin sees the Astrologer and the Ancient Woman. Today, they are known as the Old Woman Playing the Organ (seen from Tongue Gill or Easedale Tarn) and the Lion and the Lamb (seen from the road below Dunmail Raise).

F FAIRFIELD: the mountain which returned the sound of the Waggoner's footsteps—'And mighty Fairfield, with a chime | Of echoes, to his march kept time'.

G* DUNMAIL RAISE: 'From Grasmere the Traveller ascends to Wythburn by Dunmail raise gap, an opening in the shape of a huge inverted arch, the sides of which are formed by Steel fell on the left and on the right by Seat Sandal. Having passed the monumental heap of stones [King Dunmail's burial cairn, according to tradition], he will come in view of the lake and vale of Wythburn extending thro' a long mountainous vista, terminated by Skiddaw and other mountains' (*Prose Works*, ii. 272n). Speaking to Miss Fenwick about his early poem, *An Evening Walk*, Wordsworth said, 'There is not an image in it which I have not observed; and now, in my seventy-third year, I recollect the time and place where most of them were noticed. I will confine myself to one instance:

> Waving his hat, the shepherd, from the vale,
> Directs his winding dog the cliffs to scale,—
> The dog, loud barking, 'mid the glittering rocks,
> Hunts, where his master points, the intercepted flocks.

I was an eye-witness of this for the first time while crossing the Pass of Dunmail Raise.'

H WYTHBURN CHAPEL: 'Wytheburne's modest House of prayer'. The clergyman, the Reverend Joseph Sympson, was a close friend of the Wordsworths.

I* THE CHERRY TREE: formerly an inn at Wythburn, the scene of the boisterous merry-night in *The Waggoner*. The building once stood about half a mile north of Wythburn Chapel, on the same side of the old road.

J* ROCK OF NAMES: once 'an upright mural block of stone' which three Wordsworths, two Hutchinson sisters, and Coleridge carved their initials on, at a favourite meeting-spot between Keswick and Grasmere. It was blasted away when the new road was built, but a monument of its fragments stands above the highway a quarter of a mile north of the castellated water-pumping station. There is, however, no stopping on this busy highway.

K GREAT HOW: 'GREAT HOW is a single and conspicuous hill, which rises towards the foot of Thirlmere, on the western side of the beautiful dale of Legberthwaite, along the high road between Keswick and Ambleside.'—Wordsworth's note to his poem 'Rural Architecture', about schoolboys building a rock 'man', or pyramid, on top of the hill. 'These structures, as everyone knows, are common among our hills, being built by shepherds as conspicuous marks, occasionally by boys in sport' (I.F.).

L NATHDALE FELL: now called Naddle Fell (locally) or High Rigg.

M CASTLERIGG STONE CIRCLE: one of the 'circles of rude stones attributed to the Druids' (*Guide*). Wordsworth was much interested in ancient stone circles, as evidenced by his vision on Salisbury Plain near Stonehenge, recorded in *The Prelude*, xiii. 312–49. He did not write about Castlerigg as he did about the Swinside Stone Circle (in the River Duddon sonnets), but he alluded to it in his *Guide* when mentioning an island in Derwent Water and 'the spirits of the ancient Druids who officiated at the circle upon the opposite hill'.

N THRELKELD HALL: referred to in *The Waggoner*, iv, 43–56, as the place where Sir Lancelot Threlkeld hid the boy Henry

Lord Clifford, disguised as a shepherd, until he was restored to his estate in the fifteenth century. The story is the subject of 'Song at the Feast of Brougham Castle upon the Restoration of Lord Clifford, the Shepherd, to the Estates and Honours of his Ancestors.' The Wordsworths were distantly related to the Threlkelds.

o BLENCATHRA: of 'rugged feet' in *The Waggoner* (iv. 46) and 'rugged coves' in 'Song at the Feast of Brougham Castle' (line 90). In a note to the latter poem Wordsworth wrote, 'Blencathara . . . is the old and proper name of the mountain vulgarly called Saddle-back.'

P BOWSCALE TARN: mentioned in 'Song at the Feast of Brougham Castle'. Of Lord Clifford as a young man, the Minstrel sings that

> . . . both the undying fish that swim
> Through Bowscale-tarn did wait on him. . . .

> (lines 122–3)

Wordsworth added a note: 'It is imagined by the people of the Country that there are two immortal Fish, Inhabitants of this Tarn, which lies in the mountains not far from Threlkeld.'

Travel directions

Walking along Thirlmere is an anachronism—as much so as an eight-horse wagon, like Benjamin's, or its replacement, 'eight sorry carts'. You may now speed by in your choice of modern conveyance—car, Ribble bus, or tourist coach. It will be as little like Wordsworth's journeys to meet Coleridge as the present Manchester reservoir is like the old Wythburn Lake. But, if you are travelling to Keswick, pause to remember the comic and lamentable journey of Benjamin the Waggoner. If you travel by car, follow Benjamin's route by bearing right at the west end of Rydal Water, taking the old road up the hill. On this road you will pass Glow-worm Rock, the Wishing Gate (Chapter 2), and Dove Cottage (Chapter 8). After you pass Dove Cottage turn right to rejoin the main road up Dunmail Raise. Past Thirlmere, Benjamin followed the road to Keswick. The Muse, however, not given to servile attendance, struck out on her own, taking a right into St. John's Vale. There was no road into St. John's Vale from here in the Waggoner's day, but there was a footpath. In a travel guide which he did not publish, Wordsworth gave directions for this walk. The traveller, he wrote, could 'follow the stream that issues out of Wytheburn Lake [Thirlmere] till it enters St. John's Vale, which he may do if he be on foot, keeping to the side of it almost all the way. . . . Proceed a mile and a half down St. John's Vale, and then . . . cross Naddle Fell, by St. John's Chapel.' This will 'bring him into the road between Ambleside and Keswick, something better than two miles short of the latter place.' A traveller can still do this on foot by following the public footpath on the west side of the stream for two miles to Bridge House, before turning right to cross the fell. The path begins just north of where the Ambleside–Keswick road passes over St. John's Beck. There is now a road into St. John's Vale at Legburthwaite as well as a smaller paved road up to St. John's Chapel. The Muse, however, ascended the ridge by flying.

2

Bainriggs and White Moss

Guide to places

A*   GLOW-WORM ROCK : the subject of two poems by Wordsworth.

B*   MARY POINT AND SARA POINT, BAINRIGGS: the 'heath-clad' rocks which once overlooked Bainriggs Wood and the valley between Rydal Water and Grasmere. They are the subject of one of the 'Poems on the naming of Places'. Returning from their nine-month stay at Coleorton in 1807, the Wordsworths were chagrined to find that 'all the trees in Bainriggs are cut

* These places are discussed further in the second chapter of Part I: Poems and Places, p. 20.

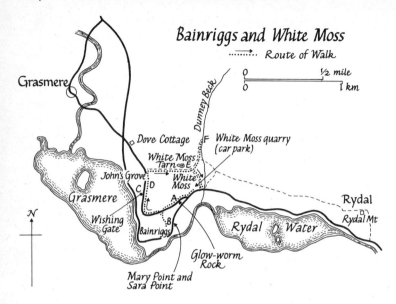

down'. The new growth obscures the view now, and the heather is gone.

c* THE WISHING GATE, OR SARA'S GATE: where, according to ancient tradition, wishes could be made which would come true. The tradition and the gate are the subject of two poems. Near here, Wordsworth met the subject of 'The Sailor's Mother', a woman who carried her dead son's legacy—'a little Singing-bird'—under her cloak. It begins,

> One morning (raw it was and wet—
> A foggy day in winter time)
> A Woman on the road I met,
> Not old, though something past her prime:
> Majestic in her person, tall and straight;
> And like a Roman matron's was her mien and gait.

Wordsworth said, 'I met this woman near the Wishing-Gate, on the high-road that then led from Grasmere to Ambleside. Her appearance was exactly as here described, and such was her account, nearly to the letter' (I.F.).

D* JOHN'S GROVE: named for the poet's brother and 'a favourite haunt with us all'. Once a fir grove with a single beech (according to Wordsworth's poem about it), it is now a beech grove with a few other species, but no firs.

E WHITE MOSS TARN: sometimes (wrongly) said to be where Wordsworth encountered the leech-gatherer of 'Resolution and Independence'. He encountered the leech-gatherer 'a few hundred yards' the other side of Dove Cottage, not gathering leeches but begging.

F WATERFALL: a possible site for 'The Waterfall and the Eglantine', the companion-poem to 'The Oak and the Broom'. Wordsworth located the scenes of both poems on the upper Rydal-Grasmere path, this one 'nearer to Grasmere'. Both are 'Poems of the Fancy' but inspired by particular scenes: 'The eglantine remained many years afterwards,' Wordsworth said, contrary to the apparent outcome of the poem, 'but is now gone' (I.F.). (See p. 122).

Walking directions

This short walk up the old Rydal-Grasmere road and back by the still older footpath on the mountain-side leaves the car park at White Moss quarry near the west end of Rydal Water. The Ribble bus stops here on request. The walk is about a mile and a half long. To begin at Grasmere, which adds another mile, see the directions below.

1. Begin at the car park in the old quarry between Rydal and Grasmere, next to where the old paved road heads up the hill.
2. Walk up the old road. About 75 yards up the road is a crag on the right, Glow-worm Rock [A].
3. Further along, when you reach the crest of the old road, just before it starts downhill, take the road to the left, leading to a small car park, and in less than ten yards turn right, up the road that quickly becomes a path. Continue straight on the path and pass through the gap in the stone fence, marked with a white dot.
4. The easiest way to Mary Point and Sara Point [B] is to turn left when just through the fence and follow a faint track that soon

leaves the fence and goes to a rocky promontory (but covered with grass where you go up) about 70 yards away, high above the lower road through Bainriggs. This is the top of one of the points. Its slightly lower twin is about 40 yards further.

5. Return to the road via the gap in the stone fence and continue down the old paved road to the left toward Grasmere.

6. When you come to a wooden gate in the stone fence to your left, you are at the site of the Wishing Gate [C].

7. Behind you, as you face the Wishing Gate and the lake, is John's Grove [D], accessible through iron gates at either end, if you wish to walk in it.

8. Continue on the road and at the junction turn right, uphill (marked 'No Through Road for Motorists'; going downhill would bring you to Dove Cottage). This road takes you up to the oldest of the three routes between Rydal and Grasmere; further on, it runs just behind Rydal Mount (not on this walk, but part of the walk on p. 245). On the level section of the road is White Moss Tarn [E], to the left.

9. Continue until you come to a stile on your left, just before a stream. To see a likely (though not certain) site that inspired a fanciful poem, cross the fence at the stile and follow the path up to the stone bridge (the Thirlmere–Manchester aqueduct). The waterfall [F] is just behind the aqueduct.

10. Return to the path by the stile and turn right, going back to White Moss Tarn. Take the rock track to your left down to the car park at the quarry.

Same walk from Grasmere. Walk to Dove Cottage and on up the hill, past the sign, 'No Through Road for Motorists'. Continue up, following the directions above from the second sentence of No. 8 to No. 10; then No. 1 to No. 7. When you reach the junction again, turn left, downhill, and return to Grasmere.

3

Greenhead Gill

Guide to places

A* RUINS: Michael's sheep-fold? Someone else's? A mining camp?
Michael's sheep-fold, whether here or elsewhere, was 'Beside
the brook . . . a straggling heap of unhewn stones!'

B BEN PLACE: home of the Dawsons. In *The Excursion* (vii.
695–890), when the Pastor is relating narratives of the dead in
the Churchyard, he tells of 'young Oswald', who is based on
George Dawson, 'the finest young man in the vale', according
to Dorothy. He was a handsome young man—'Pan or Apollo,
veiled in human form'—an excellent athlete and scholar, and a
natural leader who volunteered with nine other young men
from the area to serve in the military early in the Napoleonic
Wars. After his return, he died in 1807 in circumstances
recounted by the Pastor: he engaged in a strenuous fox-hunt in
the morning, then, in a weakened condition, bathed his father's
sheep in a cold stream, which brought on convulsions. 'The
premature death of this gallant young man', Wordsworth said,
'was much lamented, and, as an attendant at the funeral, I
myself witnessed the ceremony and the effect of it as described
in the Poem' (I.F.).

C SWAN HOTEL: known as the Swan Inn in Wordsworth's time.
Benjamin the Waggoner made it past the Swan without
pausing for a drink on his ill-fated journey (see Part I:
Chapter 1). Tradition has it that when Walter Scott visited
Wordsworth—a water-drinking bard—he would surrepti-
tiously repair to the Swan for stronger drink.

---

* This place is discussed further in the third chapter of Part I: Poems and
Places, p. 34.

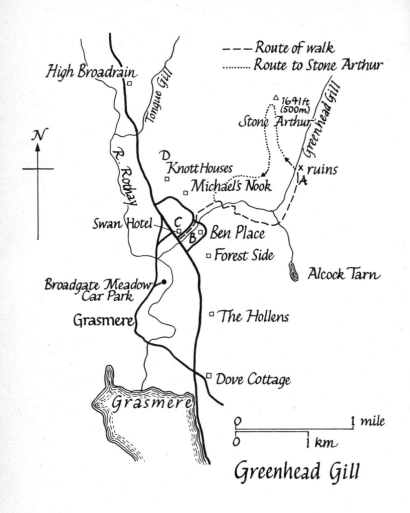

High Broadrain

Tongue Gill

——— Route of walk
·········· Route to Stone Arthur

△ 1641 ft
(500m)
Stone Arthur

Greenhead Gill

R. Rothay

D
Knott Houses

× ruins
A

Michael's Nook

N

Swan Hotel
C
B   Ben Place

Forest Side

Broadgate Meadow
Car Park

Alcock Tarn

Grasmere

The Hollens

Dove Cottage

Grasmere

0 |————————————————| 1 mile
0 |————————————| 1 km

Greenhead Gill

D   KNOTT HOUSES: site of the mansion built by the 'courteous Knight' of *The Excursion* (vii. 923–75). 'The Pillars of the Gateway in front of the mansion remained when we first took up our abode at Grasmere', Wordsworth said. 'Two or three cottages still remain, which are called Knott-houses from the name of the gentleman (I have called him a knight) concerning whom these traditions survive' (I.F.).

Walking directions

From the Swan Hotel to the stone ruin on Greenhead Gill is less than a mile, and the Broadgate Meadow car park in Grasmere is less than half a mile from the Swan Hotel. This walk becomes somewhat longer and much more strenuous if you climb from the ruins up to Stone Arthur. (See pp. 100 and 236). From Stone Arthur there are fine views of Helm Crag, Easedale, Silver How, Grasmere, Loughrigg, and far beyond.

1. Begin at the Swan Hotel (Grasmere), on the Ambleside–Keswick road, three-quarters of a mile north of Dove Cottage. Walk up the road that leaves the main road next to the Swan Hotel. At the second lane on the right (with a signpost), turn right. The 'boisterous brook' of Greenhead Gill will soon be on your right.
2. Go past a stone bridge, through a gate, across the wooden foot-bridge, and up the right side of the stream by the stone wall.
3. In less than 100 yards the path curves to the right (where the wall turns) and climbs steeply, taking you along the hillside above the Thirlmere–Manchester aqueduct (with iron gates on it).
4. Where the stone fence by the path turns right (above the aqueduct), do not follow the main path to the right, but follow the branch that leads straight ahead, up Greenhead Gill.
5. The stream bends, with the vale, sharply to the left. Continue until you come to the ruins [A] on the right side of the stream.
6. When you have explored Greenhead Gill, follow it back downstream the way you came or along the stream itself. Or, if the bracken is not too thick, you can get to Stone Arthur from the ruins by going straight up the fell opposite the ruins. At the

crest, Stone Arthur—a rock crag at the end of a long ridge higher than Stone Arthur itself—will be to your right. To descend from Stone Arthur, head towards Alcock Tarn, the high mountain lake to the left of Grasmere and across Greenhead Gill (which is out of sight), and the path will lead you down to Greenhead Gill near the Swan Hotel.

4

Helvellyn

Guide to places

A HIGH BROADRAIN: 'that lowly Parsonage | (For such in truth it is, and appertains | To a small Chapel in the vale beyond)', home of the family of the Reverend Joseph Simpson, vicar of Wythburn for over fifty years. 'The Clergyman and his family described at the beginning of this book [*The Excursion*, vii. 38–291] were, during many years, our principal associates in the Vale of Grasmere, unless I were to except our very nearest neighbours. . . . The whole that I have said of them is as faithful to the truth as words can make it' (I.F.).

B* GRISEDALE TARN: where Wordsworth last parted from his brother John and later wrote 'Elegiac Verses', part of which is inscribed on a stone below the outlet of the tarn.

C* HELVELLYN: the third highest peak in England, much frequented by Wordsworth and often mentioned in his poems. Lockhart, Sir Walter Scott's biographer, wrote, 'I have heard Mr Wordsworth say, that it would be difficult to express the feelings with which he, who so often had climbed Helvellyn alone, found himself standing on its summit with two such men as Scott and [Humphry] Davy.'

---

* These places are discussed further in the fourth chapter of Part I: Poems and Places, p. 52.

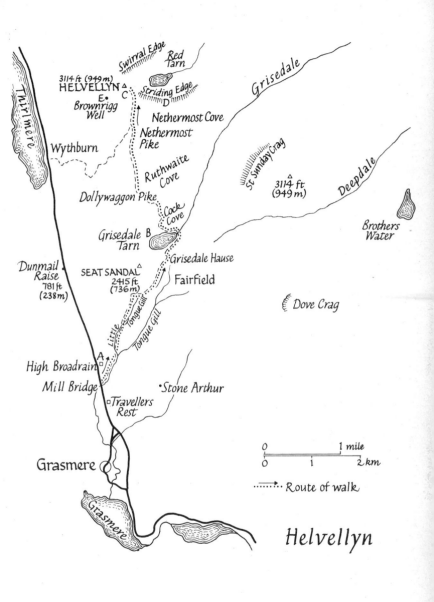

Thirlmere

Swirral Edge

Red Tarn

3114 ft (949 m)
HELVELLYN △
C
E•
Brownrigg Well

Striding Edge
D

Griesdale

Wythburn

Nethermost Cove

Nethermost Pike

Ruthwaite Cove

St Sunday Crag

3114 ft (949 m)

Deepdale

Dollywaggon Pike

Cock Cove

Brothers Water

Griesdale Tarn
B

Griesdale Hause

Dunmail Raise
781 ft (238 m)

SEAT SANDAL △
2415 ft (736 m)

Fairfield

Little Tongue Gill

Tongue Gill

Dove Crag

A
High Broadrain □

Mill Bridge

•Stone Arthur

□ Travellers Rest

0   1 mile
0   1   2 km

Grasmere

······▸ Route of walk

Grasmere

Helvellyn

D* STRIDING EDGE: where the angler fell and the dog stayed by his remains for three months—the subject of 'Fidelity'.

E* BROWNRIGG WELL: Wordsworth's 'fountain of the mists', near the top of Helvellyn.

Walking directions

If transportation can be arranged, you can avoid retracing your steps by using different routes for the ascent and descent. There are paths at Wythburn, the Swirls, and Thirlspot on the western side. Or, for more interesting views, approach Helvellyn from Patterdale or Glenridding. In 1805 Wordsworth and Scott went from Patterdale to the summit via Striding Edge, and down to Grasmere. To avoid Striding Edge, go from Patterdale to Grisedale Tarn, and then to the summit. Of this route Wordsworth wrote in his *Guide*, 'A sublime combination of mountain forms appears in front while ascending the bed of this valley, and the impression increases till the path leads almost immediately under the projecting masses of Helvellyn.' To begin and end at Grasmere, however, take the route described below, following the old packhorse trail to Grisedale Tarn. From Grasmere to the summit and back is twelve miles; from the beginning of the trail at Mill Bridge and back, ten miles.

1. Begin at Mill Bridge, on the Keswick–Ambleside road, 200 yards beyond the Traveller's Rest, one mile north of Grasmere. A signpost, 'Patterdale and Helvellyn', just north of Tongue Gill, points the way. The next farmhouse on the road to the north, with the stone farm buildings behind it, is High Broadrain [A].

2. Follow the path up Tongue Gill; when the stream branches, follow the left branch (Little Tongue Gill).

3. When you come to a grassy meadow where the trail is obscure, the stream will be to your right and a rock crag above you, to the left of the stream. (Ignore a tractor track which goes off to your left.) The path goes up to the left of the crag and across the top of it, then on to Grisedale Hause and Grisedale Tarn.

4. Cross the stream at the outlet of Grisedale Tarn and walk downstream 150 yards to the large stone topped by a black iron sign, 'The Brothers' Parting—Wordsworth' [B].

5. Return to the path which goes by the foot of Grisedale Tarn and continue on it. It leads up Dollywagon Pike, Nethermost Pike, and to the summit of Helvellyn [C].

6. From the summit, you can see Striding Edge [D] to the south and Red Tarn below it. A memorial to Gough with lines from Wordsworth and Scott, stands at the top of the path from Striding Edge. To reach Brownrigg Well [E], walk slightly south of west from the summit for 500 yards. (The shelter just below the summit has four arms, one of which points away from Red Tarn toward Pillar. Walk in that direction to reach Brownrigg Well.)

7. Retrace your steps to get back to Mill Bridge. (At about half a mile from the summit the path splits: the right branch goes to Wythburn, and the left branch goes back to Grisedale Tarn.)

5

Keswick

Guide to places

A* GRETA HALL: a two-family house, home of the Coleridges (Coleridge himself lived here from 1800 to 1803) and the Southeys (1803–43).

B* CROSTHWAITE CHURCH: parish church of Keswick, with Southey's grave and memorial, inscribed with verses by Wordsworth.

C* APPLETHWAITE: the site of property in the Wordsworth family for over 150 years. Part of it was given to Wordsworth so that he could live near Coleridge, and he later added to it by purchasing adjoining land.

* These places are discussed further in the fifth chapter of Part I: Poems and Places, p. 62.

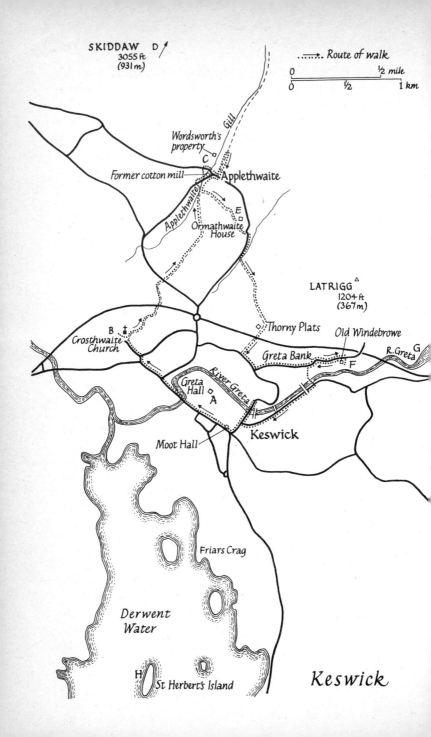

SKIDDAW D
3055 ft
(931 m)

······→· Route of walk

0   ½ mile
0   ½   1 km

Gill

Wordsworth's
property
C
Former cotton mill
Applethwaite

E
Ormathwaite
House

Applethwaite

LATRIGG
1204 ft
(367 m)

◊ Thorny Plats

Old Windebrowe

B
Crosthwaite
Church

Greta Bank

R. Greta   G

F

Greta
Hall

River Greta

A

Keswick

Moot Hall

Friars Crag

Derwent
Water

H
St Herbert's Island

Keswick

D SKIDDAW: the mountain standing in 'solitary majesty' to the north of Derwent Water. The four celebrated Greek mountains and the Castalian spring, sacred to the Muses, provoked this sonnet in celebration of an *English* mountain:

> Pelion and Ossa flourish side by side,
> Together in immortal books enrolled:
> His ancient dower Olympus hath not sold;
> And that inspiring Hill, which 'did divide
> Into two ample horns his forehead wide,'
> Shines with poetic radiance as of old;
> While not an English Mountain we behold
> By the celestial Muses glorified.
> Yet round our sea-girt shore they rise in crowds:
> What was the great Parnassus' self to Thee,
> Mount Skiddaw? In his natural sovereignty
> Our British Hill is nobler far; he shrouds
> His double front among Atlantic clouds,
> And pours forth streams more sweet than Castaly.

The comparison with Parnassus was probably suggested by Nicolson and Burn, *History and Antiquities of . . . Westmorland and Cumberland* (1777): 'the mountain *Skiddaw* . . . rises with two heads, like unto Parnassus'.

E ORMATHWAITE: owned by Raisley Calvert, Wordsworth's benefactor. From 1795 to 1804 it was the home of the Reverend Joseph Wilkinson, who drew the scenes in *Select Views in Cumberland, Westmorland, and Lancashire* (1810), for which Wordsworth wrote the text.

F* WINDY BROW (now Old Windebrowe): the Calvert farmhouse on Latrigg where William and Dorothy stayed in the spring of 1794.

G RIVER GRETA: subject of a sonnet in which it is likened to the Cocytus, a river in Hades. In a note to the poem Wordsworth explained that Greta is said to have derived from a dialect word, ' "*to greet*"; signifying to lament aloud, mostly with weeping, a conjecture rendered more probable from the stony and rocky channel. . . . The channel of the Greta, immediately above Keswick, has, for the purposes of building, been in a great measure cleared of the immense stones which, by their concussion in high floods, produced the loud and awful noises described in the sonnet.'

TO THE RIVER GRETA, NEAR KESWICK

Greta, what fearful listening! when huge stones
Rumble along thy bed, block after block:
Or, whirling with reiterated shock,
Combat, while darkness aggravates the groans:
But if thou (like Cocytus from the moans
Heard on his rueful margin) thence wert named
The Mourner, thy true nature was defamed,
And the habitual murmur that atones
For thy worst rage, forgotten. Oft as Spring
Decks, on thy sinuous banks, her thousand thrones,
Seats of glad instinct and love's carolling,
The concert, for the happy, then may vie
With liveliest peals of birth-day harmony:
To a grieved heart the notes are benisons.

H   St. Herbert's Island: scene of the 'desolate ruins of St. Herbert's Cell' and Wordsworth's poem, 'For the Spot where the Hermitage Stood on St. Herbert's Island, Derwent-Water' (*PW*, iv. 206).

Walking directions

In his *Guide* Wordsworth advises that 'The best views of Keswick Lake [Derwent Water] are from Crow Park; Frier's Crag; the Stable-field, close by; the Vicarage, and from various points in taking the circuit of the Lake. More distant views, and perhaps full as interesting, are from the side of Latrigg, from Ormathwaite, and Applethwaite. . . .' This walk of about five miles includes these 'more distant views'. Three warnings: the path to Applethwaite may be muddy; the path from Applethwaite to Old Windebrowe, through a public right of way, cuts across fields and is not always a visible footpath; and the Wordsworth rooms at Old Windebrowe usually require an appointment to be seen ('appointments welcome'; telephone Keswick 72112). Hence proper footwear, a determination to forge ahead, and an advance phone call may be in order. The Fitz Park Museum is a curious place, particularly strong in its Southey holdings. There is a large car park near the town centre and bus service by Ribble, Cumberland, National Travel, Mountain Goat, and Wright Brothers.

1. Begin at the Tourist Information Office at Moot Hall in the Market Place, and walk away from the building along Main Street. (If you walk out of the Tourist Information Office, you will need to make a U-turn.)
2. Just beyond the gates to Keswick School, at the road to the pencil factory, you can catch a glimpse of Greta Hall [A] in the school grounds at the top of the hill, though in the summer it is largely obscured by trees.
3. Cross the bridge, continue straight ahead on the road, past the Catholic Church. When the road curves, continue straight ahead on the lane to Crosthwaite Church [B] at the end, and enter the churchyard through the gate. Signs point to Southey's grave; the Southey Memorial is inside the church near the south-east corner.
4. Leave the churchyard by the gate you entered and take the footpath on your left, going away from the church. (An iron fence is on the right-hand side of the footpath; the path, not following a road, goes among trees, between playing fields, and soon up a small hill.)
5. At the right-angled bend in the path, go through the wooden gate and down the hill toward the road, under the old railway tracks, and across the road.
6. After crossing the road, walk over the foot-bridge, the stile, and across the field to the opposite gate. Do not go through this gate; go over the stile just to the right of it and follow the path across the road and straight on. The path curves left a bit at one point to go between two farm buildings.
7. Follow the farm track straight ahead until you come to the end of the fence on your left; then turn left. In about 30 yards, cross a stile and walk between fences but still in the same direction. (This path may be muddy.)
8. After crossing a stream near a farm building, you arrive at

Applethwaite [c]. Follow the road up, and when it forks, just before a bridge, take the smaller road, on the left. Cross another road: the property ahead of you, along the stream, was Wordsworth's property, called Gill, now named The Ghyll. Turn right and go over the stream to the paved road on your right. The house between the road and stream was formerly a cotton mill, built when Wordsworth owned the property above; he considered it a 'blemish'.

9. You will need to return to this spot to continue, but for a brief detour to get a better view of Wordsworth's property, continue ahead, up the hill 50 yards. Go through the gate opposite Rose Cottage and up the footpath 50 or 100 yards; from here you can overlook Applethwaite Gill and The Ghyll. Return to the junction of the two paved roads at the former cotton mill.

10. At the junction and former cotton mill, follow the road and the stream downhill, across the bridge, and return to where you crossed the stream upon arriving in Applethwaite.

11. Cross the stream. In 20 yards do *not* go through the wooden gate on your right (the way you came), but rather go over the stile to your left.

12. Go straight ahead for less than 100 yards, through a gate, then bear right, heading for the house and farm buildings, just visible over the hill. (This is a public right of way, though no footpath is visible.) Cross the bridge below the house and go through the iron gate.

13. Follow the hedge on your left to the gate and go through the gate at Ormathwaite House [E]. Continue in the same direction as before, to the road. Turn right.

14. In 300 yards, go through the wooden gate to your left. Follow the farm track through another gate, and then go over a stile to the left of the next gate. Now proceed with the wire fence on your right. Do not go through the next gate: bear left and keep the fence on your right.

15. Go past the house, turn right, and cross the bridge over the highway.

16. At the T-junction, turn left. At the signpost, 'Windebrowe and Brundeholm', turn left again and walk about half a mile to the

house where the Wordsworths stayed, Old Windebrowe [F], just beyond Windebrowe House.

17. From Old Windebrowe, start back down the road you came up, and in less than a quarter of a mile take the track to the left, which goes under a disused bridge and over the River Greta [G].

18. When you reach the road on the other side of the Greta, turn right, and follow the road along the river to the war memorial.

19. If you wish to visit the Fitz Park Museum, turn right at the war memorial; the museum is 200 yards down the road. Otherwise, turn left at the war memorial and the road will take you back to the town centre and Moot Hall.

6

Cockermouth and the North West

Guide to places

A* WORDSWORTH HOUSE: Wordsworth's birthplace and his home until he was nine years old, 1770–9. Owned then by the Lowthers for the use of their agent, it is now in the possession of the National Trust and is open to the public.

B* RIVER DERWENT: subject of a sonnet, 'To the River Derwent' (beginning, 'Among the mountains were we nursed, loved Stream!'), and of lines in *The Prelude*.

C* VIEW OF WATCH HILL: sometimes known as Hay Hill. Wordsworth's view from the terrace behind his house of the road going over the hill is described in *The Prelude*.

---

* These places are discussed further in the sixth chapter of Part I: Poems and Places, p. 70.

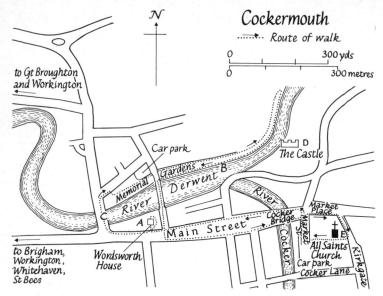

D* COCKERMOUTH CASTLE: 'The noble ruins of Cockermouth Castle', Wordsworth describes them in his *Guide*. They had been ruins long before his time, the Castle having been dismantled by Parliamentarian troops during the Civil War. Part of it, however, is still inhabited.

E CHURCHYARD, ALL SAINTS: the burial place of the poet's father, John Wordsworth. In a sonnet called 'In sight of the town of Cockermouth (Where the Author was born, and his Father's remains are laid)', Wordsworth contemplates the graves of his parents and the graves in the Grasmere churchyard of two of his children, Catharine and Thomas. It begins:

> A point of life between my Parents' dust,
> And yours, my buried Little-ones! am I;
> And to those graves looking habitually
> In kindred quiet I repose my trust.

The church, which has a Wordsworth Memorial Window (east side), was rebuilt in 1851, after a fire destroyed the earlier church. The Grammar School which Wordsworth attended was on Cocker Lane, at the site of the present Church Room, on the south side of the churchyard. Wordsworth did not much like this school; he learned more Latin in two weeks at Hawkshead, he said, than he had in two years at Cockermouth.

[*For the following places, see the map on p. xviii.*]

BRIGHAM: a village, two miles west of Cockermouth, associated with two Wordsworth sonnets, both in 'Itinerary Poems of 1833' (*PW* iv. 23–4). 'Nun's Well, Brigham' is about the well 'named from the Religious House which stood close by' (I.F.). 'To a Friend on the banks of the Derwent' was addressed to the poet's son, John, the 'Pastor and Patriot'; he was building a vicarage here but feared that it might be taken away from him. Wordsworth wrote that 'The situation is beautiful, commanding the windings of the Derwent both above and below the site of the House; the mountain Skiddaw terminating the view one way, at a distance of 6 miles—and the ruins of Cockermouth castle appearing nearly in the centre of the same view' (*Letters, c.* 15 January 1834). Wordsworth enjoyed the thought of his grand-daughter Jane 'culling flowers and gathering pebbles upon the banks of the same stream that furnished me with the like delights 60 years ago' (23 September 1833). Ten years later a railway was built a few yards from the house; now both have disappeared.

MORESBY: home of Wordsworth's son, John, who became the rector at St. Bridget's, Moresby, in 1829 and lived here until he built a vicarage at his new parish of Brigham in 1833. Wordsworth's visit to Moresby soon after the birth of his granddaughter led to the writing of several poems in 'Evening Voluntaries': 'On a High Part of the Coast of Cumberland', 'By the Sea-Side', and 'Composed by the Sea-Shore' (*PW*, iv. 2, 3, 13).

WHITEHAVEN: home of Wordsworth's uncle, Richard, who was a customs collector. The Wordsworths as children often visited here, and on the death of their father, this uncle became one of their legal guardians. 'With this coast', Wordsworth said, 'I have been familiar from my earliest childhood, and remember being struck for the first time by the town and port of Whitehaven, and the white waves breaking against its quays and piers, as the whole came into view from the top of the high ground down which the road (it has since been altered) then descended abruptly. My sister, when she first heard the voice of the sea from this point, and beheld the scene spread before her, burst into tears. Our family then lived at Cockermouth, and this fact was often mentioned among us as indicating the sensibility for which she was so remarkable' (I.F., note to 'On a High Part of the Coast of Cumberland', a poem 'composed on the road between Moresby and Whitehaven').

ST. BEES: subject of 'Stanzas Suggested in a Steamboat off Saint Bees' Heads, on the Coast of Cumberland' (*PW*, iv. 25). Wordsworth's note to the poem explains that 'St. Bees' Heads, anciently called the Cliff of Baruth, are a conspicuous sea-mark for all vessels sailing in the N.E. parts of the Irish Sea. In a bay, one side of which is formed by the southern headland, stands the village of St. Bees; a place distinguished, from very early times, for its religious and scholastic foundations.' The poem is an extended meditation on the monastery established by St. Bega in 650 A.D. and its succeeding monasteries, churches, and schools.

EGREMONT CASTLE: a 12th to 13th century ruin, the setting of 'The Horn of Egremont Castle'. The story of the horn that could be sounded only by the rightful owner of the castle was not originally associated with Egremont, though it was, Wordsworth said in a note to the poem, 'a Cumberland tradition' and was related of Hutton John, an 'ancient mansion' five miles west of Penrith.

Walking directions

This is a short walk of one mile in Cockermouth and up the Derwent. The Wordsworth House and Museum is open to the public, but the Castle is not. (Permission to see the dungeon, where Wordsworth played, may be obtained by writing in advance to The Custodian, The Castle, Cockermouth.) Cumberland and National Travel run bus services to Cockermouth.

1. Begin at the Information Centre off Market Street, by the River Cocker.
2. Walk down Market Street, turn left at Market Place, cross the Cocker Bridge, and continue down the Main Street, past the

Mayo Monument and Bridge Street, to the Wordsworth House [A] on your right.

3. On leaving the Wordsworth House, through the Museum and National Trust shop, turn right and walk to the car bridge. Cross the bridge over the Derwent [B] on the right-hand side; from it, looking upstream, you can see Watch Hill [C].

4. At the end of the bridge turn right, entering the Memorial Gardens through the green gate, and walk upstream. Go under the path leading to the footbridge and continue upstream, through the gate (opposite the brewery), around the bend in the river, and beyond the disused sluice. A fence blocks the way, but from this point you will have a view up the Derwent and an excellent view of the Castle [D] downstream.

5. Retrace your steps to the foot-bridge and cross it. Turn left at Main Street; continue over the Cocker Bridge, bear right at the intersection and pass Market Street (which leads to the car park). In less than 100 yards, go up the narrow road on the right (Kirkgate), and through the iron gates into the churchyard [E]. The grave of John Wordsworth, the poet's father, is to the left of the window facing you, which is the Wordsworth Memorial Window.

6. As you leave the church, follow the lane to your right, down the hill. It leads to the Town Hall and Information Centre.

7

Hawkshead, Esthwaite Vale, and the South

Guide to places

A*   MARKET HOUSE, the 'smart Assembly-room': built in 1790, after Wordsworth left school, on a spot where he and his school fellows bought treats at Nanny's Stone.

B*   ANN TYSON'S COTTAGE, Hawkshead: where Wordsworth lodged from 1779 to 1783, aged nine to twelve. The shorter upstairs window belongs to the room that was probably Wordsworth's; he carved his name on the window seat that was once here.

C*   SNARING WOODCOCKS: Wordsworth's nocturnal sport at Keen Ground High and Charity High, 'the two green hills . . . situated between Hawkshead and Hawkshead Moor' (T. W. Thompson, *Wordsworth's Hawkshead* (1970), p. 34). The eighteenth-century scientist and travel-writer Thomas Pennant explains how it was done: 'See on the plain part of these hills numbers of springes for woodcocks, laid between tufts of heath, with avenues of small stones on each side to direct these foolish birds into the snares, for they will not hop over the pebbles' (quoted by Mary Moorman, *William Wordsworth: The Early Years* (1957), p. 33n).

D*   HAWKSHEAD CHURCH: 'the grassy churchyard hangs | Upon a slope above the village school' (*The Prelude*, v. 392–3).

E*   HAWKSHEAD GRAMMAR SCHOOL: Wordsworth's school from 1779 to 1787, where he herded with 'A race of real children; not too wise, | Too learned, or too good; . . . | Mad at their sports

---

* These places are discussed further in the seventh chapter of Part I: Poems and Places, p. 77.

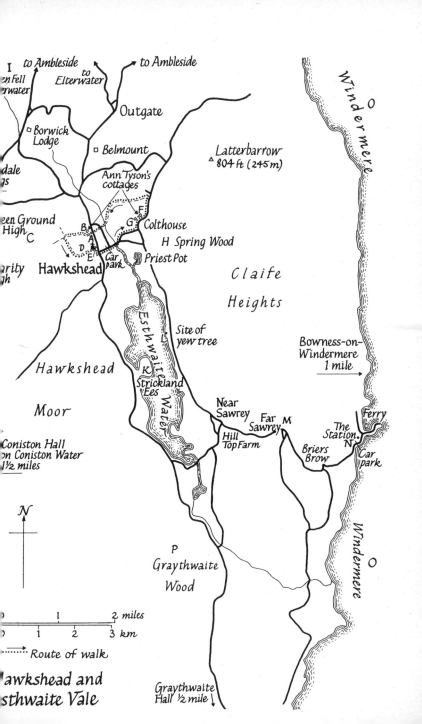

to Ambleside

to Ambleside

to Elterwater

I

en Fell
erwater

Outgate

Borwick Lodge

Belmount

Ann Tyson's cottages

Latterbarrow
△ 804 ft (245 m)

dale
gs

Green Ground
High

C

F

G

Colthouse

H Spring Wood

B

A

D

E

Car park

Priest Pot

Hawkshead

rity
gh

Claife
Heights

Esthwaite Water

Site of
yew tree

Hawkshead

Bowness-on-Windermere
1 mile →

Moor

K

Strickland
Ees

Near
Sawrey

Far
Sawrey

M

The
Station

Windermere

Coniston Hall
on Coniston Water
1½ miles

Hill
Top Farm

Briers
Brow

Ferry

N

Car
park

Windermere

N

P

Graythwaite
Wood

1   2 miles

1   2   3 km

········ Route of walk

awkshead and
sthwaite Vale

Graythwaite
Hall ½ mile ↓

like withered leaves in winds; . . . yielding not | In happiness to the happiest upon earth' (*The Prelude*, v. 406–25).

F* GREEN END COTTAGE: where Wordsworth and his brothers lodged with Ann Tyson from 1783 to 1787.

G* GREEN END HOUSE: home of Mary Rigge of Wordsworth's 'Ballad', and where Wordsworth stayed briefly.

H* SPRING WOOD: of interest because Wordsworth was *not* here (*The Prelude*, viii, 406ff.).

I WAITING FOR THE HORSES, Christmas, 1783: Mr. Gordon Wordsworth identified a place half a mile north of Borwick Lodge, north-west of Hawkshead, as the spot where Wordsworth anxiously awaited the horses to take him and his brothers to Cockermouth for the Christmas holidays, during which their father died (*The Prelude*, xii. 287–335).

J CONISTON HALL: the 'old hall' and 'neglected mansion-house' of the 1799 *Prelude*.

> There was a row of ancient trees, since fallen,
> That on the margin of a jutting land
> Stood near the lake of Coniston, and made,
> With its long boughs above the water stretched,
> A gloom through which a boat might sail along
> As in a cloister. An old hall was near,
> Grotesque and beautiful, its gavel-end
> And huge round chimneys to the top o'ergrown
> With fields of ivy.
>
> (ii. 140–8)

The entire passage describes a fishing trip which Wordsworth and his school friends took when he was thirteen years old, and a 'momentary trance' of the young poet. (See the Norton Critical Edition of *The Prelude*, edited by Jonathan Wordsworth, M. H. Abrams, and Stephen Gill (1979), pp. 17–18. A shorter, and less interesting, version appears in the 1850 *Prelude*, viii. 458–75.)

K* STRICKLAND EES, or Strickland-ears: the place where Wordsworth, aged nine, was roving when he saw a heap of garments left by a drowned schoolmaster.

L* SITE OF THE YEW TREE: scene of 'Lines Left upon a Seat in a Yew-tree', not quite a mile from the road junction at the Hawkshead car park. On the left, going from Hawkshead toward Sawrey, is a private road marked 'Broomriggs'. Ten yards farther, on the right, is a stile that leads to the probable site, now enclosed and without the yew tree.

M FAR SAWREY: where Wordsworth encountered the Discharged Soldier. The poet walked up the road at Briers Brow from the Windermere Ferry ('a long ascent') late at night, came around the bend in the road at Far Sawrey ('a sudden turning of the road'), and saw the 'uncouth shape' of the old soldier. There being no lights in the village (Far Sawrey, where 'all were gone to rest'), he took the soldier back to a cottage, probably at Brier, and left him with the labourer. There 'I return'd the blessing of the poor unhappy Man; | And so we parted' (*The Prelude*, iv. 339–468; 1805 *Prelude*, iv. 361–504).

N THE STATION: a once-famous vantage point for viewing Windermere. Wordsworth knew the spot as a boy:

> The site was long ago pointed out by Mr. West in his Guide, as the pride of the lakes, and now goes by the name of 'The Station.' So much used I to be delighted with the view from it, while a little boy, that some years before the first pleasure-house was built, I led thither from Hawkshead a youngster about my own age, an Irish boy, who was a servant to an itinerant conjurer. My motive was to witness the pleasure I expected the boy would receive from the prospect of the islands below and the intermingling water. I was not disappointed. . . .
>
> (I. F., note on 'Lines Left upon a Seat in a Yew-tree')

Later, in the 1790s, a two-storey building, Belle View, was erected to receive fashionable visitors. In 1829 a group of them entered their praise in the guest book: 'Lord and Lady Darlington, Lady Vane, Miss Taylor and Captain Stamp pronounce this Lake superior to Lac de Genève, Lago de Como, Lago Maggiore, L'Eau de Zurich, Loch Lomond, Loch Katerine, or the Lakes of Killarney.' Wordsworth paid a visit to The Station shortly thereafter, saw these lines, and responded with the following impromptu comic verses.

WRITTEN IN THE STRANGERS' BOOK AT 'THE STATION,' OPPOSITE BOWNESS

My Lord and Lady Darlington,
I would not speak in snarling tone;
Nor to you, good Lady Vane,
Would I give a moment's pain;
Nor Miss Taylor, Captain Stamp,
Would I your flights of *memory* cramp.
Yet, having spent a summer's day
On the green margin of Loch Tay,
And doubled (prospect ever bettering)
The mazy reaches of Loch Katerine,
And more than once been free at Luss,
Loch Lomond's beauties to discuss,
And wished, at least, to hear the blarney
Of the sly boatmen of Killarney,
And dipped my hand in dancing wave
Of Eau de Zurich, Lac Genève,
And bowed to many a major-domo
On stately terraces of Como,
And seen the Simplon's forehead hoary,
Reclined on Lago Maggiore,
At breathless eventide at rest
On the broad water's placid breast,—
I, not insensible, Heaven knows,
To all the charms this Station shows,
Must tell you, Captain, Lord and Ladies,
For honest worth one poet's trade is,
That your praise appears to me
Folly's own hyperbole.

The picturesque view is now largely obscured by trees, but Belle View is a picturesque ruin. It is 150 yards up an easy path marked by a sign, 'Public Footpath Claife Heights', off the road about one-third of a mile from the ferry.

o WINDERMERE: described by Wordsworth in *The Prelude*, iv. 1–17, as he saw it from the eastern ridge above the ferry when he returned from Cambridge for the summer vacation:

I overlooked the bed of Windermere,
Like a vast river, stretching in the sun.

In the same poem, ii. 54–69, Wordsworth describes the schoolboys' boat races from island to island, and in ii. 138–74, their bowling and 'strawberries and mellow cream' at the old White Lion at Bowness ("twas a splendid place' which 'to this hour . . . to me is dear | With all its foolish pomp'), and their evening boat ride across the lake, listening to a fellow student play the flute 'Alone upon the rock' of one of the islands. The round Curwen house on Belle Isle is fleetingly mentioned as 'the Hall . . . built | On the large island'. The Reverend R. P. Graves of Bowness told Wordsworth the story which the poet transformed into 'The Widow on Windermere Side' (*PW*, ii. 94).

P* GRAYTHWAITE WOODS: the woods extending from the south side of Esthwaite Water, associated with Wordsworth's poem 'Nutting'. He said that 'these verses arose out of the remembrance in the extensive woods that still stretch from the side of Esthwaite Lake towards Graythwaite, the seat of the ancient family of Sandys' (I.F.). Graythwaite Hall is two and a half miles south of Esthwaite Water.

[*For the following places, see the map on p. xviii.*]

CARTMEL PRIORY: burial place of the Reverend William Taylor, Headmaster of Hawkshead School when Wordsworth was a pupil. He died in 1786 at the age of thirty-two. When Wordsworth visited Rampside in 1794, he walked across the Leven Sands

> To seek the ground where, 'mid a throng of graves,
> An honoured teacher of my youth was laid,
> And on the stone were graven by his desire
> Lines from the churchyard elegy of Gray.

The gravestone still stands in the churchyard: as you enter through the gate from the village, the grave is fifteen yards ahead of you and fifteen yards to the right. Taylor had encouraged Wordsworth's study of poetry:

> He loved the Poets, and, if now alive,
> Would have loved me, as one not destitute
> Of promise, nor belying the kind hope

> That he had formed, when I, at his command,
> Began to spin, with toil, my earliest songs.
>
> (*The Prelude*, x. 533–6, 548–52)

FURNESS ABBEY: where the Hawkshead schoolboys rode on horseback, as described in *The Prelude*, ii. 94–137 (and recalled in x. 594–603),

>   . . . the antique walls
> Of that large abbey, where within the Vale
> Of Nightshade, to St. Mary's honour built,
> Stands yet a mouldering pile with fractured arch,
> Belfry and images, and living trees,
> A holy scene! . . .
> With whip and spur we through the chauntry flew
> In uncouth race, and left the cross-legged knight,
> And the stone-abbot, and that single wren
> Which one day sang so sweetly in the nave
> Of the old church. . . .

The abbey is also the subject of two sonnets, both called 'At Furness Abbey' (*PW*, iii. 62–3).

CHAPEL ISLAND AND LEVEN SANDS: After their visit to Furness Abbey, Wordsworth and his school friends rode their horses up the east coast of Furness, 'over the smooth sands | Of Leven's ample estuary' (x. 514–15);

> Lighted by gleams of moonlight from the sea
> We beat with thundering hoofs the level sand.
>
> (ii. 136–7)

Some years later, in August 1794, when Wordsworth returned across the sands from his visit to Cartmel Priory, he passed near Chapel Island, which then had the remains of a small Roman Catholic chapel:

> As I advanced, all that I saw or felt
> Was gentleness and peace. Upon a small
> And rocky island near, a fragment stood
> (Itself like a sea rock) the low remains
> (With shells encrusted, dark with briny weeds)
> Of a dilapidated structure, once
> A Romish chapel. . . .

Also on the sands were travellers being conducted by a guide:

> Not far from that still ruin all the plain
> Lay spotted with a variegated crowd
> Of vehicles and travellers, horse and foot,
> Wading beneath the conduct of their guide
> In loose procession through the shallow stream
> Of inland waters; the great sea meanwhile
> Heaved at safe distance, far retired. I paused,
> Longing for skill to paint a scene so bright
> And cheerful. . . .

Here Wordsworth heard the momentous news from France that Robespierre was dead (*Prelude*, x. 553–75).

PIEL CASTLE: the subject of 'Elegiac Stanzas Suggested by a Picture of Peele Castle, in a Storm, Painted by Sir George Beaumont', which begins,

> I was thy neighbour once, thou rugged Pile!
> Four summer weeks I dwelt in sight of thee:
> I saw thee every day; and all the while
> Thy Form was sleeping on a glassy sea.

Piel Island is south of Barrow-in-Furness, opposite the 'small Village' (1805 *Prelude*, x. 473) of Rampside, where Wordsworth spent a month in the summer of 1794. He stayed in his cousin's house; it was later rebuilt and is now the Clarkes Arms Hotel.

Walking directions

Wordsworth made a point of not walking to one place in this area, Spring Wood, because of its mysterious-seeming 'sparkling patch of diamond light', but in his nine years as a roving schoolboy at Hawkshead, he no doubt walked over much of the rest of the countryside. The nineteenth-century enclosures will keep us from some of his haunts, but there are still many inviting tracks and footpaths. This short walk of two miles passes through the village and hamlet. Ribble buses stop just opposite Wordsworth's Grammar School, which is open to the public.

1. Begin in Hawkshead, at the Town Hall (formerly the Market House [A]), just below the north side of Hawkshead Church.

The sign, 'Built by subscription MDCCXC', shows the portion built soon after Wordsworth was a pupil here. Go through the passageway to the right of the King's Arms Hotel, turn left and go through another passageway, and in 15 yards Ann Tyson's Cottage [B] is on the right.

2. Continue up the lane past the Cottage, and in 300 yards follow the road left, over the stream, and on to the path. Go through the iron swinging gate; you will see the church on your left and a fine view of Latterbarrow, the almost treeless end of the ridge (Claife Heights) above the church.

3. Follow the footpath to Hawkshead Church [D], well worth a visit. Just below the church (continuing down the path on the south side of the church), pass through the iron gate. Hawkshead Grammar School [E] is the first building on the left.

4. When you reach the road just beyond the Grammar School, turn right; then turn left in 70 yards at the road junction, and follow the road toward Sawrey.

5. Just over the bridge, turn left on the road to Colthouse.

6. As you enter the hamlet of Colthouse (half a mile from Hawkshead), a lane branches off to the left; Green End Cottage [F] is the house to the right of the lane, with a National Trust plaque over the door. Between the Colthouse road and Green End Cottage is the 'box'd, . . . paved' brook, and across the lane is Green End House [G].

7. On the Colthouse road again, with your back to Green End Cottage, you can see Spring Wood [H] on the nearest hill ahead of you. Continue up the Colthouse road, past Croft Foot. Follow the road left, up the hill.

8. Just over the crest of the hill, turn left, and, in 60–70 yards, left again, through the wooden gate in the stone wall, on to the public footpath.

9. Follow the hedgerow and bear right, to the end of the stone wall, where the wire fence begins. Go over the steps at the end of the stone wall.

10. Take the path to the left (it is indistinct), across the field to the far corner, bearing right.

11. Cross the wall at the steps (near the corner), and go down the

hill, through the wooden gate, across the lane, and over the stile.

12. Follow the path to the next stile, cross the stream, and walk across the field, bearing left, to the wooden gate, and continue in the same direction to the foot-bridge, over it, and on to the main road.

13. Cross the main road, but do not follow it; continue straight ahead, up the cobbled street into Hawkshead. You will enter the village centre from under an arch at the Red Lion Inn.

8

Grasmere

Guide to places

A* DOVE COTTAGE: the Wordsworths' home from late December 1799 to mid-1808, called by them Town End, the name of the hamlet. The Cottage, Museum, and Library are now owned by the Dove Cottage Trust.

B SYKESIDE: home of Agnes Fisher, described in *The Excursion* (vi. 675–777) as a woman 'surpassed by few | In power of mind and eloquent discourse' but ruled by 'avaricious thrift'. Her sister-in-law Molly Fisher was the Wordsworths' servant, 'a drollery belonging to the Cottage', according to Coleridge. The old Sykeside barn is now the Dove Cottage Trust Library, housing a valuable collection of manuscripts and books for the use of Wordsworth scholars.

C ASHBURNERS' COTTAGE: home of Thomas and Peggy Ashburner. The loss of their estate suggested Wordsworth's poem 'Repentance'. Peggy was a valued friend of Dorothy's

* These places are discussed further in the eighth chapter of Part I: Poems and Places, p. 89.

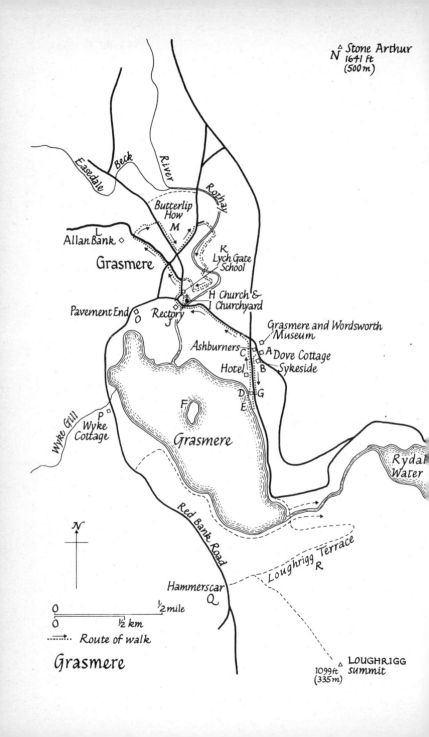

N △ Stone Arthur
1641 ft
(500 m)

Easedale Beck

River Rothay

Butterlip
How
M

Allan Bank ◇
L

Grasmere

K
Lych Gate
School

H Church &
I Churchyard

Pavement End

Rectory
J

Grasmere and Wordsworth
Museum

Ashburners
C

A Dove Cottage
B
Sykeside

Hotel

D G
E

Wyke Gill

F

P
Wyke
Cottage

Grasmere

Rydal
Water

Red Bank Road

Loughrigg Terrace
R

N

Hammerscar
Q

0   ½ mile
0   ½ km
······· Route of walk

Grasmere

1099 ft
(335 m)

△ LOUGHRIGG
summit

and Thomas supplied the Wordsworths with coal from Keswick.

D* BOATHOUSE: an 'impertinent structure' built by Mr Pearson, a 'quondam clown' whom Wordsworth knew at school at Hawkshead and who became the wealthy proprietor of a fashionable school. Wordsworth hated the boathouse: 'it is our utter detestation'. 'Every passenger will be disgusted with the sight of this Edifice, not merely as a tasteless thing in itself, but as utterly out of place. . . .' Its foundation gave way twice ('from the lake no doubt being intolerant of the intrusion'), and when it was rebuilt Wordsworth conceded that it had been improved: 'Much as one wishes it away it is not now so very unsightly' (I.F., note to *The Excursion*, vi).

E* EASTERN SHORE OF THE LAKE: the site of 'Point Rash-Judgement'—the 'uncouth' memorial name given to it by the poet ('A narrow girdle of rough stones and crags').

F* ISLAND: the subject of a Wordsworth inscription. The barn, now restored by the National Trust, was here in Wordsworth's time.

G THE SITE OF BROTHERS WOOD: where Wordsworth wrote 'The Brothers' about an incident that happened in Ennerdale. 'This poem was composed in a grove at the north-eastern end of Grasmere Lake, which grove was in great measure destroyed by turning the high-road along the side of the water' (I.F.).

H* GRASMERE CHURCH: the parish church, in Wordsworth's time, for Grasmere, Langdale, Rydal, Loughrigg, and Ambleside north of Stock Ghyll. The annual Rushbearing festival, still celebrated, is the subject of a Wordsworth sonnet, 'Rural Ceremony' (*PW*, iii. 400). A memorial to Wordsworth is near the step from the choir to the altar, on the left.

I* CHURCHYARD: site of Wordsworth's grave, the graves of other members of his family, and of Hartley Coleridge. George and Sarah Green, the Easedale couple who perished in the fells, are buried to the right of the path that goes from the back of the church to the lych gate, midway between the church and the gate. The yew trees in the churchyard were planted,

Wordsworth said, 'under my own eye, and principally if not entirely by my own hand. . . . May the trees be taken care of hereafter when we are all gone, and some of them perhaps at some far distant time rival in majesty the Yew of Lorton and those which I have described as growing in Borrowdale . . .' (I.F.).

J*   RECTORY: the Wordsworths' home from 1811 to 1813. He described it in 1800 as a 'gloomy house' ('To Joanna'); it stood in a bog, and the chimneys smoked. Two of his children died while the family lived here.

K*   OLD SCHOOLHOUSE: now a ginger-bread shop, formerly the tiny Lych Gate school which the poet's son attended and where, briefly, the poet taught.

L*   ALLAN BANK: the Wordsworths' home from 1808 to 1811. Wordsworth disapproved of the way the house 'stared' over the valley, but he was its first tenant and planted its grounds.

M   BUTTERLIP HOW, or Butharlyp Howe: a favourite walking spot for members of the Wordsworth household, mentioned often in Dorothy's journals. When Prince Leopold, later King of the Belgians, visited the Lake District, Wordsworth suggested that his host take him to this small hill: 'it commands a panorama view of this celebrated Vale'. The Wordsworths wanted to buy the land in 1810 to prevent it from falling into bad hands, but they did not have enough money.

N*   STONE ARTHUR: 'Stone William', or perhaps 'William's Rock', to Dorothy. Its towering prominence, quiet beauty, and loneliness (described in 'There is an Eminence') made it a fit emblem of her brother.

O   PAVEMENT END on Gold Rill side: home of John, a butcher, and Margaret Green, who lived here with 'seven lusty sons' when their daughter Margaret was born. The Pastor's account of the birth and death of this daughter in *The Excursion* (vii. 632–94) is, Wordsworth said, 'an exact picture of what fell under my own observation' (I.F.). The stream which runs by the house, Gold Rill Beck, is said to have been so named by Wordsworth himself because of the distinctive colour of the water after it had run through manure from the farm.

P   WYKE GILL: the scene of 'The Westmoreland Girl'. Sara
    Mackareth, upon whom the poem is based, was the daughter of
    the Parish Clerk and bell ringer at the Grasmere Church. The
    family lived at Wyke Cottage, near where the stream formerly
    flowed over the road. In the first part of the poem, a ten-year-
    old girl saves a lamb by jumping into the flooded stream; in the
    second, she, 'fulfilling her sire's office', rings his death-knell—
    'She in Grasmere's old church-steeple | Tolled this day the
    passing bell.' 'This little poem . . . I thought might interest you
    . . . as exhibiting what sort of characters our mountains breed.
    It is truth to the Letter', Wordsworth wrote to a friend.

Q* HAMMERSCAR ON THE RED BANK ROAD: where the schoolboy
    Wordsworth saw the vale, as described at the beginning of
    Home at Grasmere. De Quincey describes it as 'the very gorge
    of Hammerscar, from which the whole vale of Grasmere
    suddenly breaks upon the view in a style of almost theatrical
    surprise, with its lovely valley stretching in the distance, the
    lake lying immediately below, with its solemn bent-like island
    of five acres in size, seemingly floating on its surface . . .' (De
    Quincey, p. 122). Thomas West, the most important early
    travel writer of the Lakes, singled out this place in 1778 as the
    most 'advantageous station to view this romantic vale from'.
    The trees now unfortunately obscure the view.

R* LOUGHRIGG TERRACE: the path along the northern side of
    Loughrigg Fell, overlooking Grasmere vale, and the setting for
    the finale of *The Excursion* (ix. 569–759), where the 'little
    band | Gathered together on a green hill-side' to watch the
    sunset and listen to the Parson's prayer and meditation.

Walking directions

This is the heart of Wordsworth Country. A visit to Dove Cottage
and the Grasmere churchyard are the long-established rituals of
tourists, and they are seldom disappointed. This walk, less than two
miles, includes them as well as Wordsworth's two other houses,
Allan Bank and the Rectory (neither of them open to the public),
and other places associated with his poetry. Another walk, around
the lake (about three miles), will take you past Pavement End and

Wyke Cottage and under Hammerscar and Loughrigg Fell. For the walk described below, park at the Stock Lane car park or leave the Ribble bus near the Prince of Wales Hotel.

1. Begin at Dove Cottage [A], near the Ambleside–Keswick road, just opposite Stock Lane, which leads to Grasmere village from the south.

2. After visiting Dove Cottage and the Grasmere and Wordsworth Museum, cross the road in front of Dove Cottage and follow the sign 'Footpath to Main Road', which goes past Sykeside [B] on the left and the Ashburners' Cottage [C] on the right, both just across the road from Dove Cottage.

3. At the main road, go left 100 yards, past the Prince of Wales Hotel, to the boathouse [D] ('W.P.', for William Pearson, and '1843' above the door). Just beyond it, descend the stairs to the lake. This area has changed drastically since Wordsworth lived in Dove Cottage; the road was built since then and the level of the lake has dropped. To your left, the eastern shore [E] was once a favourite walking spot for Wordsworth. From here you can also see the island [F] to which he often rowed and, behind you and where the present road is, the site of Brothers Wood [G].

4. Turn back, on the same road, and walk past the Prince of Wales Hotel, left at Stock Lane, and into Grasmere village.

5. You will come to Grasmere church [H] on the right, with the Wordsworth graves in the churchyard [I]. Opposite the church is the Rectory [J].

6. Continue on the road past the ginger-bread shop, which was the old schoolhouse [K], bear left past the Wordsworth Hotel, and go straight past the Red Lion Hotel and telephone box, up the road ('No Through Road') and on to the private road (open to pedestrians). When you have gone up the hill a short way, you will see Allan Bank [L] to your left, about a quarter of a mile from the Red Lion. At the fork below the house, turn right, then right again in 20 yards, down the car track. At the fence, take the footpath to the right and go out by the iron gate.

7. Turn right on the road and return to Grasmere. At the junction, turn left, walk to the Broadgate Meadow car park sign (Butterlip How [M] is the hill to the left) and turn right. Cross the foot-

bridge over the River Rothay (signed 'Riverside Path'). As you cross the foot-bridge, Stone Arthur [N] is the highest rocky promontory to your left.

8. The footpath takes you behind the church to the road next to the Wordsworth Hotel; the elegant sign in front of it is Wordsworth's signature. As you leave the path, Dove Cottage is down the road to your left.

9

Easedale

Guide to places

A*   EMMA'S DELL: the spot described in 'It was an April morning'.

B*   GEORGE AND SARAH GREEN'S COTTAGE: home of a couple who perished in the fells. 'The House, in its appearance and situation', Wordsworth wrote in a letter, 'strikingly accords with the melancholy catastrophe; a brawling Brook close by, and huge stones and scattered rocks on every side'. The stone house has since been covered with rough-cast.

C*   EASEDALE TARN: 'one of the finest tarns in the country', according to Wordsworth's *Guide*.

D*   LANCRIGG: 'our favourite haunt', where Wordsworth wrote much of *The Prelude*.

Walking directions

This four and a quarter mile walk was popular enough in the late nineteenth and early twentieth centuries to require a tea hut at Easedale Tarn. Its remains are still to be seen, but moderns, like Wordsworth, apparently prefer Nature without a catering service.

* These places are discussed further in the ninth chapter of Part I: Poems and Places, p. 107.

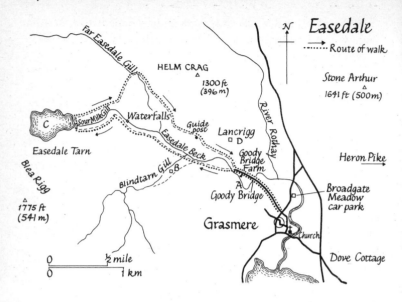

The circular walk returns by Far Easedale. The track *up* Far Easedale Gill goes ultimately to Borrowdale. Park in any of the Grasmere car parks (e.g., on the Easedale road or at Broadgate Meadow), or take the Ribble bus to the village green.

1. Begin in Grasmere at the village green. Walk up the road marked 'Easedale Tarn', which leaves the village opposite the bookseller's shop.

2. Over the crest of the hill, beyond Goody Bridge Farm, turn left and cross the signposted foot-bridge and a smaller slate foot-bridge.

3. After crossing the slate foot-bridge, walk down to the wooden gate to your left. If you look down the stream some 60 or 70 yards, you will catch a glimpse of Emma's Dell [A]. (The view is much better from just below the small waterfall; to get there you must go through or over the wooden gate and follow the path down the stream, but this is not a public footpath.)

4. Return to the slate foot-bridge and follow the path through an iron gate.

5. Beyond the second iron gate, the path crosses a stream,

Blindtarn Gill, and continues past a signpost pointing the way to Easedale Tarn. To the left, several hundred yards away, is the Greens' cottage [B].

6. As you come into full view of the tarn [C], a path branches off to the right opposite a large boulder and rubble (the remains of the tea hut). When you are ready to return, take this path to the right, and cross the stream, as it leaves the tarn, at the stepping stones.

7. Take the next path to the right, about 15 yards beyond the stepping stones. The path skirts to the left of the grassy slope and after about half a mile jogs left away from the stream. (The path is marked here, and elsewhere, by white circles painted on rocks.)

8. Descend on the path into the valley (Far Easedale), cross the wooden foot-bridge over Far Easedale Gill, and follow the path first along the stream and later along a stone fence as it goes down the valley toward Grasmere.

9. After passing a farm on your right and, a short time later, a signpost, follow the path through an iron gate, down the hill, and on to the narrow paved road.

10. Continue along the unfenced road. (About midway down it, Heron Pike is ahead of you, Stone Arthur—the rocky promontory—is to the left of it, and Helm Crag is closest, on your immediate left. The house to the left and above you, with round chimneys, is Lancrigg [D].)

11. When you pass through the iron gate you will be on the road back to Grasmere.

10

Rydal

Guide to places

A LOUGHRIGG FELL: subject of a sonnet 'suggested in front of
Rydal Mount, the rocky parapet being the summit of
Loughrigg Fell opposite. Not once only, but a hundred times,
have the feelings of this Sonnet been awakened by the same
objects seen from the same place' (I.F.).

> I watch, and long have watched, with calm regret
> Yon slowly-sinking star—immortal Sire
> (So might he seem) of all the glittering quire!
> Blue ether still surrounds him—yet—and yet;
> But now the horizon's rocky parapet
> Is reached, where, forfeiting his bright attire,
> He burns—transmuted to a dusky fire—
> Then pays submissively the appointed debt
> To the flying moments, and is seen no more.
> Angels and gods! We struggle with our fate,
> While health, power, glory, from their height decline,
> Depressed; and then extinguished: and our state,
> In this, how different, lost Star, from thine,
> That no to-morrow shall our beams restore!

B NAB COTTAGE: home of De Quincey's wife and, later, of
Hartley Coleridge. Hartley, Samuel Taylor Coleridge's son,
was a poet and author himself, a frequent visitor of the
Wordsworths throughout his life, and the subject of 'To H.C.,
Six Years Old'. He died at Nab Cottage in 1849.

C* ISLAND: the scene of Wordsworth's poems, 'Inscription
Written with a Slate Pencil' and 'The Wild Duck's Nest'.

---

* These places are discussed further in the tenth chapter of Part I: Poems and
Places, p. 114.

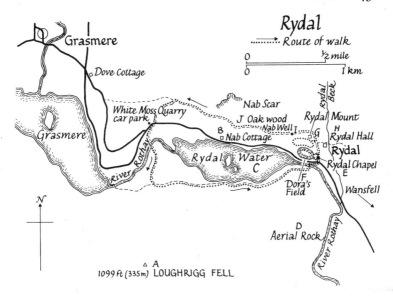

D   AERIAL ROCK: 'A projecting point of Loughrigg, nearly in front
of Rydal Mount. Thence looking at it, you are struck with the
boldness of its aspect; but walking under it, you admire the
beauty of its details' (I.F.). Aerial Rock is Wordsworth's name;
it was then called Holme-Scar, and is now Lanty Scar.

> Aerial Rock—whose solitary brow
> From this low threshold daily meets my sight;
> When I step forth to hail the morning light;
> Or quit the stars with a lingering farewell—how
> Shall Fancy pay to thee a grateful vow?
> How, with the Muse's aid, her love attest?
> —By planting on thy naked head the crest
> Of an imperial Castle, which the plough
> Of ruin shall not touch. Innocent scheme!
> That doth presume no more than to supply
> A grace the sinuous vale and roaring stream
> Want, through neglect of hoar Antiquity.
> Rise, then, ye votive Towers! and catch a gleam
> Of golden sunset, ere it fade and die.
>
> (*PW*, iii. 7)

E*   RYDAL CHAPEL: built by Lady (Ann Frederica) Fleming of Rydal Hall in 1824. The Wordsworths often attended services here, and the poet served as Chapel Warden in 1833. The Wordsworths sat in the front pew on the left as you face the pulpit; Dr Arnold of Fox How, the Headmaster of Rugby, and his family (including his son, Matthew Arnold) sat in the front pew on the right; and the Le Flemings sat above, in the gallery, with their private fireplace.

F*   DORA'S FIELD: purchased by Wordsworth in 1825 as a place to build his home if he could not continue at Rydal Mount, and later given to his daughter. In 1933 it was given by a member of the Wordsworth family to the National Trust. It still contains two poetic inscriptions by Wordsworth.

G*   RYDAL MOUNT: Wordsworth's home from 1813 until his death in 1850. His sister Dorothy died here in 1855 and his wife Mary in 1859. The house was purchased by Lady (Diana) Fleming in 1813 and then let to Wordsworth, and it remained in the Fleming family until 1969, when it was sold to a descendant of Wordsworth.

H   RYDAL HALL: home of Lady Fleming, who owned Rydal Mount. Years before Wordsworth became a tenant of Lady Fleming, he and Coleridge were reprimanded by an indignant servant for trespassing on the grounds of Rydal Hall. Wordsworth used a tradition about the building of the hall in his River Duddon sonnet XXVII (see p. 282). In that context he told Miss Fenwick, 'The present Hall was erected by Sir Michael le Fleming, and it may be hoped that at some future time there will be an edifice more worthy of so beautiful a position.' But the old hall remains. The waterfall of Rydal Beck was a well-known tourist attraction, referred to in *An Evening Walk*, lines 57–69. Of the poem, 'Lyre! though such power do in thy magic live', he said, 'The natural imagery of these verses was supplied by frequent, I might say intense, observation of the Rydal torrent' (I.F.).

I*   NAB WELL: a spring near Rydal Mount on the upper path from Rydal to Grasmere, and the subject of a long poem originally intended to be part of *The Recluse*.

j*   OAK WOOD: setting of the fanciful poem, 'The Oak and the Broom'.

Walking directions

For this walk, park your car or leave the Ribble bus at the White Moss quarry car park by the side of Rydal Water. Wordsworth's comment about the people who stop here need not necessarily be taken personally: the begging boys in his poem 'Beggars' were encountered, he said, 'near the quarry at the head of Rydal Lake, a place still a chosen resort of vagrants travelling with their families'. The walk from the quarry around Rydal Water and back is about three miles; if you wish to begin and end at Grasmere (see the directions below), it will be more than two miles longer and will cover part of the route described in 2: Bainriggs and White Moss. Wordsworth's house at Rydal Mount has been open to the public since 1970.

1. Begin at the car park in the old quarry between Rydal and Grasmere, near the head of Rydal Water.
2. Take the trail leading to the foot-bridge over the River Rothay.
3. Cross the foot-bridge and enter the wood, following the broad footpath through the wood and out by the gate in the stone wall.
4. Turn left outside the stone wall and walk to the far end of Rydal Water. Loughrigg Fell [A] is to your right at the outset; as you walk along the lake, Nab Scar is to your left across the lake. When you go beyond the stone wall, you will see the white building, Nab Cottage [B], across the lake, and the largest island [C].
5. Near the end of the lake, bear left, go through the iron gate in the stone fence (near the water) and enter Rydal Wood. Where the path forks in the wood, the right branch is more direct but the other joins it.
6. Cross the River Rothay at the foot-bridge.
7. Turn right at the main road, go 100 yards, and turn left, up the road marked Rydal Mount. A short way up the road, turn left to visit Rydal Church [E]. As you leave through the church door, walk straight ahead through the iron gate into Dora's Field.
8. On entering Dora's Field [F], follow the path uphill and along the stone wall. The inscription 'In these fair vales' (quoted,

p. 119), is in the far, upper corner, beyond the gate, embedded in a large stone protruding from the stone wall. Continue down to the lower path and follow it until you come to Wordsworth's winding stone steps to the left. The inscription about 'the living Rock' (p. 119) is carved into a stone on your left, some 40 steps up.

9. Return to the gate, and walk to the left of the chapel. Continue up the road and turn in to Rydal Mount [G], which is to your left. (Between the church and Rydal Mount, to the right, is a road and public footpath to Ambleside. It passes immediately behind Rydal Hall [H] and over Rydal Beck.)

10. As you leave Rydal Mount, turn left up the paved road, then left again, on to the footpath to Grasmere that goes behind Rydal Mount.

11. Thirty yards beyond the wooden gate at the far edge of the Rydal Mount property is a spring, Nab Well [I], next to the path. Continue on the path. After passing through three more wooden gates, you will find above and to your right an oak wood [J] and many large boulders from Nab Scar.

12. When you come to a house on the right, take the path down to the left, along the stone wall. Descend by the stone wall to the main road, turn right, and you will soon be back at the quarry car park.

Same walk from Grasmere. Walk down the east side of the lake (Grasmere), past the Prince of Wales Hotel, following the main road until it makes a sharp bend to the left. Take the footpath here to the foot of the lake, go over the foot-bridge, and up the steps. Take the path to your left. Soon you will come to a stone fence; keep it to your left and you will pass the gate mentioned in No. 3 above. Follow the directions (except 'Turn left') from No. 4 on, following the same path to the end of Rydal Water. Continue as above until No. 12. Do not descend at this point, but follow the track you have been on; it will take you back to Grasmere.

11–14

Over Kirkstone Pass

Guide to places

A*   KIRKSTONE PASS: the route from Ambleside to Patterdale, often taken by the Wordsworths, and the subject of a poem.

B   BROTHERS WATER: the lake where Wordsworth, on his way back to Grasmere in 1802, stopped and composed 'Written in March, while resting on the bridge at the foot of Brother's Water' ('The Cock is crowing . . .'). The occasion is recorded in Dorothy's journal, 16 April 1802. The lake is also mentioned in the 1805 *Prelude* (viii. 231–2): 'Brothers Water (named | From those two brothers that were drowned therein)'. In her journal for 9 November 1805 Dorothy says, 'It is remarkable that two pairs of brothers should have been drowned in that lake. There is a tradition, at least, that it took its name from two who were drowned there many years ago, and it is a fact that two others did meet that melancholy fate about twenty years since.'

C*   PATTERDALE HOTEL: an old coaching inn where Wordsworth and Sir Walter Scott stayed before their ascent of Helvellyn. It is referred to in Clarke's *Survey of the Lakes* (1787) as 'the little alehouse called Nell-House'. This is probably where Wordsworth was staying when he stole the rowing boat [G].

D*   BROAD HOW: Wordsworth's property from 1806 to 1834. He originally planned to build a house here or to add two rooms to the old, existing farmhouse, dated 1670 and now called Wordsworth's Cottage. The present house called Broad How was built shortly after Wordsworth sold the property.

* These places are discussed further in the eleventh chapter of Part I: Poems and Places, p. 127.

Ullswater and Martindale

0 _____ 1 mile
0 _____ 1 km

to Matterdale
and Keswick

to Penrith

Gowbarrow Fell
1579 ft
(481m)

GOWBARROW PARK

Hallsteads

Lyulph's
Tower

Aira Force

Aira Force
Valley

K   L

Car park

Sandwick Bay   N

Hallin Fell

Sandwick

Bridgend   Hallinbank   Howt

U l l s w a t e r

Aira Point

End of Gowbarrow
Parks on Clarke's
map, 1789

Scalehow Force

Glencoyne
Beck

Silver
Point

Scalehow Beck

Old quarry

Wintercrag   O   Old Church
St Martin

Glencoyne
Wood

F

Black
Crag

Site of
daffodils

Stybarrow
Crag   G   Devil's Chimney

J

G

Low Moss
sheepfold

Boardale Beck

Purse
Point   H   Blowick

Glen-
ridding

M A R T I N D A L E

Pier

Place Fell
2156 ft
(657m)

Round How

P

Dale Head

Side Farm

Rowley Gutter

Wordsworth
Cottage

1641 ft
(500m)

D

C   Goldrill
Br.

E   Chapel in the Hause
BOARDALE HAUSE

Patterdale Hotel

Broad How

(For legend see
facing page)

Sheepfold

to Brothers Water B 1 mile
and Kirkstone Pass A 4 miles

Q
Kidsty Pike | 3m

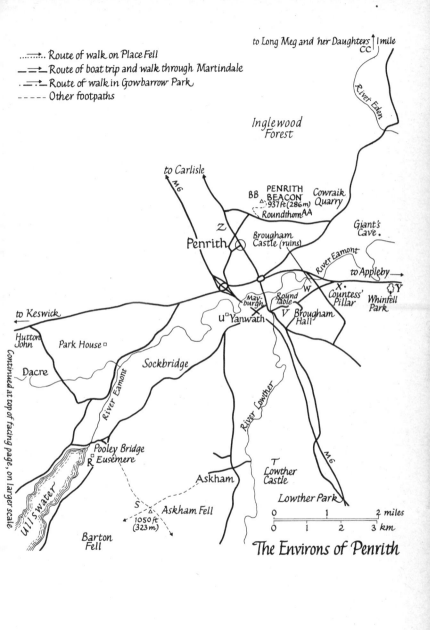

to Long Meg and *her Daughters* ↑ 1 mile
CC

..........➤.. Route of walk on *Place Fell*
━ ═ ⤴ Route of boat trip and walk through *Martindale*
.━.═.⤴ Route of walk in *Gowbarrow Park*
─ ─ ─ ─ Other footpaths

Inglewood
Forest

River Eden

to Carlisle

M6

BB PENRITH
△ BEACON
937 ft (286 m)
Roundthorn AA

Cowraik
Quarry

Giant's
Cave.

Z
Penrith

Brougham
Castle (ruins)

River Eamont

to Appleby →

W
May-
burgh *Round*
Table

X.
Countess'
Pillar

Y
Whinfell
Park

to Keswick ←

U Yanwath

V Brougham
Hall

Hutton
John

Park House □

River Eamont

Dacre

Sockbridge

River Lowther

Continued at top of facing page, on larger scale

Pooley Bridge
R □ Eusemere

Askham

T
Lowther
Castle

M6

S
△
1050 ft
(323 m)

Askham Fell

Lowther Park

Ullswater

Barton
Fell

0   1   2 miles
0   1   2   3 km

The Environs of Penrith

E*† CHAPEL IN THE HAUSE: an isolated, ruined chapel where an old man took refuge during a storm in the summer of 1805. The incident is the basis for an important episode in *The Excursion*—the death of the Solitary's ancient friend. Wordsworth's description of it in his *Guide* is quoted on p. 140.

F   LAKESIDE PATH: 'From Blowick a narrow track conducts along the craggy side of Place-fell, richly adorned with juniper, and sprinkled over with birches, to the village of Sandwyke . . .' (*Guide*).

G* PURSE POINT, DEVIL'S CHIMNEY, OR STYBARROW CRAG: the most likely spots from where Wordsworth as a schoolboy stole a boat, rowed out into Ullswater, and was driven back by the appearance of a huge cliff, which must have been either Place Fell, looming over the rocks and trees along the shore, or Black Crag. (Black Crag over Stybarrow Crag was suggested by Ernest de Selincourt; Place Fell over Purse Point or Devil's Chimney, by Mary R. Wedd.) The episode is one of the most famous passages of *The Prelude* (i. 357–400).

H   BLOWICK: a farm, one of Dorothy's and William's favourite spots for viewing Ullswater. 'No persons but such as come to Patterdale, merely to pass through it, should fail to walk as far as Blowick. . . . The axe has here indiscriminately levelled a rich wood of birches and oaks, that divided this favoured spot into a hundred pictures. It has yet its land-locked bays, and rocky promontories; but those beautiful woods are gone, which *perfected* its seclusion; and scenes, that might formerly have been compared to an inexhaustible volume, are now spread before the eye in a single sheet,—magnificent indeed, but seemingly perused in a moment!' (*Guide*). It is once again partly wooded.

I* SIDE FARM: formerly called Side, home of Wordsworth's close friends, Mr and Mrs Charles Luff. The Wordsworths often stayed here when they visited Patterdale. Dorothy described this house in a letter of 3 August 1808, after the Luffs had bought another estate (Holme Ground in Tilberthwaite) and thought of moving there:

   † These places are discussed further in the twelfth chapter, p. 136.

The Luffs' place is a paradise, but Mrs. L wants to be doing and is all agog to go to Holm Ground, for which desirable change a few hundred pounds are wanting. There is no one convenience, nay, luxury wanting at Patterdale, we cannot help wondering how so many things have been collected together—glasses, glass jugs all in style, Mahogany tables, dumb waiter and all kitchen conveniences complete. The garden and outside of the house called for unmingled approbation, for that is all done by attention and labour. The vegetables are the best in the country, the shrubs thriving, the walks neat and the house almost covered with trailing plants. I said to her what a delightful place—'a little pottering spot!' was her reply.

The yew tree in front of the house is probably the one referred to in Dorothy's journal of 8 November 1805: 'Mrs Luff's large white Dog lay in the moonshine upon the round knoll under the old Yew Tree—a beautiful and romantic image—the dark Tree with its dark shadow, and the elegant Creature as fair as a Spirit.' De Selincourt noted that Wordsworth used this image for *The White Doe of Rylstone* (*PW*, iii. 554).

J†‡ SHORE OF ULLSWATER, BETWEEN STYBARROW CRAG AND GLENCOYNE BECK: site of the 'never-ending line' of daffodils, about which Wordsworth wrote the famous poem, 'I wandered lonely as a cloud'.

K‡ AIRA FORCE VALLEY: the subject of Wordsworth's short poem, 'Airey-Force Valley'.

L† LYULPH'S TOWER: 'A pleasure-house built by the late Duke of Norfolk upon the banks of Ullswater', according to Wordsworth in his footnote to 'The Somnambulist', which was inspired by this building and the surrounding area. John Britton and E. W. Brayley (*The Beauties of England and Wales* [1802], iii. 162) wrote in Wordsworth's time that the Tower was built 'about twenty years ago, and called *Lyulph's Tower*, from a tradition that a chieftain, named Lyulph, was the owner of these possessions about the time of the Conquest. This is merely intended as an occasional residence for his Grace, who generally resides here a few weeks in the summer season,

‡ These places are discussed further in the thirteenth chapter, p. 141.

surrounded by a small band of chosen friends, and living in all the pristine magnificence of British hospitality.'

M   SITE OF THE JOYFUL TREE: a tree in *The Excursion*, vi. 831–54. The Pastor tells of Ellen, who on May Day danced around 'The Joyful Tree', a 'wide-spread elm', bearing her 'secret burthen' of an unborn child. The story of Ellen (lines 787–1052) actually took place in Hawkshead, though in the poem it apparently takes place in Grasmere, the setting of the Pastor's narration. But the tree Wordsworth used for the story came from Ullswater (it is located on a map by James Clarke, 1787).

N†   SANDWICK BAY: where Wordsworth, Dorothy, and Charles Luff left their rowing boat to begin the walk through Martindale recounted in Wordsworth's *Guide* (see Part I: Chapter 12).

O†   OLD CHURCH OF ST. MARTIN: 'the chapel, with its "bare ring of mossy wall", and single yew-tree', near the 'one-arched bridge' (*Guide*).

P†   DALE HEAD: farmhouse where Wordsworth was entertained, and the gathering place for sportsmen at the annual chase of red deer.

Q   KIDSTY PIKE: the mountain referred to in 'The Brothers', lines 139–45.

> On that tall pike
> (It is the loneliest place of all these hills)
> There were two springs which bubbled side by side,
> As if they had been made that they might be
> Companions for each other: the huge crag
> Was rent with lightning—one hath disappeared;
> The other, left behind, is flowing still.

'The impressive circumstance here described, actually took place some years ago in this country, upon an eminence called Kidstow Pike, one of the highest of the mountains that surround Hawes-water. The summit of the Pike was stricken by lightning; and every trace of one of the fountains disappeared, while the other continued to flow as before' (W.W., note).

R   EUSEMERE: a house near Pooley Bridge built by Thomas Clarkson, the great abolitionist and friend of Wordsworth, who often visited here until Clarkson moved in 1804. The sonnet, 'Clarkson! it was an obstinate hill to climb . . .', celebrates the passage of the bill abolishing the slave trade in 1807.

S   BARTON FELL MOOR: the scene at the beginning of 'Resolution and Independence'—

> I was a Traveller then upon the moor;
> I saw the hare that raced about with joy.

> (lines 15–16)

Wordsworth said, 'I was in the state of feeling described in the beginning of the poem, while crossing over Barton Fell from Mr Clarkson's, at the foot of Ullswater [Eusemere], towards Askam. The image of the hare I then observed on the ridge of the Fell' (I.F.). The leech-gatherer whom the poet meets was encountered not on Barton Fell but in Grasmere (see p. 32).

T   LOWTHER CASTLE: home of Lord Lonsdale, Wordsworth's noble friend who arranged for his appointment as Distributor of Stamps. Of Lowther Castle Wordsworth wrote,

> Lowther! in thy majestic Pile are seen
> Cathedral pomp and grace, in apt accord
> With the baronial castle's sterner mien. . . .

'Hourly the democratic torrent swells', Wordsworth observed gloomily in the sonnet, but it was a fire rather than a democratic torrent that caused the ruin of the castle in 1957. Only the shell remains.

> Fall if ye must, ye Towers and Pinnacles,
> With what ye symbolise; authentic Story
> Will say, Ye disappeared with England's Glory!

Wordsworth's father was the agent for Lord Lonsdale's father, a much-hated man known as 'the bad earl'. When John Wordsworth died, the earl refused to pay the money he owed the Wordsworths, thus keeping an inheritance from the children. The debt was later paid by the new Lord Lonsdale, and Wordsworth became a loyal political supporter of the family's interests.

U YANWATH: home of one of the few spades honoured in verse—

> Spade! with which Wilkinson hath tilled his lands,
> And shaped these pleasant walks by Emont's side. . . .

The spade belonged to Thomas Wilkinson, Quaker, poet, and gardener. He built his house, The Grotto, here on the Eamont. Wordsworth described him as the 'Arbiter Elegantiarum, or Master of the grounds at Lowther'.

V BROUGHAM HALL: known as Birdnest, after its earlier owners, the Birds. Wordsworth's cousin, Captain John Wordsworth, lived here before Henry Brougham (who became Lord Chancellor) inherited it in 1810. Wordsworth supported Lord Lonsdale's interests against Brougham in the bitterly fought Westmorland election of 1818. Brougham's origins (Scottish), the pronunciation of his name ('broom'), and his campaign colour (blue, in contrast to Lord Lonsdale's yellow) figure in Wordsworth's humorous polemical poem, 'The Scottish Broom' (*PW*, iv. 377), not published during his lifetime.

W§ BROUGHAM CASTLE: a ruined twelfth-century castle and the subject of lines in *The Prelude*. It is also the setting of 'Song at the Feast of Brougham Castle', in which a minstrel celebrates the restoration of Lord Clifford's estates in the fifteenth century.

X§ COUNTESS' PILLAR: the subject of Wordsworth's Sonnet XXIV in *Yarrow Revisited*. The pillar, which stands two miles east of Penrith, was erected in 1656 by the Countess of Pembroke, in memory of her mother, the Countess of Cumberland, who lived in Brougham Castle.

Y§ SITE OF HART'S-HORN TREE: subject of Wordsworth's Sonnet XXII in *Yarrow Revisited*, 'Hart's-horn Tree, near Penrith'. The Hart's-horn Tree was one and three-quarter miles beyond the Countess' Pillar, but it was gone when Wordsworth wrote his sonnet about it.

§ These places are discussed further in the fourteenth chapter, p. 147.

z§ PENRITH: 'where I used to pass my summer holidays under the roof of my maternal Grandfather', William Cookson (I.F., note to 'Nunnery'). The Cookson's draper shop in the Market Square still stands as a draper's shop (Arnison's), but it has been rebuilt since Wordsworth's time. The Cookson family, and often the Wordsworth children, lived upstairs. Just below the Market Square, in King Street, is the Robin Hood Inn, where Wordsworth stayed while caring for his dying friend, Raisley Calvert, in December and January 1794–5.

AA§ ROUNDTHORN: probably the eminence in the sonnet, 'Suggested by a view from an Eminence in Inglewood Forest' (*PW*, iii. 276).

BB§ PENRITH BEACON: the large hill by Penrith, unwooded in Wordsworth's time, with a square, stone signal-tower on the summit. Wordsworth's memorable 'spot of time' in *The Prelude*, xii. 209–86, occurred on the Beacon, when the lost, five-year-old boy came upon the place where a murderer had been hanged, saw the gibbet, and then saw a girl carrying water and struggling against the wind at a small tarn. According to Mr Gordon Wordsworth, the mouldering gibbet was at Cowdrake Quarry (or Cowraik Quarry, as it is called on the 1860 Ordnance Survey maps).

CC§ LONG MEG AND HER DAUGHTERS: standing stones north-east of Penrith, and the subject of a sonnet. 'The daughters of Long Meg, placed in a perfect circle eighty yards in diameter, are seventy-two in number above ground; a little way out of the circle stands Long Meg herself, a single stone, eighteen feet high' (W.W., note to the sonnet).

Travel directions

PLACE FELL
This walk is about seven miles, beginning with a 1600-foot ascent of Place Fell, with fine, panoramic views from the top, then going downhill to the beautiful lakeside walk. If you want to walk to Blowick to heed Wordsworth's advice—'No persons . . . should fail to walk as far as Blowick'—without going up Place Fell, follow the path past Side Farm (instead of going up to Boardale Hause) and

walk about three-quarters of a mile. Park in Patterdale or in one of the two large car parks in Glenridding, one mile to the north. Ribble and Mountain Goat run bus services over Kirkstone Pass to Glenridding.

1. Begin at the Patterdale Hotel [C]. Walk away from the lake along the road for 250 yards, turn left at the first road beyond the White Lion, and cross Goldrill Bridge. Beyond the bridge, you will pass Broad How [D] and the old farmhouse called Wordsworth's Cottage.

2. From this cottage, follow the signs to Boardale Hause: first bear left, then right, through the gate, and go uphill to the footpath on the fellside. Take the path to the right which follows the wall and, in about 100 yards, crosses Rooking Gill. Follow this rocky path uphill to the pass, Boardale Hause.

3. Enter the Hause with the sheep-fold to your right. Bear left around the rocky knoll. You will soon find the ruins of the Chapel in the Hause [E] (similar to the sheep-fold, but smaller). Follow the path up Place Fell, which is ahead of you as you stand by the chapel ruins with your back to the sheep-fold. (At Boardale Hause, the paths go in many directions. You will not go wrong if you remember that, as you cross Boardale Hause from Patterdale, Place Fell is to your left.)

4. Continue on the path toward Place Fell. From the summit, look behind you, toward Kirkstone Pass, for a good view of Brothers Water [B].

5. Proceed to the tall cairn (an Ordnance Survey triangulation column) and descend by a path which goes to the left of the small tarn. Where the path branches at the far end of the tarn, take the well-worn left branch.

6. One mile from the summit you will arrive at the sheep-fold at Low Moss. Several paths cross here: take the path to the left about 80 yards beyond the sheep-fold, near the foot of the opposite hill. Follow this path above Scalehow Beck, past the ruin, and down the gully past Scalehow Force.

7. Below Scalehow Force this path joins the lakeside path [F] from Sandwick to Patterdale. Turn left, cross Scalehow Beck and continue toward Patterdale.

8. In one and a half miles, the rocky point jutting into the lake is

Silver Point. The next, smaller one, half a mile further along, is Devil's Chimney [G]. Soon you will pass above the farm buildings of Blowick [H].

9. At Side Farm [I], turn right between the farm buildings and walk to the Patterdale road. The Patterdale Hotel is to your left.

MARTINDALE

This walk begins with a 30-minute boat ride from Glenridding to Howtown. (Call Kendal 21626 for times of departure.) The walk itself, from Howtown to Glenridding, is about eight miles. Ribble or Mountain Goat bus services go to Glenridding. If you are driving, park at the Glenridding Pier or, if full, at the National Park car park, a short distance to the north. The Wordsworths' description of this walk is printed in Part I: Chapter 12. This follows their route very closely, but not exactly. The price we pay for not having a rowing boat and a servant to row it back is that we must land beyond Sandwick Bay, at Howtown, and where we keep to the public footpaths in Sandwick and Martindale, we deviate from Wordsworth's route by not more than a few dozen yards.

1. Begin at the Glenridding Pier and car park. Take the boat to Howtown. On the boat ride, Place Fell is on the right, and Stybarrow Crag [G] and the site of Wordsworth's daffodils [J] are on the left. Aira Point and Lyulph's Tower [L] are further down the lake on the left.

2. Disembark at Howtown and follow the lakeside footpath that goes back, to the right, towards Patterdale. When the path reaches Sandwick Bay [N], it leaves the shore and goes through a field. Follow the sign. Cross the bridge at Sandwick and follow the road, ignoring the signs to Patterdale.

3. Cross the first bridge to the left (to Bridge End). In 100 yards, go through the gate marked 'Footpath to Howtown', over another bridge, and over the wall to the right at the signpost. Follow the yellow arrows across the field and go behind the farm house (Hallinbank).

4. Past Hallinbank, go through the gate and follow the cart track (not the footpath) down to the paved road.

5. Continue straight ahead (as nearly as possible) on the paved road. A stone fence will be on your right and you will soon pass

a telephone box. In half a mile the road passes the Old Church of St. Martin [O] and goes over the 'one-arched bridge'. Continue on the road to the end, at Dale Head.

6. Go to Dale Head and take the signposted footpath which goes up to the ridge.

7. At the crest of the ridge the footpath goes to the other side of the fell. Follow it. (Or, if you have an Ordnance Survey map, you may want to walk along 'the top of the hill' for a while, as William and Dorothy did, in the direction you have been going, before going down to join the path to Boardale Hause.)

8. At Boardale Hause (the mountain pass that separates Boardale and Patterdale), find the Chapel in the Hause [E], a pile of stones resembling a ruined sheep-fold. (Directions: As you approach the hause, or pass, you may see the stones behind two rocky knolls, about 200 yards from the drop into Patterdale on one side and about 250 yards from the drop into Boardale on the other side. If you fail to see it, go to the large ruined sheep-fold in the hause overlooking Patterdale. Stand with the sheep-fold on your right and your back toward Patterdale, then walk around the base of the rocky knoll above you to your left. You should soon come upon the ruined chapel; it will be smaller than the sheep-fold.)

9. Go through the hause towards Patterdale and Glenridding, and descend on the path going down the hillside to the right.

10. Cross the foot-bridge at the foot of the path, between the stone walls, pass through the gate, and turn right, immediately, through another gate leading to Side Farm.

11. At Side Farm [I], turn left and follow the road between the buildings to the main road. Turn right at the main road and walk back to Glenridding.

AIRA FORCE AND GOWBARROW PARK

Aira Force is among the most famous waterfalls in the Lake District, and Gowbarrow Park affords spectacular views of Ullswater and the surrounding fells; as one might expect, they are very popular places. The easiest way to get here is by car, or tourist coach. Coaches stop here only briefly in spite of Wordsworth's observation that 'in Gowbarrow Park the lover of Nature might wish to linger for hours'. The walk described below is about three miles.

1. Begin at the far end of the Aira Force car park, which is just north of where the road from Matterdale joins the road along Ullswater.

2. Cross Aira Beck at the wooden foot-bridge, go up the steps, and follow the left branch of the path up Aira Force valley [K] to the stone foot-bridge just below Aira Force.

3. Cross the foot-bridge and walk up to the higher stone foot-bridge at the top of the waterfall.

4. Cross the upper stone foot-bridge and follow the path that ascends to your right as you leave the bridge. (You will now be walking back towards Ullswater.)

5. Continue on the path with the fence to your left, pass through the wooden gate, and follow the path which curves left above another fence, behind Lyulph's Tower [L].

6. After following the fence behind Lyulph's Tower for 150–200 yards, take the path that branches upwards, to your left, ascending the hill under the crag.

7. Continue on this path, ignoring the branch in half a mile which goes higher up the hill. You will pass a crag and a stone cairn on your right (an excellent look-out); the path then turns away from the lake. In 200 yards you will come to a smaller path (next to a small, perhaps temporary, stone cairn), branching to the right down the fell, descending fairly steeply at first. Go down this path. (The main path continues up the fell.)

8. Near the foot of the gully the footpath turns right, through the wood, then curves down to run along the base of the larch wood.

9. Continue on this path (ignoring the steps that cross it at one point) until you are again behind Lyulph's Tower. Bear left, cross the stile, descend into Aira Force valley, cross the wooden foot-bridge, and return to the car park.

PENRITH AND ENVIRONS

The shop called Arnison's at the north end of the Market Square in Penrith [z] was once owned by Wordsworth's grandfather, William Cookson. Before her marriage, Wordsworth's mother lived with her family above the shop, and after the deaths of their parents the

Wordsworth children sometimes lived there as well. A few doors south of the Market Square, in King Street, is the Robin Hood Inn, where Wordsworth, aged twenty-four, looked after a dying friend.

The scene of a memorable ride on horseback, Penrith Beacon [BB], is a private and enclosed plantation, but the public has access to the superb view from the top, where the stone beacon has stood since 1719. The footpath begins at the end of Fell Lane. It is just over a mile from the Market Square to the summit.

The ruins of Brougham Castle [W], one and a half miles south-east of Penrith, are well preserved and open to the public. The castle is at the junction of the Rivers Eamont and Lowther, just off highway A66 and clearly signposted.

Less than a mile further east on A66 is the Countess' Pillar [X], on the south side of the road, just beyond the electric power lines. There is a convenient parking spot on the opposite side of the highway.

Lowther Castle [T] has fallen to ruins, but Lowther Park, four miles south of Penrith on A6, is open to the public as a wildlife park.

Long Meg and her Daughters [CC], a large and impressive stone circle, is six miles north-east of Penrith. To find it, follow A686 from the roundabout on the south side of Penrith. In four miles, after crossing the River Eden and entering Langwathby, turn left at the first road, drive through Little Salkeld, and follow the signs to the druid circle.

15

Borrowdale

Guide to places

A   LODORE: subject of Southey's famous poem, 'The Cataract of Lodore', and of Wordsworth's lines in his early poem, *An Evening Walk*:

> Where Derwent rests, and listens to the roar
> That stuns the tremulous cliffs of high Lodore. . . .

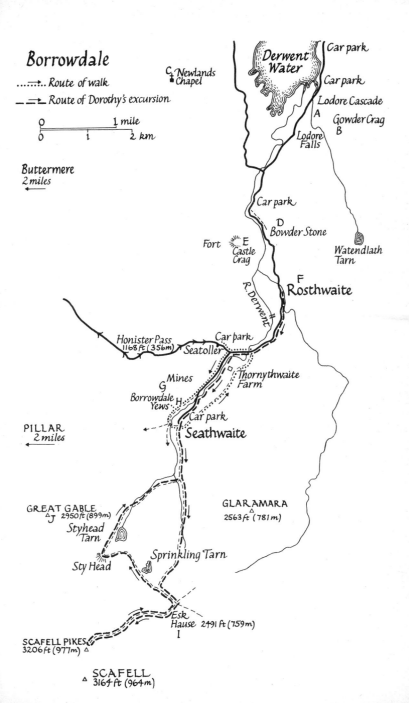

Borrowdale

......→... Route of walk

— —→— Route of Dorothy's excursion

0   1 mile
0   1   2 km

Derwent Water

Car park

Car park

Lodore Cascade

A

Gowder Crag

B

Lodore Falls

C Newlands Chapel

Buttermere
2 miles

Car park

D Bowder Stone

Fort E Castle Crag

Watendlath Tarn

F Rosthwaite

R. Derwent

Honister Pass
1168 ft (356 m)

Seatoller

Car park

Car park

Mines

G

Borrowdale
Yews H

Thornythwaite Farm

PILLAR
2 miles

Car park

Seathwaite

GREAT GABLE
△ J 2950 ft (899 m)

Styhead Tarn

Sty Head

Sprinkling Tarn

GLARAMARA
△
2563 ft (781 m)

Esk Hause 2491 ft (759 m)
I

SCAFELL PIKES
3206 ft (977 m) △

△ SCAFELL
3164 ft (964 m)

B GOWDER CRAG: where peat was moved by the 'blooming Lass' who served as the Wordsworths' 'Charioteer' on their trip from Grasmere to Bootle, described in the poem, 'Epistle to Sir G. H. Beaumont'. As a girl she led the sledge 'From the peat-yielding Moss on Gowdar's head'. An earlier poet (Richard Cumberland, in 'Ode to the Sun', 1775) had written of his ethereal emotions as his 'giddy tread | Press[ed] the moss on Gowdar's head'. Wordsworth's use of the same phrase for a less elevated purpose was his little joke at Cumberland's expense.

C NEWLANDS CHAPEL: 'My daughter and I left Rydal Mount upon a tour through our mountains . . . in the month of May, 1826, and as we were going up the vale of Newlands I was struck with the appearance of the little Chapel gleaming through the veil of half-opened leaves; and the feeling which was then conveyed to my mind was expressed in the stanza that follows' (I.F.).

> How delicate the leafy veil
>   Through which yon house of God
> Gleams 'mid the peace of this deep dale
>   By few but shepherds trod!
> And lowly huts, near beaten ways,
>   No sooner stand attired
> In thy fresh wreaths, than they for praise
> Peep forth, and are admired.

('To May', lines 81–8)

D BOWDER STONE: 'the huge mass of Bowder Stone, lying like a stranded Vessel whose hour of danger is no more' (*Prose Works*, ii. 345).

E CASTLE CRAG: 'springing out from the midst of [the rocks & woods], crowned with the antiquated circle of a Roman encampment' (*Prose Works*, ii. 345).

F ROSTHWAITE: where William and Dorothy spent the night on a tour in 1812, William sharing a bed with a Scotch peddler ('which however he did not seem to mind', according to an acquaintance). In 1818 Dorothy started here on her excursion to the top of Scafell Pikes with her friend, Miss Barker, who lived, I suspect, in what is now the Scafell Hotel.

G   MINES: the plumbago lead mines, above the yew trees. 'The discovery of the vein of black lead unsettled the peaceful spirit of Borrowdale & broke in upon the even tenor of its pastoral & rural labours' (*Prose Works*, ii. 346).

H* BORROWDALE YEWS: 'the fraternal Four of Borrowdale', subject of the poem, 'Yew-trees'.

I* ESK HAUSE: called Ash Course by Dorothy and by Wordsworth in the *Guide*. Dorothy intended to walk only this far, but she and her friend continued from here to the top of Scafell Pikes and then to Sty Head, from where they viewed Wasdale and looked back toward Scafell: 'the depth of the ravine appeared tremendous: it was black, and the Crags were awful' (*Prose Works*, ii. 367).

J   GREAT GABLE: 'The Great Gavel [a variant of 'gable'], so called, I imagine, from its resemblance to the gable end of a house, is one of the highest of the Cumberland mountains. It stands at the head of the several vales of Ennerdale, Wastdale, and Borrowdale' (W.W., note to 'The Brothers', line 310).

[For the following places, see the map on p. xviii.]

BUTTERMERE: home of the famous Maid of Buttermere, Mary Robinson, the beautiful daughter of the innkeeper. Travellers made a point of stopping at the Fish Inn to admire her as she served meals. One John Hatfield, who pretended to be Alexander Augustus Hope, MP, and brother to the Earl of Hopetoun, won her heart and married her in 1802. Soon after the marriage, however, he was exposed as a fraud: there was no seat in Parliament, no noble relation, and he was already married to another woman. He fled but was captured and hanged in Carlisle for forgery. The story was the subject of newspaper reports (sent to *The Morning Post* by Coleridge), a dramatic monologue, a novel, and a cartoon by James Gillray. In *The Prelude*, Wordsworth refers to

a Story drawn
From our own ground, the Maid of Buttermere,

---

* These places are discussed further in the fifteenth chapter of Part I: Poems and Places, p. 158.

And how the Spoiler came, 'a bold bad Man'
To God unfaithful, Children, Wife, and Home,
And wooed the artless Daughter of the hills,
And wedded her, in cruel mockery
Of love and marriage bonds.

He and Coleridge (the 'Friend') were served by her on their tour in 1799 as well as later, after her desertion and fame.

O Friend! I speak
With tender recollection of that time
When first we saw the Maiden, then a name
By us unheard of; in her cottage Inn
Were welcomed, and attended on by her,
Both stricken with one feeling of delight,
An admiration of her modest mien,
And carriage, mark'd by unexampled grace.
Not unfamiliarly we since that time
Have seen her; her discretion have observ'd,
Her just opinions, female modesty,
Her patience, and retiredness of mind
Unsoil'd by commendation, and the excess
Of public notice.

(1805 *Prelude*, vii. 320–39)

PILLAR: mountain at the head of Ennerdale (four miles west of Seathwaite), scene of the event described in 'The Brothers'. 'The poem arose out of the fact, mentioned to me at Ennerdale, that a shepherd had fallen asleep upon the top of the rock called The Pillar, and perished as here described, his staff being left midway on the rock' (I.F.). The Priest points out the place to the remaining brother, who has returned twelve years later:

You see yon precipice;—it wears the shape
Of a vast building made of many crags;
And in the midst is one particular rock
That rises like a column from the vale,
Whence by our shepherds it is called, THE PILLAR.

Wordsworth and Coleridge heard the story during their visit to Ennerdale in 1799: the young man was said to have fallen off Proud Knott on the east side of Pillar.

Walking directions

The famous Bowder Stone stands not far from the road up Borrowdale, between Lodore and Rosthwaite. There is a car park north of the stone and a walk of a quarter of a mile to the stone. Further up the valley, it is possible to park just below the Borrowdale Yews at Seathwaite, but by parking at Seatoller, one can get to the yews by the pleasant three and a quarter mile circular walk described below. The walk follows the road for a short distance at the beginning and the end. The yews of Wordsworth's poem, 'Yew-trees', are wrecks compared to what they were in his day, but they are magnificent now in their decay. Be sure to walk up and look at them at close range. The other yew, 'the pride of Lorton vale', of the same poem, is in High Lorton, north of Crummock Water, behind the Yew Tree Hall. It has survived better than the fraternal four of Borrowdale, but it is evident that much has been lost over the years. The Cumberland bus service travels between Keswick and Seatoller.

1. Begin at the car park at Seatoller. Walk down the road (towards Keswick) for 75 yards; then turn right and walk up the road towards Seathwaite. In three-quarters of a mile, you will come to a bridge where the road crosses a stream. Turn right on the footpath that leaves the road just before the bridge.

2. Walk up the footpath, with the stream to your left. When you have covered more than half the distance between the bridge and the farm buildings, you will pass a low, spreading yew next to the river and to the left of the path. The path then crosses a stream bed and the four famous yew trees are up the hill about 40 yards above the path. Leave the path and walk up to the dark green yews, now declining but still with huge trunks. Three are together, and one stands to the left by itself.

3. After looking at the yews, return to the footpath, continue upstream, and cross the River Derwent at the foot-bridge.

4. Just above the farm buildings is a sign, 'Path to Borrowdale via Thorneythwaite'. It follows the foot of the fell down the opposite side of the valley you walked up. Follow it until you come to an iron gate from where you can see the roofs of Thorneythwaite Farm 100–150 yards ahead of you, through the

trees. Turn right and follow the stone fence (on your left) to the paved farm road. Follow it to the Borrowdale road.

5. At the Borrowdale road, turn left and return to Seatoller.

16

Dungeon Ghyll Force and the Langdales

Guide to places

A LOUGHRIGG TARN: 'Diana's Looking-glass', the subject of 'Epistle to Sir G. H. Beaumont', lines 164–94, and of 'Upon Perusing the Foregoing Epistle Thirty Years after Its Composition'. A short and late poem in triplets, 'So fair, so sweet, withal so sensitive', was suggested by the sight of the shadow of a daisy on a stone, observed by the side of the tarn in 1844.

B LANGDALE CHURCHYARD: burial place of Revd Owen Lloyd, clergyman at the Langdale Chapel and subject of Wordsworth's 'Epitaph in the Chapel-Yard of Langdale, Westmoreland', carved on Lloyd's tombstone in front of the church, under the yew tree. A picture of the chapel in Wordsworth's and Lloyd's time hangs in the porch of the present church. This churchyard, rather than Grasmere's, is the place where the Poet and his friends are interrupted by a wagon bearing a giant oak in *The Excursion*, vii. 541–5:

> . . . near the quiet churchyard where we sate,
> A team of horses, with a ponderous freight
> Pressing behind, adown a rugged slope,
> Whose sharp descent confounded their array,
> Came at that moment, ringing noisily.

C* DUNGEON GHYLL FORCE: the waterfall of 'The Idle Shepherd-Boys'.

D STICKLE TARN: where Wordsworth, standing under Harrison

---

* These places are discussed further in the sixteenth chapter of Part I: Poems and Places, p. 165.

Stickle, heard an echo which is dramatically described in *The Excursion*, iv. 402–12. 'There is in *The Excursion*, an allusion to the bleat of a lamb thus re-echoed, and described without any exaggeration, as I heard it, on the side of Stickle Tarn, from the precipice that stretches on to Langdale Pikes' (I.F. note on 'To Joanna').

E*   LANGDALE PIKES: Pike of Stickle and Harrison Stickle, the 'two huge Peaks', the 'lusty twins', the 'prized companions' of the Solitary, who watches them from his secluded home at Blea Tarn (*The Excursion*, ii. 688–725). They are visible from most of Blea Tarn valley but not in fact from Bleatarn House. The sonnet, 'How clear, how keen, how marvellously bright', was 'suggested on the banks of the Brathay by the sight of Langdale Pikes' (I.F.).

F*   LINGMOOR FELL: where the Poet and Wanderer make their 'steep ascent' to the ridge, look down on Blea Tarn, and make their way down, winding from crag to crag, to visit the Solitary in *The Excursion*, Book ii.

G*   BLEA TARN: described from above in *The Excursion*, ii. 327–48. Wordsworth quoted this passage later in his *Guide to the Lakes*. Books ii, iii, iv, and the beginning of v of *The Excursion* are set in this valley.

H*   BLEATARN HOUSE: a farmhouse, the 'one bare dwelling' in the valley, where Wordsworth's Solitary lives and where the Wanderer and Poet spend the night in *The Excursion*.

I*   WATERFALL: perhaps the site of the lean-to described in *The Excursion*, ii. 412–28, where the Poet and Wanderer find the Solitary's damp copy of *Candide*, 'dull product of a scoffer's pen' (line 484). The site is conjectural: all one can see now is the ruins of 'one old moss-grown wall' which clearly once 'met in an angle' with the 'upright mass of rock' on the right-hand side of the stream, as you face the waterfall. Wordsworth describes a lean-to that children built in such an angle 'By thrusting two rude staves into the wall | And overlaying them with mountain sods'. This waterfall may also be the site of the 'hidden nook' where the Poet, Wanderer, and Solitary have their long talk in Book iii, although the waterfall does not fit the description

E LANGDALE PIKES

D Stickle Tarn

Stickle Ghyll

Dungeon Ghyll

C Dungeon Ghyll Force

Dungeon Ghyll New Hotel

Dungeon Ghyll Old Hotel

Car park

Car park

Camp ground

Wall End

Side House

Gate

GREAT LANGDALE

Robinson Place

Harry Place

Great

Oak Howe

Langdale

Beck

B Ch St.

Side Pike

Lingmoor Tarn

Oakhowe Crag

Stile

Gate in fence

H House

Bleatarn House

stile

G Blea Tarn

Car park

J

Summit 1530 ft (466m)

Gate and stile

LINGMOOR FELL

L Bield Crag

Bleamoss Beck

Dale End

Ha

to Wrynose Pass and River Duddon

R. Brathay

K Fell Foot

LITTLE LANGDALE

Little Lang- dale Tarn

Ivy M

The Langdales

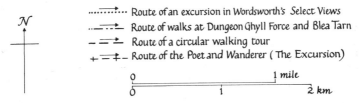

......▸.... Route of an excursion in Wordsworth's *Select Views*

...═▸ Route of walks at Dungeon Ghyll Force and Blea Tarn

─ ═▸ Route of a circular walking tour

+ ═ + ─ Route of the Poet and Wanderer (*The Excursion*)

0   1 mile

0   1   2 km

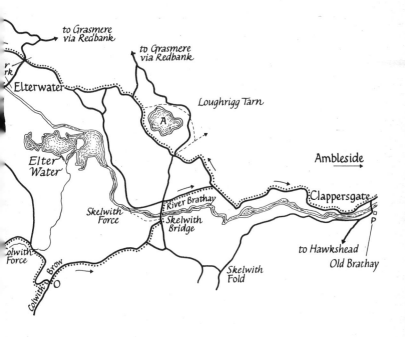

N

to Grasmere
via Redbank

to Grasmere
via Redbank

Elterwater

Loughrigg Tarn

A

Elter
Water

Ambleside

Clappersgate

River Brathay

Skelwith
Force

Skelwith
Bridge

to Hawkshead

Old Brathay

olwith
Force

Colwith Brow

O

Skelwith
Fold

exactly. Wordsworth may have used this location but described a different waterfall, just as he may have imagined the mass of rock [J] on the other side of the valley to be in this location.

J*   MASS OF ROCK: large fragments of rock, fallen from the crag above, which perhaps inspired the scene in *The Excursion*, iii. 50–91, where the Poet, Wanderer, and Solitary find 'A mass of rock, resembling . . . | A stranded ship', three stones 'not unlike | To monumental pillars', and 'A fragment, like an altar, flat and smooth'.

K   FELL FOOT: the site of the Parsonage in *The Excursion*, though the action and setting of the Pastor's part of the poem are largely in Grasmere vale. After the Poet, Wanderer, and Solitary leave Blea Tarn, 'we descend into . . . Little Langdale, towards the head of which stands, embowered or partly shaded by yews and other trees, something between a cottage and a mansion or gentleman's house such as they once were in this country. This I convert into the Parsonage . . .' (I.F.). Wordsworth's friend, the artist William Green, described it in 1819 as 'the ancient building called Fellfoot . . . embowered in trees' (*Tourist's New Guide*, i. 249, 251). Most of the trees are gone, but the building remains.

L   BIELD CRAG: scene of the death of the 'poor, ill-fated Shepherd of Bield Crag' who fell down the screes to his death in a winter storm while looking for a lost sheep on 'that smooth blue steep | That sinks abruptly from the grassless crown | Of yon huge height'. Wordsworth wrote the tale for *The Excursion* but did not include it in the published poem. (See *PW*, v. 461–3).

M   IVY HOW (now Iving Howe): a farm which Wordsworth purchased in 1818 to divide up into a number of freeholds. These were sold to members of the family and friends to provide additional votes for Lord Lonsdale's party. Mary described it as 'a sweet sunny place with beautiful rocks'.

N   HACKETT: a farmhouse, high on the hill,

> A house of stones collected on the spot,
> By rude hands built, with rocky knolls in front,
> Backed also by a ledge of rock, whose crest

> Of birch-trees waves over the chimney top;
> A rough abode. . . .

In *The Excursion*, v. 670–837, the Pastor and the Wanderer tell of its inhabitants. 'In this nothing is introduced but what was taken from nature and real life', Wordsworth said. 'The cottage is called Hackett, and stands, as described, on the southern extremity of the ridge which separates the two Langdales; the Pair who inhabited it were called Jonathan and Betty Yewdale. Once when our children were ill, of whooping-cough I think, we took them for change of air to this cottage, and were in the habit of going there to drink tea on fine summer afternoons . . .' (I.F.). On one such outing for tea, a friend of the Wordsworths brought his flute, stationed himself on a nearby rock, and played to everyone's delight (including, reputedly, the cows'). The occasion prompted the sonnet, 'The fairest, brightest, hues of ether fade' (*PW*, iii. 5).

o COLWITH BROW: where the Wordsworths passed on their way from Grasmere to Bootle and were hailed from Hackett by Betty Yewdale, as described in the 'Epistle to Sir G. H. Beaumont', lines 203–22.

p OLD BRATHAY: home of Charles Lloyd, former pupil of Coleridge, author of a novel *(Edmund Oliver)* whose hero is an unflattering portrait of Coleridge, acquaintance of Wordsworth (they did not much like one another), and brother-in-law of the youngest Wordsworth brother (Christopher). Lloyd was not always at Old Brathay—he spent some time in a mental institution near York—but his son Owen grew up here and became the clergyman at the Langdale Chapel [B]. The story of the Jacobite and Hanoverian in *The Excursion*, vi, led Wordsworth to comment in 1843 on the Lake District as a place of concealment: 'Such was particularly the case with two brothers of the name of Weston[1] who took up their abode at Old Brathay, I think about 70 years ago. They were highwaymen, and lived there some time without being discovered, though it was known that they often disappeared in

---

[1] An alias. Their real name was Gilbert, according to Joseph Budworth in *A Fortnight's Ramble to the Lakes* (1792), p. 130.

a way and upon errands which could not be accounted for. Their horses were noticed as being of a choice breed. . . . They, as I have heard, and as was universally believed, were in the end both taken and hanged' (I.F.).

Travel directions

AN EXCURSION IN WORDSWORTH'S *SELECT VIEWS*

Wordsworth describes a round-trip excursion from Ambleside up Great Langdale to Dungeon Ghyll Force, past Blea Tarn into Little Langdale, and back to Ambleside. The entire trip may now be made by car, although when Wordsworth wrote this, one could travel beyond Chapel Stile only by foot or on horseback. For a better walking route today, see the circular walking tour (10 miles) below. For shorter walks, drive along this route and stop for the walks described below at Dungeon Ghyll Force and Blea Tarn. Here are Wordsworth's directions (the route is marked on the map):

Great Langdale [is] a Vale which should on no account be missed by him who has a true enjoyment of grand separate Forms composing a sublime Unity, austere but reconciled and rendered attractive to the affections by the deep serenity that is spread over every thing. There is no good carriage road through this Vale; nor ought that to be regretted; for it would impair its solemnity: but the road is tolerable for about the distance of three miles from Ambleside, namely along the Vale of Brathay, and above the western banks of Loughrigg Tarn [A], and still further, to the entrance of Langdale itself: but the small and peaceful Valley of Loughrigg is seen to much greater advantage from the eastern side. When therefore you have quitted the River Brathay enquire at the first house for the foot road, which will conduct you round the lower extremity of the Tarn, and so on to its head, where, at a little distance from the Tarn the path again leads to the publick road and about a mile further conducts you to Langdale Chapel [B].—A little way beyond this sequestered and simple place of worship is a narrow passage on the right leading into a slate-quarry [Thrang Quarry, much enlarged now] which has been finely excavated. Pursuing this road a few hundred yards further, you come in view of the noblest reach of this Vale, which I shall not attempt to describe. Under the Precipice adjoining to the Pikes [E] lies invisibly Stickle Tarn [D], and thence descends a conspicuous Torrent down the breast of the Mountain. Near this Torrent is Dungeon Gill Force [C]. . . . If the Traveller has been zealous enough to advance as far as Dungeon-gill Force, let him enquire for Blea Tarn [G]; he may return by that circuit to Ambleside. Blea Tarn is not an object of any beauty in itself, but it is situated in a small, deep circular Valley of peculiar character; for it contains only one Dwelling-house and two or three cultivated fields. Passing down this Valley, fail not to look back now and then, and you will see Langdale Pikes [E], from behind the rocky steeps that form its north-eastern boundary, lifting themselves, as if on tip-toe, to pry into it. Quitting the Valley you will descend into little Langdale, and thence may proceed by Colwith Force and Bridge . . . [on to] Skelwith-Bridge. . . .

(Prose Works, ii. 269–70)

From Skelwith Bridge, Wordsworth recommends returning to Ambleside via Skelwith Fold for a view no longer accessible, but a better way for cars is through the village of Skelwith Bridge, then right, and on to Ambleside by the same side of the River Brathay. 'The whole of this excursion', Wordsworth writes, 'may be as much as 18 miles, and would require a long morning to be devoted to the accomplishment.' He also recommends this 'charming excursion' in his *Guide*, where his less-detailed directions are in the reverse order, to allow a better view of the Langdale Pikes.

DUNGEON GHYLL FORCE

Wordsworth advises that 'Dungeon Gill Force . . . cannot be found without a Guide, who may be taken up at one of the Cottages at the foot of the Mountain'. But the following directions may serve as well. The Ribble bus service runs from Ambleside to the Dungeon Ghyll Old Hotel, but you should get off at the Dungeon Ghyll *New* Hotel. If you are driving, park in the National Trust car park just past the Dungeon Ghyll New Hotel. The walk to the waterfall is about half a mile. (This walk is included in the circular walking tour of Wordsworth's Langdales, below.)

1. Begin at the National Trust car park west of the Dungeon Ghyll New Hotel. Next to a large rock near the entrance to the car park, a sign points out the path to Dungeon Ghyll Force.
2. Go up the hill; a stone fence will be on your left. Go through the wooden gate, turn right, and in a few yards go through the iron gate. Then turn right and follow the wall (with it on your right) until you reach a stile 50 yards beyond the seat.

3. Cross the fence at the stile; then cross the stream (Dungeon Ghyll), and follow the path up the left side of the stream.

4. In about 300 yards from where you crossed the stream you will be near the corner of a stone fence on your left. Take the path which branches to the right and leads to a promontory from which you can see Dungeon Ghyll Force [C]. If you want a better view of the waterfall and rock bridge, climb down the rock steps (on the promontory), descending to the stream, and walk across the boulders. If the stream is not in spate, you can follow it up to the pool under the stone bridge, where the lamb is rescued in the poem. This may require wading through the water. You can also see the chockstone wedged between the walls of the ravine by walking further up the hill from the promontory.

5. To return to the car park, follow the same route by which you came.

BLEA TARN

If you drive to Blea Tarn, you can park on the south side of the valley and walk to the mass of rock [J] or along the road to Bleatarn House [H] and the waterfall [I] near it. These places, as well as the view of the valley seen by the Poet and Wanderer from the top of the ridge, are included in the following walk of about three miles, and most of this walk is included in the circular walking tour of Wordsworth's Langdales, below.

1. Begin at the car park, cross the road, follow the path that is parallel to the foot of Blea Tarn, and cross the stream. Continue straight on, to the other side of the plantation of trees and rhododendrons, until you come to the mass of rock [J] above the path and at the foot of the cliff.

2. Continue on the path, through the tree plantation, and on until you come to the road. Turn right and walk down the road for over a quarter of a mile beyond the gate and cattle grid, and then go up the fellside with a wire fence and Side Pike to your left.

3. When the path reaches a stone wall, follow the path to the right until it goes through the fence at a gate. Go through the gate and continue up the ridge to the summit, now with the stone wall on your right. The best view of Blea Tarn [G] and Bleatarn House is

on the other side of the crumbling wall and the fence (on open-access National Trust property), but the ridge itself affords fine views of the Langdales, lakes, and surrounding mountains.

4. Just below the summit cairn (there are several others along the ridge), the ruined stone wall makes a right-angled turn and there is a stile over the wire fence. Cross at the stile and follow the stone wall down to the gate and another stile, on your right. Cross at this stile and bear left, uphill briefly, on the path, and then descend on the path marked by small cairns, keeping the gully and stream to your right.

5. Further down, the path goes through a stone wall. Below it, when you are about half way between the wall and the road, leave the path and find a waterfall [I] in the stream on your right, not far above the road. (Or, take the path to the road, and then follow the stream from the road up to the waterfall.) Follow the stream down to the road at Bleatarn House [H], turn left on the road, and return to the car park.

ROUTE OF THE POET AND WANDERER

In Book ii of *The Excursion* the old Wanderer decides to introduce the Poet to his friend, the Solitary, who lives in the mountains. Wordsworth told Miss Fenwick, 'In the Poem, I suppose that the Pedlar [Wanderer] and I [the Poet] ascended . . . up the vale of Langdale, and struck off a good way above the chapel [B] to the western side of the vale.' Thus they followed the road from Chapel Stile to somewhere near Robinson Place and crossed Great Langdale Beck. 'We ascended the hill [Lingmoor Fell, F] and thence looked down upon the circular recess in which lies Blea Tarn [G], chosen by the Solitary for his retreat.' There is now, as then, no footpath up this part of Lingmoor Fell ('We scaled, without a track to ease our steps, | A steep ascent' [ii. 323–4]), and there is no right of way. The map indicates a likely route for them, to the east of the stream leading from Lingmoor Tarn (there is a gate on the public footpath near where it crosses this stream) and well to the west of the vertical cliffs of Oakhowe Crag, but this route now goes through thick juniper on the fellside. Once on the ridge, the Poet sees 'a tumultuous waste of huge hill tops . . . savage region!' On the other side of the present crumbling wall and the fence, he looks down on the 'urn-like' valley of Blea Tarn. After a rest 'upon a bed of heath', they go down to Bleatarn House [H]:

> So, to a steep and difficult descent
> Trusting ourselves, we wound from crag to crag,
> Where passage could be won.
>
> (ii. 403–5)

They spend the night in Bleatarn House (now a bed and breakfast farmhouse) and the next day, with the Solitary, they leave Blea Tarn by the road going south into Little Langdale, come to a house (Fell Foot [K]) which Wordsworth 'converts' into a Parsonage, and 'as by the waving of a magic wand' (I.F.) they find themselves in Grasmere vale.

A CIRCULAR WALKING TOUR OF WORDSWORTH'S LANGDALES

This ten-mile walk begins and ends at the village of Elterwater, where there are car parks and Ribble bus service.

1. Begin at the bridge in Elterwater, next to the car park. Cross the bridge and follow the signposted footpath up the left side of the stream. (For the first few hundred yards, the footpath is on the road.) Cross again at the foot-bridge by the Langdales Hotel in Chapel Stile, and walk to the Langdale church [B], which is ahead of you as you leave the bridge.

2. Leave the churchyard by the gate to your right (as you face the village), go down the hill to the 'Give Way' sign, walk right on the road for 150 yards, and turn left through the gate, on to a farm road which soon turns right, following the stone wall. Cross the bridge over the stream.

3. Turn right after leaving the bridge and follow the path up Great Langdale. In half a mile, the path turns away from the stream, passes Oak Howe Cottage, then goes between ruined stone walls and back near the stream (but with a wall between the path and the stream).

4. At Side House, turn right and follow the farm road across the stream and the main road. Cross the road, bear left, and walk into the National Trust car park.

5. Next to a large rock near the entrance to the car park is a sign pointing out the path to Dungeon Ghyll Force. Follow it.

6. Go up the hill; a stone fence will be on your left. Go through the wooden gate, turn right, and in a few yards go through the iron gate. Then turn right and follow the wall (with it on your right) until you reach a stile 50 yards beyond the seat.

7. Cross the fence at the stile; then cross the stream (Dungeon Ghyll), and follow the path up the left side of the stream.

8. In about 300 yards from where you crossed the stream you will be near the corner of a stone fence on your left. Take the path which branches to the right and leads to a promontory from which you can see Dungeon Ghyll Force [C]. Rock steps (on the promontory) lead down to the stream for the best view, and you can wade or go from rock to rock a few yards further upstream to see the pool where the lamb is rescued in the poem. The path above, which continues up the hill, leads to a higher view of the waterfall and chockstone wedged between the walls of the ravine.

9. Follow the path downstream the way you came up, but at the iron gate turn right and follow the path to the Dungeon Ghyll *Old* Hotel. Turn left past the back of the hotel, where the stone wall turns, go through the gate, out to the road, and across the bridge. Follow the road to the right, then to the left, sharply, at the post box.

10. In 150–200 yards, when the road bends right, go left through the gap in the stone fence, just beyond the gate, into the camping ground. Keep the stone fence to your right (it soon turns right) until it ends, cross four fences at the stiles, and go up the fellside with a stone fence to your right.

11. Where the road crests and enters the Blea Tarn valley, go over the fence at the stile, walk to the left along the road for over a quarter of a mile, and then go up the fellside with a wire fence and Side Pike to your left.

12. When the path reaches a stone wall, follow the path to the right until it goes through the fence at a gate. Go through the gate and continue up the ridge to the summit, now with the stone wall on your right. The best view of Blea Tarn [G] and Bleatarn House is on the other side of the crumbling wall and the fence (on open-access National Trust property).

13. Just below the summit cairn (there are several others along the

ridge), the ruined stone wall makes a right-angled turn and there is a stile over the wire fence. Cross at the stile and follow the stone wall down to the gate and another stile, on your right. Cross at this stile and bear left, uphill briefly, on the path, and then descend on the path marked by small cairns, keeping the gully and stream to your right.

14. Further down, the path goes through a stone wall. Below it, when you are about half way between the wall and the road, leave the path and find a waterfall [I] in the stream on your right, not far above the road. (Or, take the path to the road, and then follow the stream from the road up to the waterfall.) Follow the stream down to the road at Bleatarn House [H], turn left on the road, and walk to the car park.

15. Opposite the car park, follow the path that is parallel to the foot of Blea Tarn, and cross the stream. Continue straight on, to the other side of the plantation of trees and rhododendrons, until you come to the mass of rock [J] above the path and at the foot of the cliff.

16. Return to the stream and follow the path down the right side of it. In a few hundred yards the path turns away from the stream; it later goes above a ruined stone building, and on to the road.

17. Turn left on the road, following it past Fell Foot [K] and Little Langdale Tarn. As you walk by this lake, the crag on Lingmoor Fell ahead and to your left is Bield Crag [L].

18. At the top of the hill beyond Little Langdale Tarn, turn left on the road marked 'Unsuitable for Motor Vehicles'. In slightly more than one mile this road joins a better road, and then another. Continue ahead for 300 yards to the bridge in Elterwater.

17

River Duddon

Guide to places

A* THREE SHIRE STONE: the approximate scene of the beginning
    sonnets of *The River Duddon*. 'In my own fancy I have fixed its
    rise near the noted Shire-stones placed at the meeting-point of
    the counties, Westmoreland, Cumberland, and Lancashire.
    They stand by the wayside on the top of the Wrynose Pass, and
    it used to be reckoned a proud thing to say that, by touching
    them at the same time with feet and hands, one had been in the
    three counties at once' (I.F.).

B   COCKLEY BECK: the cottage of Sonnet V.

C* HARDKNOTT CASTLE: one of 'several Roman stations among
    these mountains. . . . The ROMAN FORT here alluded to ["that
    lone Camp on Hardknot's height"], . . . is most impressively
    situated half-way down the hill on the right of the road that
    descends from Hardknot into Eskdale' (W.W. note on Sonnet
    XVII).

D* STEPPING STONES: where children test their courage and old
    men note their infirmities (in Sonnet IX) and where lovers
    court (Sonnet X). There are several sets of stepping stones
    across the Duddon. The set that fits the sequence of the poems
    and development of the river (when 'struggling Rill insensibly
    is grown | Into a Brook of loud and stately march') is between
    Cockley Beck and Birks Bridge, but the set that is most
    beautiful, that has a 'high rock' nearby, and that is said by local
    tradition to be Wordsworth's steps is at Seathwaite.

E   BIRKS BRIDGE: perhaps the site of the 'sunless cleft' where
    faeries engaged in 'secret revels' (Sonnet XI). The gorge over a

---

* These places are discussed further in the seventeenth chapter of Part I:
Poems and Places, p. 176.

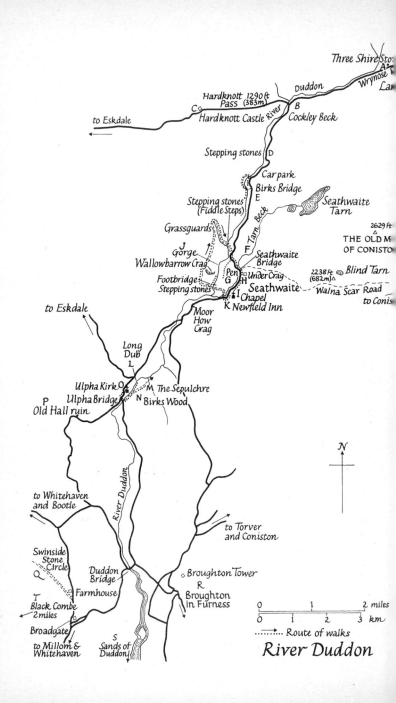

Three Shire Sto
A
Wrynose La

Duddon

Hardknott 1290 ft
Pass (383m)
C
Hardknott Castle
River
B
Cockley Beck

Stepping stones D

Car park
Birks Bridge
E

Stepping stones
(Fiddle Steps)

Seathwaite
Tarn

Grassguards

Tarn Beck

2629 ft
△
THE OLD M
OF CONISTO

J
Gorge
Wallowbarrow Crag

F
Seathwaite
Bridge

Under Crag

2238 ft
(682m)△

Blind Tarn

Footbridge
Stepping stones

Pen
G H
Seathwaite
Chapel
K Newfield Inn

Walna Scar Road
to Conis

to Eskdale

Moor How
Crag

Long
Dub
L

to Eskdale

Ulpha Kirk O
Ulpha Bridge
P
Old Hall ruin

M The Sepulchre
N Birks Wood

River Duddon

N

to Whitehaven
and Bootle

to Torver
and Coniston

Swinside
Stone
Circle
Q

Duddon
Bridge
Farmhouse

Broughton Tower
R
Broughton
in Furness

T
Black Combe
2 miles

Broadgate

to Millom &
Whitehaven

S
Sands of
Duddon

0   1   2 miles
0   1   2   3 km
......·.. Route of walks

River Duddon

quarter of a mile downstream from Birks Bridge supplies many 'Hints for the Fancy' (Sonnet XII)—'Wild shapes . . . | Niagaras, Alpine passes, and anon | Abodes of Naiads, calm abysses pure, | Bright liquid mansions. . . .' From here, 'Turn from the sight . . . we must', since the rocks prevent further passage.

F TARN BECK: the 'Tributary Stream' of Sonnet XIX, running through the valley of Seathwaite, which Wordsworth particularly admired. 'After all, the traveller would be most gratified who should approach [the Duddon] neither at its source, as is done in the Sonnets, nor from its termination; but from Coniston over Walna Scar [by footpath]; first descending into a little circular valley, a collateral compartment of the long winding vale through which flows the Duddon.' This 'recess' is described at length in the third paragraph of Wordsworth's note to Sonnets XVII and XVIII.

G* PEN: the 'green hill' which is vantage point for the 'Open Prospect' (Sonnet XIII). From here the poet sees fields, 'one small hamlet' (Seathwaite), the 'barn and byre' of Newfield, and the 'spouting mill' which once stood on Tarn Beck.

H* UNDER CRAG: the birthplace of the Reverend Robert Walker (1709–1802), known as Wonderful Walker, the curate of Seathwaite for sixty-six years, subject of Duddon Sonnet XVIII, of *The Excursion*, vii. 315–60, and of Wordsworth's fine 'Memoir' in his notes on the Duddon sonnets.

I* SEATHWAITE CHAPEL: Wonderful Walker's school and church (Sonnet XVIII), since rebuilt.

J WALLOWBARROW GORGE: the passage which the Duddon cleaves 'through this wilderness' in Sonnet XIV, and the 'deep chasm' of Sonnet XV. 'The wild and beautiful scenery . . . gave occasion to the Sonnets from the 14th to the 20th inclusive. From the point where the Seathwaite brook [Tarn Beck] joins the Duddon, is a view upwards, into the pass through which the river makes its way into the plain of Donnerdale. The perpendicular rock on the right bears the ancient British name of THE PEN; the one opposite is called WALLA-BARROW CRAG.

... The *chaotic* aspect of the scene is well marked by the expression of a stranger, who strolled out while dinner was preparing, and at his return, being asked by his host, "What way he had been wandering?" replied, "As far as it is *finished!*" The bed of the Duddon is here strewn with large fragments of rocks fallen from aloft. ... That there is some hazard in frequenting these desolate places, I myself have had proof; for one night an immense mass of rock fell upon the very spot where, with a friend, I had lingered the day before' (W.W., note on Duddon Sonnets XVII and XVIII).

K*   NEWFIELD INN: a farmhouse, in Wordsworth's time, which served as an inn (Sonnet XIII).

L*   LONG DUB: the 'hidden pool' and 'steep rock' which the poet associates with a traditional tale of a 'love-lorn Maid' who drowns herself (Sonnet XXII), and the 'pool smooth and clear' of the 'Sheep-washing' sonnet (XXIII).

M*   THE SEPULCHRE: the enclosed Quaker burial ground, with no tombstones ('the blank earth, neglected and forlorn'), of Sonnet XXIX.

N*   BIRKS WOOD: perhaps the 'rough copse' through which the Duddon wheels in Sonnet XXX.

O*   ULPHA KIRK: the church, with its 'wave-washed Church-yard', of Sonnet XXXI. 'From this Church-yard [the traveller] will have as grand a combination of mountain lines and forms as perhaps this country furnishes' (*Prose Works*, ii. 262).

P*   OLD HALL RUIN: the 'shapeless heap' of an 'embattled House', 'massy Keep', and 'ancient Hold' of Sonnet XXVII. The notion in the sonnet that its warriors deserted it because it was inhabited by ghosts was not in fact associated with this ruin. Wordsworth said that he used 'a tradition belonging to Rydal Hall, which once stood, as is believed, upon a rocky and woody hill on the right hand as you go from Rydal to Ambleside, and was deserted from the superstitious fear here described [in the sonnet], and the present site fortunately chosen instead' (I.F.).

Q*   SWINSIDE STONE CIRCLE: 'that mystic Round of Druid frame | Tardily sinking by its proper weight | Deep into patient Earth, from whose smooth breast it came!' (Sonnet XVII). 'The country people call it *Sunken Church*' (W.W., note to the sonnet). It is mentioned in *An Evening Walk*, line 171, and alluded to, along with Furness Abbey, in *The Prelude*, ii. 101–2 ('some framed temple where of yore | The Druids worshipped'), as the destination of horse rides when he was a schoolboy at Hawkshead.

R BROUGHTON: where Wordsworth 'during my college vacation, and two or three years afterwards, . . . was several times resident in the house of a near relative'. The relative was his cousin Mary, who married John Smith of Broughton and died a relatively young woman. His visits and her death are alluded to in Sonnet XXI.

S SANDS OF DUDDON: where 'in radiant progress toward the Deep . . . *now* expands | Majestic Duddon, over smooth flat sands | Gliding in silence with unfettered sweep!' (Sonnets XXXII and XXXIII).

T BLACK COMBE: a 'huge Eminence,—from blackness named, | And, to far-travelled storms of sea and land, | A favourite spot of tournament and war!' ('Inscription Written on the Side of Black Comb'). 'Black Comb stands at the southern extremity of Cumberland: its base covers a much greater extent of ground than any other mountain in these parts; and, from its situation, the summit commands a more extensive view than any other point in Britain' (W.W., note to his poem, 'View from the Top of Black Comb'). It was Wordsworth's 'grim neighbour' when he and part of his family spent several weeks near Bootle in 1811; the trip is the subject of 'Epistle to Sir G. H. Beaumont'.

Travel directions

Wordsworth sometimes approached his favourite river from the source, sometimes from the mouth, and sometimes—the best way, he thought—from Coniston, by foot, over Walna Scar. Even now it is not an easy place to get to. A bus service does exist: Mountain Goat runs over the two mountain passes by the far upper Duddon and the Post Bus runs on the lower Duddon and up to Cockley

Beck. The precipitous roads over Wrynose Pass and Hardknott Pass are single-lane and therefore sometimes very congested. Perhaps the best way, apart from Wordsworth's route on foot, is by car from the mouth at Duddon Bridge. But Wordsworth's sonnet sequence, *The River Duddon*, begins at the source and moves downstream to the sea. The stopping places and walks listed below follow that direction and include most of the specific places referred to in the poem.

WRYNOSE PASS
With luck, you may find a spot to pull off the road to see the Three Shire Stone [A], catch glimpses of the obscure origins of the Duddon, and look down on the upper Duddon valley.

BIRKS BRIDGE
For a walk of about a mile, park at the car park 200 yards upstream from Birks Bridge at the Dunnerdale Forest car park. Cross the river at the new bridge near the car park, and walk downstream to Birks Bridge [E]. Pass Birks Bridge without crossing it and continue, around the bends in the river, as far as you can go to a narrow gorge, with sheer crags going down to the river on the right side. (The first crag which you come to on the right is passable; go on to the next crag.) This gorge is more than a quarter of a mile below Birks Bridge. The path may be wet at spots and is not always distinct, but it is worth pursuing. Return, cross Birks Bridge, and walk up the river to the car park.

SEATHWAITE
To climb the Pen [G] for its fine views of Wallowbarrow Crag, the lower Duddon valley, Newfield Inn [K], the church [I], and Under Crag [H], park along the road near the Grassguards bridleway crossing (signposted) and walk down the road toward Seathwaite, less than a quarter of a mile, to the cattle grid. Just over the grid, a small path leaves the road to the right. Follow it over the first hill (Hollin House Tongue) and walk to the summit of the Pen. (The path becomes indistinct near the top.) Return the same way. (Or, include this in the longer walk below.)

   To see the stepping stones [D] and walk into the Wallowbarrow Gorge [J], park opposite Seathwaite Church [I] or near Newfield

Inn [K]. Take the footpath across the road from the church to the stepping stones; it goes immediately through a gap in a stone fence, follows and crosses Tarn Beck [F], and leads to the foot-bridge over the Duddon. The stepping stones are 70 yards downstream from the foot-bridge. Cross the river either at the stepping stones or the foot-bridge. Walk upstream into the gorge and return to the foot-bridge.

A longer walk of four miles (more if you climb the Pen) takes you above the Duddon on both sides, crossing the Duddon at the stepping stones or bridge at Seathwaite and at stepping stones below Grassguards. If the river level is high, it may not be possible to cross the river below Grassguards. You may want to check the water level at the stepping stones near Seathwaite before setting off.

1. Follow the directions in the previous paragraph to the Wallowbarrow Gorge, return to the foot-bridge, and bear right, up the small hill. The path takes you through three wooden gates and by some farm buildings.
2. In the farmyard bear right (not sharply) and go up the farm track with a stone wall on your right. The track takes you through more wooden gates toward Wallowbarrow Crag, which will be on your right as you go uphill and past it.
3. Follow the cart track which runs from Stoneythwaite Farm to Grassguards (nearly a mile).
4. After passing the farm buildings at Grassguards and crossing the stream, turn right (do not go straight ahead, through the gate) and follow the stream down to the Duddon. Cross the river at the stepping stones (Fiddle Steps), and follow the footpath to the right, which leads to the road.
5. Go right on the road, and just over the cattle grid you will see the small path to the Pen, which goes up to the right. (If you climb the Pen, return the same way.) Continue on the road to Seathwaite, which is less than a mile away.

ULPHA BRIDGE

This walk, to Long Dub [L], The Sepulchre [M], and back to Ulpha Kirk [O], which is on the road, is less than two miles.

1. Park at the bridge. At the east end of the bridge (the cattle grid is on the east side), go through the gap in the stone fence and walk

along the river, upstream. In about a quarter of a mile the path arrives at a wooden gate.

2. To see Long Dub, you must leave the public footpath and follow the river upstream (on Forestry Commission property, open to pedestrians) for 250–300 yards rather than go through the wooden gate. Long Dub is a long, deep pool with a sheer rock face on one side. Return to the wooden gate.

3. Pass through the gate and up through Birks Wood [N]. Go through a wider wooden gate and follow the farm road to the right. At the next gate you will see The Sepulchre, a stone enclosure containing several pines and unmarked graves.

4. Retrace your steps and return to Ulpha Bridge. Cross the bridge and follow the road to the right for 250 yards to Ulpha Kirk [O].

5. Return again to the bridge.

OLD HALL RUIN

To get to Old Hall ruin [P], go from Ulpha Kirk past Ulpha Bridge, but not over it, and continue uphill (towards Bootle) for more than a mile. The ruin is just beyond Old Hall Farm.

SWINSIDE STONE CIRCLE

The stone circle [Q] is two miles due west of Duddon Bridge and may be reached by walking up the farm road marked 'Swinside' for one mile.

To approach the stone circle from Duddon Bridge, travel southwest from Duddon Bridge on the road to Whitehaven. In one and a half miles from the bridge, turn right on the road to Broadgate. Park at Broadgate or further up the road and walk the rest of the way to the farm road marked 'Swinside' and up it to the stone circle.

To approach the stone circle from Ulpha Bridge, five miles away, go up the road to Bootle, past the Old Hall ruin, turn left (towards Duddon Bridge), then right (towards Whitehaven), and then left (towards Millom) at the guideposts. The farm road to Swinside goes up to the right in one and a quarter miles from the last intersection. Park off the side of the road nearby or continue down the road a quarter of a mile to Broadgate, where there are more parking places.

GLOSSARY

beck: brook or stream.

bield: 'A word common in the country, signifying shelter, as in Scotland' (W.W., note to 'Epistle to Sir G. H. Beaumont').

dungeon: 'fissures or caverns, which in the language of the country are called dungeons' (W.W., note to 'To Joanna').

fell: mountain.

force: 'Force is the word used in the Lake District for Waterfall' (W.W., note to 'The Somnambulist').

ghyll, gill: '*Ghyll*, in the dialect of Cumberland and Westmoreland, is a short and, for the most part, a steep narrow valley, with a stream running through it' (W.W., note to 'The Idle Shepherd-boys').

hause: 'A narrower and lower neck between two heights; a *col*; the name in the English Lake district and on the Scottish Border' *(OED)*.

how: hill.

intake: 'The word *intake* is local, and signifies a mountain-inclosure' (W.W., note to *An Evening Walk*, line 99); i.e., land enclosed with a stone wall.

sheepfold: 'It may be proper to inform some readers that a sheepfold in these mountains is an unroofed building of stone walls, with different divisions. It is generally placed by the side of a brook, for the convenience of washing the sheep; but it is also useful as a shelter for them, and as a place to drive them into, to enable the shepherds conveniently to single out one or more for any particular purpose' (W.W., note to 'Michael').

syke: small stream.

tarn: 'Tarn is a *small* Mere or Lake, mostly high up in the mountains (W.W., note to 'Fidelity'). 'A tarn is a lake, generally (indeed always) a small one; and always, as I think, (but this I have heard disputed) lying above the level of the inhabited valleys and the large lakes; and subject to this further condition, as first noticed by Wordsworth, that it has no main feeder' (De Quincey, p. 251n).

-thwaite (as in Crosthwaite): 'A piece of ground; *esp.* one cleared from forest or reclaimed from waste' *(OED)*.

SELECT BIBLIOGRAPHY

Armitt, M. L., *Rydal* (Kendal, 1916).

Britton, John, E. W. Brayley, *et al.*, *The Beauties of England and Wales*, Vols. iii, ix, xv (London, 1801–16).

Budworth (Palmer), Joseph, *A Fortnight's Ramble to the Lakes* (London, 1792).

Clarke, James, *A Survey of the Lakes of Cumberland, Westmorland, and Lancashire*, 2nd edn. (London, 1789).

De Quincey, Thomas, *Recollections of the Lakes and the Lake Poets*, ed. David Wright (Harmondsworth, 1970).

Gilpin, William, *Observations on ... the Mountains and Lakes of Cumberland and Westmoreland*, 2 vols., 3rd edn. (London, 1808).

Grasmere: A Short History, compiled by members of the Women's Institute, ed. Rachel Macalpine (Kendal, 1979).

Gray, Thomas, 'A Journal of His Tour', in *Poems*, ed. W. Mason (York, 1775), pp. 350–79.

Green, William, *The Tourist's New Guide*, 2 vols., (Kendal, 1819).

Housman, John, *A Topographical Description of Cumberland, Westmoreland, Lancashire* (Carlisle, 1800).

Howe, H. W., *Greta Hall: Home of Coleridge and Southey*, revised by Robert Woof (Norfolk, 1977).

Hutchinson, Sara, *Letters*, ed. Kathleen Coburn (Toronto, 1954).

Hutchinson, William, *An Excursion to the Lakes* (London, 1776).

Knight, William, *The English Lake District as Interpreted in the Poems of Wordsworth*, 2nd edn. (Edinburgh, 1891).

Knight, William, and Harry Goodwin, *Through the Wordsworth Country*, 3rd edn. (London, 1892).

Moorman, Mary, *William Wordsworth: The Early Years* (Oxford, 1957).

Moorman, Mary, *William Wordsworth: The Later Years* (Oxford, 1965).

Nicholson, Norman, *The Lakers: The Adventures of the First Tourists* (London, 1955).

Nicolson, Joseph, and Richard Burn, *The History and Antiquities of the Counties of Westmorland and Cumberland*, 2 vols. (London, 1777).

Noyes, Russell, *Wordsworth and the Art of Landscape* (Bloomington, Indiana, 1968).

Ordnance Survey, *The English Lakes: NW, NE, SW, SE Sheets*, 1:25 000 Outdoor Leisure Maps (Southampton, 1982).

Rawnsley, Eleanor F., *Grasmere in Wordsworth's Time* (Kendal, n.d.).

Rawnsley, H. D., *Lake Country Sketches* (Glasgow, 1903).

Rawnsley, H. D., *Literary Associations of the English Lakes*, 2 vols. (Glasgow, 1901).

Reed, Mark L., *Wordsworth: The Chronology of the Early Years* (Cambridge, Mass., 1967).

Reed, Mark L., *Wordsworth: The Chronology of the Middle Years* (Cambridge, Mass., 1975).

Robertson, Eric, *Wordsworthshire* (London, 1911).

Thompson, T. W., *Wordsworth's Hawkshead*, ed. Robert Woof (London, 1970).

Transactions of the Cumberland and Westmorland Antiquarian and Archaeological Society, new series (Kendal, 1901–).

Tutin, J. R., *The Wordsworth Dictionary of Persons and Places* (Hull, 1891).

Wainwright, A., *A Pictorial Guide to the Lakeland Fells*, 7 vols. (Kendal, 1955–66).

West, Thomas, *A Guide to the Lakes*, 3rd edn. (London, 1784).

Wordsworth, Christopher, *Memoirs of William Wordsworth*, 2 vols. (London, 1851).

Wordsworth, Dorothy, *Journals*, ed. E. de Selincourt, 2 vols. (New York, 1941).

Wordsworth, Dorothy, *Journals*, ed. Mary Moorman (London, 1971).

Wordsworth, Mary, *Letters*, ed. Mary E. Burton (Oxford, 1958).

Wordsworth, William, *Benjamin the Waggoner*, ed. Paul F. Betz (Ithaca, 1981).

Wordsworth, William, *Guide to the Lakes*, ed. E. de Selincourt (Oxford, 1970).

Wordsworth, William, *Home at Grasmere*, ed. Beth Darlington (Ithaca, 1977).

Wordsworth, William, *Prose Works*, ed. Alexander B. Grosart, 3 vols. (London, 1876).

Wordsworth, William, *Prose Works*, ed. W. J. B. Owen and J. W. Smyser, 3 vols. (Oxford, 1974).

Wordsworth, William, *Poetical Works*, ed. E. de Selincourt and H. Darbishire, revised edn., 5 vols. (Oxford, 1952–9).

Wordsworth, William, *The Prelude*, ed. E. de Selincourt, 2nd edn. revised by H. Darbishire (Oxford, 1959).

Wordsworth, William and Dorothy, *Letters*, ed. E. de Selincourt, 2nd edn. revised by C. L. Shaver, M. Moorman, and A. G. Hill (Oxford, 1967—).

Wordsworth, William and Mary, *Love Letters*, ed. Beth Darlington (Ithaca, New York, 1981).

INDEX OF WORDSWORTH'S POEMS

Poems are listed by title or, if there is no title, by first line. Page references in *italics* indicate where the poem, or part of the poem, is quoted.

INDEX OF LAKE DISTRICT PLACES

Page references in **boldface** indicate where the place names appear on a map.

OXFORD

MORE OXFORD PAPERBACKS

Details of a selection of other books follow. A complete list of Oxford Paperbacks, including The World's Classics, Twentieth-Century Classics, OPUS, Past Masters, Oxford Authors, Oxford Shakespeare, and Oxford Paperback Reference, is available in the UK from the General Publicity Department, Oxford University Press (JN), Walton Street, Oxford OX2 6DP.

In the USA, complete lists are available from the Paperbacks Marketing Manager, Oxford University Press, 200 Madison Avenue, New York, NY 10016.

Oxford Paperbacks are available from all good bookshops. In case of difficulty, customers in the UK can order direct from Oxford University Press Bookshop, 116 High Street, Oxford, Freepost, OX1 4BR, enclosing full payment. Please add 10 per cent of published price for postage and packing.

GUIDE TO THE LAKES

William Wordsworth

Edited by Ernest de Selincourt

A naïve clergyman, according to Matthew Arnold, once asked Wordsworth if he had written anything else, apart from his best-selling *Guide to the Lakes*. It was first published in 1810 as an anonymous introduction to a book of drawings. Later republished as a separate volume, it had gone through five editions by 1835. Ernest de Selincourt's edition of Wordsworth's final text was first published in 1906, with an introduction, detailed notes, a map, and eight illustrations reproduced from books which appeared in Wordsworth's lifetime. Four further contemporary illustrations and an index have also been included in this edition. The text is studded with many complete poems, and will delight anyone interested in Wordsworth and his work, and anyone visiting the Lake District.

'the archetypal book for the Lake District connoisseur . . . a classic of committed prose about a passionately loved landscape' Melvyn Bragg in *The Times*

LETTERS OF WILLIAM WORDSWORTH

A New Selection

Chosen and edited by Alan G. Hill

Drawn from the new and enlarged edition of *The Letters of William and Dorothy Wordsworth* (of which Professor Hill is General Editor), this selection includes 162 letters that illuminate the personality and concerns of the poet.